advanced
Gold
exam maximiser

Sally Burgess
with Richard Acklam

176320

Contents

Introduction to the *Exam Maximiser*	p.4
Exam overview	p.6

UNIT 1

Reading: multiple choice Paper 1, Part 3	p.8
Vocabulary: deducing from context and using a dictionary	p.10
Grammar plus: verb patterns (1)	p.10
Listening: sentence completion Paper 4, Part 3	p.11
Speaking: Paper 5, Part 1	p.12
English in Use: error correction (extra word) Paper 3, Part 3	p.13
Writing: compulsory question Paper 2, Part 1	p.14

UNIT 2

Reading: multiple matching Paper 1, Part 4	p.16
Speaking: Paper 5, Part 2	p.18
Vocabulary: words with similar meaning	p.19
Grammar check: modal verbs (1)	p.20
Listening: multiple choice Paper 4, Part 4	p.20
Grammar plus: noun phrases	p.21
English in Use: error correction (extra word) Paper 3, Part 3	p.22
Writing: information sheet Paper 2, Part 2	p.23

UNIT 3

Reading: multiple matching Paper 1, Parts 1 and 4	p.24
Vocabulary: expressions with *carry*	p.26
Grammar check: articles	p.26
Speaking: Paper 5, Part 3	p.27
Vocabulary: compound adjectives	p.28
Grammar plus: verb tenses (1)	p.28
Writing: formal and informal letters Paper 2, Part 1	p.29
Grammar check: relative clauses/pronouns	p.30
English in Use: gapped text Paper 3, Part 6	p.31

UNIT 4

Grammar check: gerund v. infinitive	p.32
Vocabulary: similes	p.33
Reading: multiple matching Paper 1, Parts 1 and 4	p.33
Grammar plus: modal verbs (2)	p.36
Speaking: Paper 5, Part 2	p.37
Vocabulary: noun collocations (with *of*)	p.38

UNIT 5

Speaking: Paper 5, Parts 3 and 4	p.39
Grammar check: conditionals	p.40
Writing: review Paper 2, Part 2	p.40
Reading: gapped text Paper 1, Part 2	p.42
Grammar plus: conditionals (advanced features)	p.44
Vocabulary: science and medicine	p.45
Vocabulary: collocation (body)	p.45
English in Use: error correction (spelling and punctuation) Paper 3, Part 3	p.46

UNIT 6

Grammar plus: futures (advanced features)	p.47
Reading: multiple matching Paper 1, Parts 1 and 4	p.48
Grammar check: modifiers and intensifiers	p.50
English in Use: word formation Paper 3, Part 4	p.51
Vocabulary: language of gender	p.52
Writing: Paper 2, Part 1	p.52
English in Use: register transfer Paper 3, Part 5	p.54

UNIT 7

Speaking: weak forms	p.55
Vocabulary: word + prepositions (1)	p.55
Grammar check: hypothetical meaning	p.55
Reading: multiple choice Paper 1, Part 3	p.56
Grammar plus: substitution and ellipsis	p.58
English in Use: multiple-choice cloze Paper 1, Part 1	p.60
Vocabulary: commonly confused words	p.61
Writing: leaflet Paper 2, Part 2	p.61

UNIT 8

Reading: multiple choice Paper 1, Part 3	p.62
Grammar plus: verb patterns (2)	p.64

Vocabulary: synonyms — p.65
Listening: multiple matching Paper 4, Part 4 — p.65
Grammar check: reported speech — p.66
Vocabulary: word formation (prefixes) — p.66
English in Use: multiple-choice cloze
Paper 3, Part 1 — p.67
Writing: competition entry Paper 2, Part 2 — p.68

UNIT 9

Vocabulary: expressions with *make/get/keep/
gain/resolve* — p.69
Listening: multiple matching Paper 4, Part 4 — p.70
Grammar plus: emphasis (1) — p.70
Speaking: comparing and contrasting
Paper 5, Part 2 — p.71
Vocabulary: leisure activities — p.72
Grammar check: verb tenses (2) — p.73
English in Use: error correction (spelling and punctuation) Paper 3, Part 3 — p.74
Writing: report Paper 2, Part 1 — p.75

UNIT 10

Vocabulary: computers — p.77
Grammar plus: *it* as preparatory subject/object — p.77
Speaking: Paper 5, Part 2 — p.78
Listening: note-taking Paper 4, Part 1 — p.79
English in Use: open cloze Paper 3, Part 2 — p.80
Grammar check: making comparisons — p.81
Vocabulary: words from other languages — p.81
English in Use: gapped text Paper 3, Part 6 — p.82
Writing: article Paper 2, Part 1 — p.82

UNIT 11

Listening: sentence completion Paper 4, Part 2 — p.84
Grammar check: linking words — p.85
Vocabulary: expressive description — p.85
Reading: multiple matching Paper 1, Part 4 — p.86
Grammar plus: relative clauses — p.88
English in Use: register transfer Paper 3, Part 5 — p.89
Writing: brochure Paper 2, Part 2 — p.90

UNIT 12

English in Use: word formation Paper 3, Part 4 — p.91
Reading: gapped text Paper 1, Part 2 — p.92
Speaking: Paper 5 — p.94
Grammar plus: emphasis with inversion — p.96

Listening: note-taking Paper 4, Part 2 — p.97
Vocabulary: sound and light — p.97
Grammar check: questions — p.98

UNIT 13

Grammar check: passives — p.99
Grammar plus: participle clauses — p.100
English in Use: open cloze Paper 3, Part 2 — p.100
Vocabulary: language of business — p.101
Vocabulary: phrasal verbs with *up/down* — p.102
English in Use: multiple-choice cloze
Paper 3, Part 1 — p.103
Writing: application Paper 2, Parts 1 and 2 — p.104

UNIT 14

Vocabulary: word + prepositions (2) — p.106
Grammar check: countable/uncountable nouns — p.106
English in Use: word formation Paper 3, Part 4 — p.107
Reading: multiple choice Paper 1, Part 3 — p.108
Grammar plus: reported speech
(advanced features) — p.110
Vocabulary: text-referring words — p.111
Listening: sentence completion Paper 4, Part 2 — p.111
Writing: report Paper 2, Parts 1 and 2 — p.112

UNIT 15

Listening: multiple choice Paper 4, Part 4 — p.113
Reading: gapped text Paper 1, Part 2 — p.114
Vocabulary: idiomatic language connected with talking/communication — p.116
Grammar plus: passives (advanced features) — p.116
English in Use: error correction (extra word)
Paper 3, Part 3 — p.117
Writing: Paper 2, Part 2 — p.118
Grammar check: *have/get something done* — p.118
Vocabulary: revision — p.119

PRACTICE EXAM — p.120

ANSWER KEY — p.145

Introduction to the *Exam Maximiser*

What is the *Advanced Gold Exam Maximiser*?

The *Advanced Gold Exam Maximiser* is specially designed to maximise students' chances of success in the Certificate in Advanced English examination.

The *Exam Maximiser* offers:

- **further practice** exercises to complement the Vocabulary, Grammar Plus and Grammar Check sections of the *Advanced Gold Coursebook*.
- **the facts** on the papers and questions in the Certificate in Advanced English examination. The *Exam overview* on pages 6 and 7 gives you information on each of the five papers.
- **step-by-step guidance** with the strategies and techniques you need to get a good grade in the exam. There are lots of **Hot tips!** to help you get extra marks.
- **exam-style exercises** so that you can practise using the techniques.
- **sample answers** to Paper 2 (Writing) questions, showing you things you should try to do and things you should avoid doing in the exam. There are also typical teachers' corrections and examiners' comments as well as sample answers for you to grade.
- **examples of responses** in Paper 5 (Speaking), showing how you should approach this paper and how to overcome any difficulties.
- **practice with transferring rough work to answer sheets** used in the exam. This means that you know exactly what to expect in each paper and ensures that there are no unpleasant surprises.
- **help with using time effectively** in the exam so that you can avoid losing marks because you run out of time.
- **a complete practice exam** so that you know what it actually feels like to do the Certificate in Advanced English exam.

Who is the *Advanced Gold Exam Maximiser* for and how can it be used?

The *Exam Maximiser* is extremely flexible and can be used by students in a variety of situations and in a variety of ways. Here are some typical situations:

1
> You are doing a CAE course with other students probably over an academic year. You are all planning to take the exam at the same time.

You are using the *Advanced Gold Coursebook* in class. Sometimes you will also do the related exercises or even a whole unit from the *Exam Maximiser* in class, though your teacher will ask you to do exercises from it at home as well. You will use the entire *Exam Maximiser* or you and your teacher will use it selectively, depending on your needs and the time available.

2
> You have a short period in which to prepare for the CAE exam.

The level of your English is already nearing CAE exam standard, though you have not been following a CAE coursebook. You now need examination skills. You will use the *Exam Maximiser* because you need practice in the exam tasks and how to approach them.

3
> You are re-taking the CAE exam as unfortunately you were not successful in your first attempt.

You may be having to re-take the exam because you were not sufficiently familiar with the exam requirements. You will use the *Exam Maximiser* to develop your exam techniques and to build up your confidence.

4 You are preparing for the exam on your own.

- Perhaps you are in a class where the teacher is using the *Advanced Gold Coursebook* as a general English course. This means there are probably students in your class who are not actually taking the exam. Your teacher will recommend use of the *Exam Maximiser* for homework, so that everyone can revise and practise the important grammar, vocabulary and skills they have learnt. However, you can also use it on your own to prepare for the exam.
- You are not attending a CAE class, but wish to take the exam and prepare for it independently. You will get the practice and preparation you need by using the *Exam Maximiser*.

For the student: how to use this book

To be successful in the Certificate in Advanced English exam you need to:

- revise and extend the vocabulary you already know.
- organise your learning in an effective way.
- understand what the exam is testing and how best to tackle each task.
- practise doing exam tasks in the set times to get used to the exam conditions.

This book helps you to do all of these things through appropriate support, information and advice.

Graded support

The texts and tasks in the *Exam Maximiser* reflect the level and complexity of the exam right from the start of the book. Graded tasks in the early units focus on specific aspects of the language or skill that is being tested, so as to build your confidence.

Information and advice

- ***About the exam*** boxes give you information about the nature and timing of each Paper and task in the Certificate in Advanced English exam. Use them to make sure you are well aware of what you need to do.
- ***Exam Strategy*** boxes extend your exam skills, and are followed by tasks which practise the strategies outlined and assess their effectiveness for you. Use them to improve your approach to exam tasks.
- ***Hot tip!*** boxes give you ways to gain those vital extra marks in the exam … and to avoid losing them!
- ***Learner training*** boxes give you advice on ways to organise your learning of vocabulary and skills.

Vocabulary and grammar practice

All units of the *Exam Maximiser* offer you the chance to do further practice with the important vocabulary and grammar points presented in the *Advanced Gold Coursebook* through varied exercises and activities. You can either use the further practice material immediately after you have studied a vocabulary or grammar area in class or use the *Exam Maximiser* for revision once you have finished a unit in the *Coursebook*. Another approach is to use the *Exam Maximiser* in the last month before the exam as a complete self-contained revision course.

The Practice Exam

The complete Practice Exam gives you an opportunity to find out how it really feels to take the Certificate in Advanced English exam.

Exam overview

Paper	Content	Test focus
Paper 1 Reading (1 hour 15 minutes)	There are four parts, each containing a text and comprehension tasks. The texts come from newspapers, magazines, journals, non-literary books, leaflets, brochures etc. There are approximately 3,000 words to read and no more than 50 questions. There are three main types of task: **Parts 1 & 4:** Multiple matching You match prompts in a list to sections of a text. There are between 12 and 18 questions in Part 1 and between 12 and 22 questions in Part 4. The text in Part 4 usually covers two pages. **Part 2:** Gapped text You are given a number of paragraphs that have been removed from a text. You have to decide where these paragraphs should go. There is one paragraph that does not belong to the text. There are either 6 or 7 questions. **Part 3:** Multiple choice You choose between four options to finish sentences or answer questions about the text. There are between 5 and 7 questions.	Questions test your ability to find specific information. Questions test your ability to: • understand how texts are structured. • predict how a text develops. • recognise words that indicate text structure. Questions test your ability to understand: • detail. • opinion and attitude.
Paper 2 Writing (2 hours)	There are two parts, each containing one task. You are expected to write approximately 250 words for each task. **Part 1:** A compulsory task in which you read information and write one or more texts. **Part 2:** You choose one of four tasks. One of these tasks always relates to work situations.	Tasks test your ability to: • apply the information given in the task. • select and summarise that information. • compare pieces of information from the task. • write articles, reports, reviews, competition entries, leaflets, information sheets, contributions to brochures, letters, personal notes and messages. Tasks test your ability to write articles, reports, reviews, competition entries, leaflets, information sheets, contributions to brochures, letters, personal notes and messages.
Paper 3 English in Use (1 hour 30 minutes)	There are six parts and 80 questions. **Part 1:** Multiple-choice cloze A text of about 200 words with 15 gaps, followed by 15 four-option multiple-choice questions. **Part 2:** Open cloze A text of about 200 words with 15 gaps which you must fill with an appropriate word.	Questions test your ability to find specific information. Questions test your knowledge of grammar.

EXAM OVERVIEW

Paper	Content	Test focus
	Part 3: Error correction A text of about 200 words containing errors. There are two types of error: • an extra word in some lines of the text • a punctuation or spelling error in some lines of the text You read the rubric to determine which type of errors you should look for.	Questions test your ability to proofread and find punctuation and spelling or grammar errors.
	Part 4: Word formation Two short texts of up to 130 words each in which there is a total of 15 gaps. You are given the stem of the word you must use to complete each gap.	Questions test your ability to form words from a stem.
	Part 5: Register transfer This consists of two texts of approximately 150 words each. You must transfer information from one text to 13 gaps in the other text, using different words.	Questions test your ability to express information using a different register.
	Part 6: Gapped text A text of about 300 words from which six phrases or sentences have been removed. You choose from 10 options to complete the text.	Questions test your ability to understand cohesion and coherence.
Paper 4 Listening (Approximately 45 minutes)	There are four parts and between 30 and 40 questions. **Part 1:** A monologue lasting about two minutes. You must complete sentences or notes. You hear the recording twice. **Part 2:** A monologue lasting about two minutes. You must complete sentences or notes. You hear the recording **once**. **Part 3:** A conversation between two or three speakers lasting about four minutes. You must complete sentences or answer multiple-choice questions. You hear the recording twice. **Part 4:** Five short, related extracts of about 30 seconds each. You either: a) complete a two-part multiple-matching task in which you select the correct option from a list of eight. OR b) answer two multiple-choice questions about each extract. You hear the recording twice.	Questions test your ability to understand specific information. Questions test your ability to understand specific information. Questions test your ability to understand the main ideas, the supporting detail and the speakers' attitudes. Questions test your ability to: • identify who is speaking. • understand what the speakers are talking about or trying to do. • recognise the speakers' attitudes.
Paper 5 Speaking (Approximately 15 minutes)	A conversation divided into four parts between two candidates and an interlocutor. Another examiner will be in the room with you to assess your performance. **Part 1:** The interlocutor asks you to exchange information with the other candidate or to answer questions. (Approximately 3 minutes) **Part 2:** The interlocutor asks each candidate to talk about some visual prompts. Each candidate speaks for about 1 minute and comments briefly on the other candidate's prompts. **Part 3:** The interlocutor asks you and the other candidate to talk together about some visual prompts (e.g. photographs, drawings or diagrams) and to solve a problem. **Part 4:** The interlocutor develops the topic in Part 3 by asking you to discuss and give opinions on more general questions.	This part tests your ability to exchange personal and factual information. This part tests your ability to compare and contrast visual prompts and to speculate about them. This part tests your ability to negotiate, collaborate and reach agreement. This part tests your ability to explain, summarise and develop a discussion.

UNIT 1
What a spectacle!

Reading: multiple choice

▶ **Paper 1, Part 3**

About the exam: In Paper 1, Part 3 you answer multiple-choice questions after reading a text.

Strategy

Read the whole text through once quickly to get an idea of the main areas referred to.

Read each question and locate the part(s) of the text which relate(s) to it.

Read the relevant part(s) of the text carefully and underline key words and phrases.

Consider the possible options for each question carefully. The incorrect options will be wrong for different reasons:
- they are not referred to in the text, but may be true.
- they contradict what is in the text.
- they are partially (but not completely) true.
- they are irrelevant to the question.

Select the best option.

▶ Hot tip! ◀

Sometimes a question may ask you to infer the attitude of the writer to the subject of the text. To do this you will need to look for evidence throughout the text. The choice of vocabulary will often give you clues.

1 The man in the picture has had serious problems with the legal authorities in his country. Why? Read the text and find out if you were right.

Money for Art's Sake

J. S. G. Boggs is a young artist with a certain flair and panache. What he likes to do, for example, is to invite you out to eat at an expensive restaurant, run up[0] a bill of, say, eighty-seven dollars, and then, while sipping coffee after dessert, reach into his satchel and pull out a drawing he's already been working on for several hours before the meal. The drawing, on a small sheet of high-quality paper, might consist, in this instance, of a virtually perfect rendition of the face-side of a one-hundred-dollar bill.

He then pulls out a couple of precision pens from his satchel – one green ink, the other black – and proceeds to apply the finishing touches to his drawing. This activity invariably causes a stir. Guests at neighbouring tables crane their necks. Passing waiters stop to gawk[1]. The head waiter eventually drifts over, stares for a while, and then praises the young man on the excellence of his art. 'That's good,' says Boggs, 'I'm glad you like this drawing, because I intend to use it as payment for our meal.'

At this point, a vertiginous chill descends upon the room – or, more precisely, upon the head waiter. He blanches[2]. You can see his mind reeling as he begins to plot strategy. Should he call the police? How is he going to avoid a scene? But Boggs almost immediately re-establishes a measure of equilibrium by reaching into his satchel, pulling out a real hundred-dollar bill – indeed, the model of the very drawing he's just completed – and saying, 'Of course, if you want, you can take this ordinary hundred-dollar bill instead.' Colour is already returning to the head waiter's face. 'But as you can see,' Boggs continues, 'I'm an artist, and I drew this. It took me many hours to do it, and it's certainly worth something … So you have to make up your mind whether you think this piece of art is worth more or less than this standard one-hundred-dollar bill. It's entirely up to you.'

As a conceptual artist, Boggs feels a work isn't complete until he has spent one of his bills; not only spent it, in fact, but often also received change – in real currency – and a receipt. A 'successful transaction', as he explains, is one that makes people think about such concepts as value and beauty and leads them to their own conclusions, independent of any establishment – whether governmental or cultural.

But mightn't his money still be counterfeit? Boggs always makes impish[3] changes on his bills – signing his own name instead of the Secretary of the Treasury's, for instance, or substituting the faces of celebrated American women (a current project) for the men gracing US currency. Governments, however, don't take kindly to this. Boggs has been prosecuted, unsuccessfully, for counterfeiting in both England and Australia; the Australian government was even required to pay him more than $20,000 in damages.

UNIT 1 **What a spectacle!**

In the United States, things have gone less well. In 1990, just before a major exhibition of his work opened, Boggs became embroiled[4] with the U.S. Secret Service. Its agents moved to prevent publication of the show's catalogue as it was then conceived, with actual-size, full-colour reproductions of Boggs's drawings. In the end, the catalogue, 'J. S. G. Boggs Smart Money (Hard Currency)', was printed using enlarged images.

This was just the beginning for Boggs: when 'Smart Money' moved on to another gallery, Secret Service agents threatened to confiscate everything but had no search warrant. In December 1992, Boggs was preparing to embark on[5] 'Project Pittsburgh' and spend a million dollars' 'worth' of a new series of drawings. The Secret Service raided his studio and office at Carnegie Mellon University, where he was a visiting lecturer in Art and Ethics. They confiscated 1,300 items. They did not, however, arrest Boggs, whose suit to regain his material is currently on appeal.

According to Kent Yalowitz, the lawyer who has taken Boggs' case on, 'The government has never tried to explain to the courts why they think he's breaking the law or why they have a right to seize his work.' Yalowitz points out that, unlike counterfeiters, Boggs has never tried to defraud anyone with his notes, nor has anyone ever complained of fraud in any of Boggs' transactions. Yalowitz said he's offered the government a compromise[6] solution: 'So long as no one complains of being defrauded by Boggs or anyone else using one of his drawings, the government should not interfere with his work.'

'What's driving them so crazy?' Boggs asks for his part. 'It must be the way these bills of mine subvert the whole system, calling into question the very credibility of the country's entire currency.' Boggs commissioned Thomas Hipschen, the master engraver whose portraits adorn the new denominations[7] of American currency, to make a steel-engraved portrait. This portrait – of Boggs – now also adorns a series of $100,000 bills, which the artist foresees using to pay his legal expenses.

2 Now answer the multiple-choice questions below.

1 How do other guests and restaurant staff react initially to J. S. G. Boggs's behaviour?
   A They are worried by it.
   B They are curious about it.
   C They are impressed by the quality of his work.
   D They try not to take any notice.

2 The head waiter is relieved when he realises that
   A Boggs's drawing is worth more than the cost of the meal.
   B Boggs is not willing to pay the bill with legal currency.
   C Boggs is not going to cause an embarrassing incident.
   D Boggs takes the concepts of value and art seriously.

3 What is Boggs's main objective?
   A To trick people into accepting his drawings as payment.
   B To get people to question established values.
   C To obtain real currency as change.
   D To provoke a reaction from the government.

4 How have governments outside the United States reacted to Boggs's art?
   A They have tried unsuccessfully to convict him of counterfeiting.
   B They have asked him not to change the images on the original notes.
   C They have fined him as much as $20,000 for exhibiting his drawings.
   D They have shown quite a lot of sympathy for his work and ideas.

5 What difficulties has Boggs had with the authorities in the United States?
   A They have forced him to make changes to a catalogue for one of his exhibitions.
   B They have confiscated all the work from his exhibition 'Smart Money'.
   C They have charged him with fraud for trying to pay with his drawings.
   D They have charged him with counterfeiting for reproducing images on US currency.

6 How does Boggs hope to pay his lawyers?
   A With a real $100,000 bill.
   B With a portrait by another famous artist.
   C With his latest piece of work.
   D With the change from a transaction with one of his drawings.

7 What does the writer think about Boggs?
   A He is breaking the law and should be punished.
   B He is a little eccentric but interesting.
   C He is mentally unbalanced but amusing at the same time.
   D He is being unfairly victimised by the authorities.

9

Vocabulary: deducing from context and using a dictionary

Find each of the following numbered words or expressions in the text 'Money for Art's Sake' on pp.8–9. Study the context in which each word or expression occurs in the text and find the matching definition in the box below.

EXAMPLE *run up*[0] cause oneself to have (bills or debts) h)

gawk[1]
blanches[2]
impish[3]
embroiled[4]
embark on[5]
compromise[6]
denominations[7]

a) to look at something in a foolish way
b) values (of coins and notes)
c) mischievous
d) to start (especially something new)
e) involved in an argument or other difficult situation
f) an agreement where both parties agree to accept some of the other's demands
g) to become white or pale with fear
h) to cause oneself to have (bills or debts)

Grammar plus: verb patterns (1)

Study the Grammar Reference and the section on verb patterns on page 8 of the *Advanced Gold Coursebook*.

1 Look at the sentences a)–e) below and match them to the verb patterns 1–5.

a) Unemployment has **increased** slowly over the last decade.
They're going to **increase** university fees by 5 per cent next year.
b) Our dog **smiles**.
c) She **explained** the situation to us very clearly.
d) He **held** her hand all the way through the film.
e) She **threw** the cat the ball.

1 a **transitive verb with one direct object**
2 a **transitive verb with two objects (indirect and direct)**
3 a verb with a second **prepositional object**
4 an **intransitive verb**
5 a verb that can be both **transitive** and **intransitive**

2 The verbs in some of the sentences below can only be followed by a second object if this is prepositional. Find the sentences and correct them. You may need to change the word order.

EXAMPLE *He borrowed me some money.* ✗
*He borrowed some money **from me**.*

1 He warned us that we could be breaking the law.
2 Could you describe us your ideal holiday?
3 Steve said he would invite us to see his new flat.
4 A strange thing happened me the other day.
5 It surprised me that he managed to stay so calm.
6 He didn't explain us the problem very clearly.
7 My sister sent me a book for my birthday.
8 Something woke him in the middle of the night.
9 He made her a table in his carpentry class.
10 She told me a very long story about her boyfriend.
11 Tim taught me a new song on the guitar.
12 Could you suggest us a good restaurant near here?
13 He shouted me something as the train was leaving the station.
14 They were kind enough to provide us a meal when we arrived.
15 They recommended us his latest play.
16 I'm going to buy him a new sweater.

3 In some of the sentences below the object can be left out because the meaning is obvious from the context. Place a tick (✓) next to those sentences. In the other sentences write an object in the gap.

EXAMPLE *I can't find anywhere to park.* ....✓............
They found ......*the cat*...... *under the stairs.*

1 My mother always hated *sewing* ....
2 I'm so clumsy! I keep *dropping* ....
3 I wish I could *sing* ....
4 They plan to *sail* .... from here to Brazil.
5 Shall I *close* .... ? It's quite cold in here.
6 It's my turn to *pay* ....
7 He has never learnt to *drive* ....
8 I spent the whole morning *drawing* ....

10

Listening: sentence completion

▶ **Paper 4, Part 3**

About the exam: In Part 3 of Paper 4 you will hear a conversation between two or three speakers, of approximately four minutes. It could be a radio broadcast, a meeting, an interview etc. You will either have to complete sentences with missing information (a maximum of three words) or answer multiple-choice questions. There will be between six and twelve questions. Each question is worth one mark. You will be tested on your understanding of specific information, general meaning and the attitude of the speakers. There is time before you hear the recording to read the questions. You will hear the recording twice.

Strategy
Read through the information about the recording and the questions. Try to predict what you will hear.

— **Hot tip!** ◀—

In sentence completion try to predict what grammatical form goes in each gap. For example: *Her original training was as a …* must be completed by a noun, but *Her mother's method of teaching is to encourage Elena to …* must be completed by an infinitive.

1 You are going to listen to part of a radio programme about famous works of art. First look at the incomplete sentences below and decide:

- which of the two works of art is discussed in detail on the programme.
- what grammatical form you will need to use to complete each gap.

2 Now listen to the recording and complete the sentences. Remember! You only need to use between one and three words in each gap.

1 Ann and Joseph both put the 'Mona Lisa' ……………………… of the list.
2 Ann says the Norwegians believe 'The Scream' is ……………………… than the 'Mona Lisa'.
3 Nearly ……………………… visited the Louvre last year.
4 Ann thinks many people would recognise 'The Scream' but would not know who ……………………… .
5 Parodies and reproductions of famous works of art are ……………………… in Ann's opinion.
6 Joseph thinks seeing too many reproductions of the 'Mona Lisa' makes it hard for us to ……………………… .
7 Two things that make it difficult to see the 'Mona Lisa' in the Louvre are the bullet-proof glass and the ……………………… .
8 When the painting was shown in Tokyo each visitor only got to see it for about ……………………… .
9 The varnish on the 'Mona Lisa' makes the landscape ……………………… properly.
10 Joseph thinks we are obsessed with the 'Mona Lisa' because it is surrounded by a lot of ……………………… .
11 Ann thinks that for people living today 'The Scream' is a more ……………………… than the 'Mona Lisa'.

Speaking

▶ **Paper 5, Part 1**

About the exam: Paper 5 is the part of the exam where your speaking is tested. It takes 15 minutes and you are paired with another candidate. There are two examiners, one who conducts the test and one who just listens to your English. In the first part of the test you will be asked if you know the other candidate. If you DO, you may then be asked to tell the examiners about your partner. If you DON'T, you will be told to ask your partner about certain things.

> *Strategy*
>
> Practise talking about your region or town, your home and family, your hobbies and interests, your work or studies, reasons for learning English and your short-term and long-term future plans.

Hot tip!

If you know the other candidate, don't say things like 'She is a very nice girl' or 'He is a very good student'. You do not need to recommend the other candidate to the examiner.

1 Look at this list of questions to ask the other candidate and match them with one of the six boxes.

Do you enjoy your work?
What other languages would you like to learn?
What do you like doing in your spare time?
Have you got any brothers or sisters?
Have you always lived there?
What do you think you will be doing five years from now?
What's it like living there?
Do you live in a house or an apartment?
What kind of music do you like?
Do you need any special qualifications to do that?
Would you like to live anywhere else?
Are there any interesting places to visit in your area?
Are you doing anything special this summer?
Where were you born?

A Your country, region or town
Where are you from?

B Your home and family
Do you have a big family?

C Your hobbies and interests
Do you have any hobbies?

D Your work or studies
Are you working or studying at the moment?

E Reasons for learning English
Why are you learning English?

F Future plans
Have you got any special plans for the future?

2 Here is a transcript of a Paper 5, Part 1. You only have one candidate's part. Imagine you are the other candidate and complete the transcript using the questions from Exercise 1 and your own answers to the other candidate's questions.

You: 1 .... ?
Zofia: I'm from Poland originally but I live in England now. What about you?
You: .... 2 .... ?
Zofia: Yes, three brothers. Two of them are back in Poland but the eldest is living in the States. Do you have a big family?
You: .... 3 .... ?
Zofia: I like reading, going out with friends and aerobics. Do you have any special interests?
You: .... 4 .... ?
Zofia: I work. I'm a trainee manager in the London branch of a Polish bank. Do you work too?
You: .... 5 .... ?
Zofia: Well, I like it and, of course, it's essential for my job. What about you?
You: .... 6 .... ?
Zofia: Yes, I'm planning to visit my brother in the States. And you? Are you going anywhere exciting?
You: .... 7 .... ?
Zofia: I'd like to improve my English and do an MBA at a British university. What do you expect to be doing five years from now?
You: ....

UNIT 1 **What a spectacle!**

English in Use: error correction (extra word)

▶ **Paper 3, Part 3**

About the exam: In Paper 3, Part 3 you will read a text of about 16 lines. You will have to look at each line and decide if it contains an error. In one kind of task you look for extra or unnecessary words in each line. If a line does not have an extra word, tick the appropriate space on the answer sheet. If there is an extra word, write it in the appropriate space on the answer sheet.

Strategy:
1 Read the text through once quickly to get a general idea of what it is about.
2 Read the text again. Think about the grammar of each sentence and check that each of the following 'grammar words' needs to be there:
   - articles (*the, a, an*)
   - auxiliaries (*do, have, are* etc.)
   - comparatives (*as, than, more* etc.)
   - conjunctions (*because, although* etc.)
   - prepositions (*to, up, by* etc.)
   - personal pronouns (*she, it, them* etc.)
   - modifiers (*too, quite, so* etc.)
   - relative pronouns (*who, which, that* etc.)

— Hot tip! ◀—

Try reading each sentence aloud to yourself (quietly!). This will help you to pick up any words that make the sentence ungrammatical.

Read the following text and look carefully at each line. In most lines, there is one unnecessary word. It is either grammatically incorrect or does not fit in with the sense of the text. For each numbered line 1–16, find this word and then write it in the answer box. Some lines are correct. Indicate these lines with a tick (✓). The exercise begins with two examples (0 and 00).

LEARNING CIRCUS SKILLS

0	You no longer have to <u>be</u> run away to the circus to learn the skills of the big top.	0	be
00	If you ever used to dream about flying on a trapeze, taming lions or making people	00	✓
1	laugh you can go along to one of several schools around Britain to learn how.	1	
2	The most largest, *The Circus Space*, is in London. The school offers courses in all the	2	
3	circus skills from fire-eating to lion taming. The people from all over London come to	3	
4	*The Circus Space* for to throw knives at boards and scare themselves	4	
5	silly on the trapeze. It comes as something of a shock when you are find out how	5	
6	difficult it is to master you even the basics of these skills. Complete concentration is	6	
7	too important because without it you can hurt yourself. The classes are completely	7	
8	absorbing, and the experience of being told what have to do is surprisingly relaxing,	8	
9	especially if you are one of those people who they spend much of the day having	9	
10	to make decisions. Giving up control and just concentrating hard on something	10	
11	physical is a very fulfilling. Although you don't need to be particularly fit to start	11	
12	learning some of the more static circus disciplines, but you will need to achieve quite	12	
13	a high level of fitness if you had want to take trapeze work to an advanced level.	13	
14	Those of already in shape and who have a good sense of balance, like skiers and	14	
15	horse riders, have an advantage. All equipment it is provided but you need to	15	
16	wear trainers with ankle support and thick tights to protect the skin on your legs.	16	

13

Writing: compulsory question

▶ **Paper 2, Part 1**

About the exam: Part 1 of Paper 2 is compulsory. You will have to read the task and all the linked material i.e. text and notes. The task will involve writing about 250 words but this may be broken into smaller parts. You may be asked to write formal letters, informal letters, reports, articles, notes or any combination of these.

> *Strategy*
>
> Read the instructions very carefully and underline key words/phrases. Make sure you know:
> - who you are writing to *or* for.
> - whether you need to use formal or informal language.

> ◀ **Hot tip!**
>
> Always check that you have done EVERYTHING you were asked to do. You can lose marks if you do not follow the instructions fully.

1 Look at the Paper 2, Part 1 question on p.14 of the *Advanced Gold Coursebook*. Read the answer a student wrote in response to this.

Dear Sarah and Pete,

This is just a quick note to thank you for letting us to use your circus tickets. We know how much you were both looking forward to it and wish you could use the tickets yourselves. I hear that Irish folk group you like will be in town the next month. Marcus knows someone who's sister used to playing with them so he might to be able to get free tickets. Would you like to go?

All the best,

Nadja

Dear Sir/Madam,

My partner and I attended a performance of the Chipperhall Circus on Tuesday 23rd November. I am very sorry to inform you that we were both angered and disappointed by our experience.

Firstly, your circus is not representing good value for money. We were given our tickets but if we would have bought them we would have asked for our money back. We could barely see some of the acts as there was a large pillar in front of our seats. What is more, although you state on your leaflet that performances last two hours, the one we saw was a lot more shorter. We had been waiting since twenty minutes before the performance began and we were on our way home before 9 p.m.

A second criticism we have concerns standards of safety. We were all horrified to see that one of the lions managed getting outside the ring. People sitting in the front rows must have being absolutely frightened.

Finally, I wish to draw your attention to the poor facility your circus provides. There was a so long queue for drinks at the interval that we eventually gave up. I wonder do you imagine two inexperienced bar staff are sufficient to deal with several hundred customers. We were also infuriated to discover that we had to walk through very muddy ground outside the marquee to reach the car park. I doubt that I will ever be able to wear the shoes I was wearing that night again.

Your circus may performed internationally but if last Tuesday was at all typical, I am certain those who have attended these shows have been as disappointed as we were.

Yours sincerely,

Nadja Höbling

Nadja Höbling

2 Here is what the student's teacher wrote about the student's answer.

> You have understood what you were asked to do and have organised the content of the note to your friends and the letter to the circus well. I was glad to see that you used less formal language in the note than you did in the letter. You have also used your own words rather than copying the wording used in the task. Well done! Unfortunately there are a number of grammatical errors. Please correct them and hand your work in again.

Find the errors the teacher has mentioned and correct them. There are FIVE errors in the note and ELEVEN errors in the letter.

UNIT 1 **What a spectacle!**

3 Read the task below and answer these questions.

1 When and why did your friend want the season tickets returned?
2 What aspects of the auditorium particularly impressed you?
3 How many items were on the concert programme?
4 What aspects of the concert itself particularly impressed you?

TASK

A friend and her husband recently lent you their season tickets so that you could attend the opening performance at a new concert hall in your city. You went along and thoroughly enjoyed every aspect of the evening. It is now Saturday 4th December and you have just realised that your friend's season tickets are still in your wallet. Write a short note to accompany the tickets, which you plan to post to her. Also write a letter to the local newspaper praising the new concert hall and the performance you attended. Read the original note your friend sent you with the tickets and the Inaugural Concert Programme, on which you have written some notes. Then using the information, write the note to your friend (50 words) and the letter to the local newspaper (200 words).

Dear ....,
Jack and I will be out of town this weekend and won't be able to attend the opening of the new concert hall. I know what a great music lover you are so I thought you might like to use our season tickets. Could you try to get them back to me before Friday 3rd as there is another concert then and we'd quite like to go if Jack has time?
Sophia

Inaugural Concert
Friday 26th November 8.30 p.m.

excellent views of the stage from all over the auditorium and extremely comfortable seats

WELCOME TO THE GUSTAV KRAUS MEMORIAL CONCERT HALL! WE ARE SURE YOU WILL BE AS EXCITED BY YOUR FIRST EXPERIENCE OF THIS MAGNIFICENT AUDITORIUM AS WE ARE BY PERFORMING HERE FOR YOU. PLEASE TAKE THE TIME DURING THE TWO INTERVALS TO WALK AROUND A BIT AND ENJOY ALFREDO POWER'S EXTREMELY ORIGINAL ARCHITECTURAL DESIGN.

fantastic!

TO MAKE YOU FEEL ESPECIALLY WELCOME YOU ARE INVITED TO JOIN US AFTER THE PERFORMANCE FOR A GLASS OF CHAMPAGNE IN THE BAR OUTSIDE THE DRESS CIRCLE.

not just 'a glass of champagne' — as much as you could drink!

Tonight's performance begins with one of the best known concertos of the classical era: Beethoven's 5th in E Flat known also as 'The Emperor'. We are delighted to have with us again the brilliant pianist Suzanna O'Hara to perform this magnificent work. She will stay with us for the second item on tonight's programme: Chopin's Grande Polonaise. Finally, we bring you up-to-date with a medley of film sound track music, some of which I know will be familiar to you all.

my favourite piece of music

something for everybody

Yevgeny Rodriguez
MUSICAL DIRECTOR

pianist and orchestra performed two encores!

4 Finally, plan your answer. Think about these issues:

- In the note to your friend should you thank her, apologise to her or both?
- Who will read your letter and what effect do you want it to have on them?
- How can you express the ideas in the programme and your notes in different words?
- Which linking words should you use in your letter?

5 Now write a draft and check for spelling and grammatical errors.

15

UNIT 2 It takes all sorts

Reading: multiple matching

▶ Paper 1, Part 4

About the exam: Paper 1, Part 4 is a multiple-matching task. You are required to read a group of short texts or sections of text. You will be required to match each question with the relevant information from the text. There may be more than one correct answer for some questions.

> **Strategy**
> 1 Read the instructions carefully.
> 2 Skim the text(s) to get a general idea of the content.
> 3 Read all the questions, highlighting key words and phrases.
> 4 Make a note of any answers you are confident about.
> 5 Go back to the questions you are not sure about. Take each one in turn. Decide which sections they might refer to. Scan those sections carefully for 'parallel expressions'.
> 6 Check you have answered all the questions.

1 Read the texts all the way through quickly and decide which of the carnivals you would most like to experience.

2 Read the questions 0–16. A student has already underlined key words and phrases. Skim the texts looking for 'parallel expressions' (phrases which give the same information as the question but in different words). The 'parallel expressions' for questions 1 and 2 have been highlighted in the text.

3 Now answer questions 1–16 choosing from the list of carnival locations on the right. Write the letter in the space provided. There is an example (0) that has been done for you.

Which carnival or carnivals:		
begins and ends at a different time of year to the others?	**0** *D*	**A** Venice
was not celebrated for a number of years?	**1** ...	
has a wild celebration to mark the end of the festivities?	**2** ...	**B** Trinidad
was a copy of the carnival celebration of another group?	**3** ... **4** ...	
involves commercial interests?	**5** ... **6** ...	**C** New Orleans
is described in an entirely positive light?	**7** ...	
also commemorates human rights?	**8** ... **9** ...	**D** London
receives mixed reactions from local people?	**10** ... **11** ...	
has been subject to official control because of violence?	**12** ... **13** ...	**E** Tenerife
involved friendly rivalry between groups of people?	**14** ... **15** ...	
includes performers from other countries?	**16** ...	

the world's great street parties

Rio is definitely tops, but if you can't make it to Brazil why not try one of these carnival locations?

A VENICE Most scholars trace Venice's carnival to the 15th-century 'Compaigne della Calza', private clubs whose members identified themselves with different coloured stockings. These clubs, which were originally created so that groups of friends could meet together, eventually took to competing in masked balls on 'Martedi Grasso' ('Fat Tuesday'), the prelude⁰ to Lent.

From these humble beginnings Carnival was born. It rapidly evolved into one of the wildest, most debauched and longest celebrations in Europe. Throughout the 18th century the festivities began as early as 26th December and continued for over two months.

Carnival faded after the fall of the Italian republic in 1797, and died out altogether under Mussolini, when the wearing of masks in public was made illegal. It was resurrected in 1979, by a group of non-Venetians, prompted¹, say the cynics, by hotel owners, whose only slack period was during the dark, wintry days of February.

Since then, business has boomed². About half a million visitors now pile into Venice for the festivities, with 100,000 squeezing into the city for the main carnival weekend.

Those Venetians who are not sick to death of the carnival make a great effort to dazzle these visitors. Some organise balls, others party in groups. One of the most famous local ensembles dresses as the 'tarocchi', or tarot cards, reputedly introduced through Venice from the Orient. Their costumes, visions of black and gold, are some of Carnival's most stunning.

B TRINIDAD Trinidad's carnival has a unique history. French settlers in the late 18th century celebrated Mardi Gras with masked balls and parades. The parties were then mimicked by their slaves. In 1838, when the islands were emancipated, the former slaves took over, adopting the carnival as a means of celebrating their new freedom. Originally called the Canboulay (from 'cannes broulées' or burnt sugar cane liquor) the festival was a wild and violent affair, with booming drums, arson and much fighting. Repeated attempts were made to stop the Canboulay.

In 1890, the government eventually approved the celebrations, policing them and making them safe in the process. It was a success – today, Trinidad's carnival is a peaceful, but still raucous affair. The main party centres on the Savannah area in Port of Spain, where calypso and steel-band competitions can be found.

Each band has its own 'pan yard', where it practises nightly in the weeks leading up to the festival. The 'pans' were once made from pretty much anything the bands could salvage. Since the 1950s they have been provided by large companies that sponsor the bands. This sponsorship has also put an end to the violent conflicts that often erupted between the bands in the past.

C NEW ORLEANS New Orleans' Mardi Gras* also traces its origins to French settlers. Students returning from a Parisian Mardi Gras in 1827 decided to stage their own New World version. It caught on³, and the big New Orleans families began holding regular Mardi Gras masked balls. In 1833, Bernard Xavier, a rich plantation owner, raised funds from among his wealthy friends to put on a large-scale public parade. The first float appeared in 1839, and since then the carnival has just kept growing, spawning⁴ strange Mardi Gras sub-cultures such as the Indian parades, in which groups wear fantastically coloured outfits that honour the swamp Indians who once helped the early slaves to freedom. Each Indian band has a 'spy boy' who dances some distance ahead, looking out for other Indian groups. If he sees one, he relays a signal to the flag boy at the front of the group, who then tells the Big Chief. He will then decide whether to dance on or dance away. If they dance on, and there is a meeting clash, trouble sometimes results.

During the two final nights' celebrations, Bourbon Street becomes the last word⁵ in craziness. People crowding the balconies of the elegant old French Quarter houses hurl strings of glass beads to the revellers below, who bite and scratch and claw to claim them as prizes.

French expression used in English meaning 'fat Tuesday'.

D LONDON London's Notting Hill Carnival attracts more than two million visitors every year and is acknowledged as one of the top three carnivals – together with Rio and Trinidad – for the quality of its performance art and creative talent. It takes place not in February or March like other carnivals, but on the August bank holiday weekend.

Notting Hill is one of the most cosmopolitan carnivals. The dancers, musicians and masqueraders hail from around the world. Nations such as Afghanistan, Kurdistan, Bangladesh and the Philippines have all been represented alongside Caribbean, African and South American countries.

Nevertheless, a certain amount of ambivalence characterises public perceptions of the Carnival. In the early years, when a few thousand Trinidadians paraded along Portobello Road in west London accompanied by steel drums, it was regarded as a quaint⁶ folk festival, at best. After a riot between black youths and the police in 1976, it became a metaphor for violence and thereafter was seen principally as a public order problem. Despite the growth of Carnival into a major international event that reflects London's rich cultural diversity, both these impressions linger⁷.

E TENERIFE Spain's largest carnival is that of Santa Cruz de Tenerife. 'It's very much an outdoor event,' says carnival director Damaso Arteaga. 'People party from 11 p.m. until dawn in the open-air plazas.'

The festival draws people from all over the world to Santa Cruz. Visitors have plenty of opportunity to enjoy the local Canarian cuisine, typified by fish and 'papas arugadas' (wrinkled potatoes) in full-flavoured sauces.

Also typical of the Tenerife carnival is the local, Latin-flavoured music, from 'murgas' (street bands) to 'rondallas' (choral groups) and 'comparsas', dance teams of at least 50 wildly adorned locals. All the groups take part in a huge parade on the Tuesday, which is shown on television all over Spain.

Like other Spanish fiestas the Tenerife carnival includes the 'Burial of the Sardine', a mock⁸ funeral for a large fish made of stone, wood and cardboard. The surreal ceremony, a mixture of the sacred and the profane, takes place on the Wednesday. You might think this would mark the end of the festivities, but the party starts up again on the Friday night and continues throughout the weekend. Finally, on the Sunday night, a magnificent fireworks display brings the carnival to a close, after ten days of almost non-stop dancing in the street.

4 Find the following numbered words or expressions in the texts about Carnival on p.17. Two definitions are given below for each of these. Study the context in which each word or expression occurs in the text. Decide in each case which is the best definition a) or b) and tick it.

EXAMPLE *prelude⁰* a) something that is followed by something larger or more important ✓ b) a former action or case that may be used as an example for present or future action

prompted¹ a) blamed b) urged
boomed² a) grown rapidly b) become more serious by stages
caught on³ a) came up from behind to reach the same point b) became popular or fashionable
spawning⁴ a) encouraging b) bringing into existence
last word⁵ a) the most modern example b) difficulty or trouble that makes the total unbearable
quaint⁶ a) very strange, unnatural, mysterious and/or frightening b) unusual and attractive especially in an old-fashioned way
linger⁷ a) be slow to disappear b) move or wait quietly or secretly as if intending to do something wrong and not wanting to be seen
mock⁸ a) not real but very similar to the real thing b) a worthless but sometimes amusing copy of something intended to deceive

5 Now use some of the words and expressions from Exercise 4 to complete this text. You may need to change the words or expressions a little to fit grammatically into the sentences.

The fireworks displays on New Year's Eve 1999 were among the best people have ever seen. Without a doubt the industry is (1) .... A Chinese invention, fireworks rapidly (2) .... all over the world. Big public spectacles in capital cities (3) .... more modest displays in villages and towns. In some places competing firms of firework manufacturers stage (4) .... battles above the heads of astonished on-lookers. The smoke from the explosions often (5) .... for hours afterwards. Unfortunately, there are sometimes accidents and injuries and this has (6) .... some governments to ban the sale of fireworks altogether.

Speaking

▶ **Paper 5, Part 2**

About the exam: In Part 2 of Paper 5 each candidate is given the opportunity to talk for about one minute without interruption. Each candidate is asked to react to a different set of pictures. Candidates should pay attention while their partner is speaking, as they are asked to comment briefly (for about 20 seconds) after their partner has spoken.

Strategy
Listen very carefully to the instructions the examiner gives you and make sure you do all the things s/he asks you to do.

Hot tip!
The examiner always pauses after giving the instructions. If you are not sure what you have to do, ask her/him to repeat the instructions. You will not lose marks for this, though you may if you do not do what you are asked to do.

1 Listen to two candidates doing a Part 2 task. First you will hear Gerda and then Alberto. They are both talking about pictures 1 and 2 below. Do both candidates:

- follow the instructions and do exactly what they are asked?
- use a good range of vocabulary and grammar?
- sound interested and involved in what they are saying?
- speak for one minute?

2 Listen again and note down:

- key vocabulary the candidates use
- useful expressions

Vocabulary: words with similar meaning

Study the Vocabulary section on words with similar meaning on p.22 of the *Advanced Coursebook*. Then read the text below and decide which word best fits each space. Circle the letter you choose. There is an example (0) that has been done for you.

MIDSUMMER NIGHT'S EVE

In Europe, Midsummer Night's Eve, also known as St John's Eve, occ... 23rd. It (0) _D_ from the pagan celebrations of the summer solstice which ... held on June 21st. On that night throughout Europe bonfires were lit along hillsides to (1) ... the shortest night of the year. It must have looked as if some kind of violent insurrection was taking (2) ... down the coast of Scotland and England, but these signal fires in fact had a very important purpose. Bones of farm animals (3) ... the previous autumn were burned and, when the fires had (4) ... , the remaining ash was put to good use: it was spread on the fields to enrich the land and (5) ... a good harvest. The word 'bonfire' is (6) ... from 'bone fire'.

In Brazil too St John's Eve means bonfires and fireworks. Another quaint tradition involves the (7) ... of small paper hot-air balloons, although they are (8) ... by law in the cities because of the fire (9) ... . Bonfires mark the beginning of spring rather than the summer in Sweden and are lit on the last night of April. In the Swedish Midsummer's Eve (10) ... , held on June 24th, a large pole, decorated with flowers and leaves, is placed in the ground.

Thistles also have a (11) ... role in the celebration of Midsummer's Night in Europe. In the past they were thought to (12) ... witches. The pretty, prickly plant was nailed over barn doors and used in wreaths, the circular shape being a (13) ... of the turning of the seasons. Wheels laced with straw and soaked in pitch were lit from the bonfires and then rolled down hills.

There is less risk of fire in a tradition (14) ... to many Slavic countries. Young women and girls float little baskets of flowers and lighted candles down streams. Local boys swim out to (15) ... a basket, find the girl it belongs to and claim a dance at the town's Midsummer's Eve Party.

0	A terminates	B initiates	C conceives	(D) originates
1	A celebrate	B honour	C commemorate	D commiserate
2	A space	B place	C site	D location
3	A revived	B assassinated	C slaughtered	D sacrificed
4	A doused	B extinguished	C smothered	D gone out
5	A assure	B safeguard	C ensure	D endanger
6	A derived	B developed	C evolved	D decayed
7	A landing	B launching	C propelling	D ejecting
8	A barred	B outlawed	C sanctioned	D prohibited
9	A certainty	B peril	C jeopardy	D hazard
10	A tradition	B custom	C ceremony	D practice
11	A decisive	B serious	C trivial	D significant
12	A deflect	B ward off	C attract	D avert
13	A sign	B password	C logo	D symbol
14	A unique	B common	C mutual	D prevalent
15	A salvage	B rescue	C set free	D liberate

19

...eck: modal verbs (1)

...ese sentences using a modal verb
...he underlined words.

1 I suppose it is possible that he was here earlier ➡ *I suppose he might have been here earlier.*

I suppose it is possible that he was here earlier.
2 Did you know how to ride a bicycle when you were a child?
3 Friends and relatives are allowed to visit patients between five and seven o'clock every evening.
4 It was unnecessary to buy a computer as I won one in a competition.
5 Why don't you take up swimming if you want to get fit?
6 I know for sure that it is Helen in the photograph.
7 It's a very bad idea to carry heavy shopping if you have a shoulder injury.
8 I forbid you to leave the table until you have finished your meal.
9 I was obliged to stay at home all evening waiting for an important phone call.
10 There's a chance that I'll be out when you come, so I'll leave the keys under the mat.

2 Rewrite these sentences in reported speech.

1 'You must leave all notes and books at the back of the room,' said the invigilator.
2 'You can stay in my flat while I'm away,' Sally said.
3 'Will you be home by ten thirty?' asked Pete.
4 'May I smoke?' the woman asked.
5 'I have to look after my nephews this weekend,' said Mark.
6 'I can't lift those boxes in my condition,' said the man.
7 'I must go,' said Alice.
8 'You needn't write to accept the invitation,' my friends said.

3 Now continue each of the sentences you have just written in Exercise 2 by adding one of the following clauses.

EXAMPLE 1 *The invigilator said that we had to leave all our notes and books at the back of the room ... b) but the boy next to me had a tiny dictionary in his sock.*

a) ... because she had a dentist appointment at 3 o'clock.
b) ... but the boy next to me had a tiny dictionary in his sock.
c) ... but that I should give them a ring if I was going to be late.
d) ... so he wouldn't be coming to the party.
e) ... as long as I didn't mind looking after her cats.
f) ... but there was a sign saying 'no smoking' right behind her.
g) ... and the foreman asked him what the matter was.
h) ... and I told him I didn't know.

Listening: multiple choice

▶ **Paper 4, Part 4**

About the exam: In Paper 4, Part 4 you hear five short extracts in which people talk about a similar subject. You answer two questions about each extract. Sometimes the questions are multiple-choice questions. You hear each extract twice.

> **Strategy**
>
> Before listening read through the instructions and each of the questions. Try to predict what you are going to hear each speaker talk about. Listen for the specific information the questions refer to.

━━━ **Hot tip!** ◀━━━

Once you've heard the tape twice and decided on your answer, don't change your mind! Candidates often change their answers wrongly at this stage.

 You will hear five short extracts in which different people give advice to foreign business people visiting their countries or regions. For questions 1–10 choose the correct option A, B or C.

1 Business visitors to Australia should try to:
  A say what they mean.
  B give the impression of agreeing with their hosts.
  C listen carefully to what people say.

2 Men travelling alone by taxi in Australia should:
A make sure the driver knows who is boss.
B shake the driver's hand on getting into the taxi.
C not sit in the back seat.

3 In the Middle East meetings:
A are never held on Fridays.
B are never held before 12 o'clock.
C are never held during the ninth month of the Islamic calendar.

4 Visitors to the Middle East should:
A learn to write Arabic script before leaving home.
B have business cards printed in Arabic and English.
C write their names on their business cards in Arabic.

5 Business visitors to Spain may be surprised:
A that people eat lunch with their families.
B that lunch is the main meal.
C that many restaurants do not open before nine in the evening.

6 An unacceptable gift to take to your host or hostess in Spain would be:
A chocolates
B flowers
C chrysanthemums

7 In Thailand, losing one's temper in public:
A is regarded as extremely bad manners.
B is inevitable, considering the heavy traffic.
C is something visitors often do.

8 Thai people would always avoid:
A pointing at things with their heads.
B touching other people's feet.
C touching other people's heads.

9 In Venezuela punctuality:
A is something locals find strange about business travellers.
B is necessary as everyone has a lot of work to do.
C is not expected of locals or foreigners.

10 If you are invited to a Venezuelan's home for a meal, you should:
A write a short letter saying that you accept the invitation.
B send flowers the day after.
C send flowers before and write to thank your hosts afterwards.

Grammar plus: noun phrases

Study the Grammar Reference and the section on noun phrases on p.23 of the *Advanced Gold Coursebook*.

Noun phrases are formed in the three ways shown in the box below. Study these and then make noun phrases to replace the underlined words in the sentences below.

- **NOUN + NOUN** e.g. a fifteen-minute break, a firework display, a silver bracelet, a table leg
- **NOUN + 'S + NOUN** e.g. Simon's brother, a children's pool, duck's eggs
- **NOUN + PREPOSITION + NOUN** e.g. a piece of bread, a book about indoor plants, a glass of wine

1 My sister is allergic to milk taken from cows.
2 You can't get into the enclosure where club members sit without a special pass.
3 There's a fair where handicrafts are displayed and sold on next weekend. Would you like to go?
4 Apart from class tests there will be an exam that goes on for three hours at the end of the year.
5 We ate two huge slices of a cake made with chocolate each.
6 When she saw her reflection in a window in a shop she realised she only wearing one earring.
7 I sometimes go swimming at the school for boys across the road.
8 The whiskers that a cat grows help it to judge whether a space is wide enough for it to get through.
9 Five of the National Parks found in Spain are in the Canary Islands.
10 He slammed the drawer in a desk shut as she came into the room.
11 This summer I'm having a holiday that lasts two months.
12 The cousin of my mother lives in Canada.
13 There's an exhibition where books are displayed on 23rd April each year.
14 I'm saving up to buy a sweater made of cashmere.

English in Use: error correction (extra word)

▶ **Paper 3, Part 3**

About the exam: In Paper 3, Part 3 there are two possible task types. In one you are asked to read a text and locate and correct spelling and punctuation errors. In the other you look for words that should not be there in each line of the text.

Strategy
Look carefully at the instructions and the examples to see which of the two task types you have been asked to do.

Hot tip!
If you have not found errors in 11 out of the 16 lines, check each line of the text again. Usually there are no more than five correct lines.

Read the following text and look carefully at each line. Some of the lines are correct, and some have an extra incorrect word which should not be there. If a line is correct, put a tick (✓) at the end of the line. If a line has a word that should not be there, put a line through it.

WHO IS FATHER CHRISTMAS?

0	Although it is not a very clear how contemporary Father Christmas's 'look'
00	came about, it is certain that it is the result of a continuous amalgamation
1	of many old folk customs and beliefs from the varied sources. First and
2	foremost, there is the image of the three kings are bringing gifts to the baby
3	Jesus. A second source is the Roman custom of giving to children presents
4	for good luck during the pagan festival which celebrating the winter solstice.
5	Last but not least, there is Saint Nicholas, a 4th-century bishop and the patron saint
6	of children, sailors and the poor whose saint's day it is December 6. Traditionally, Saint
7	Nicholas was depicted as like a tall dignified figure riding a white horse, giving
8	sweets to children and helping for the poor. The familiar image of a good-humoured
9	round-bellied Santa Claus, is complete with sleigh, reindeers and sack of toys, seems
10	to have be a 19th-century American invention. Built up on the Dutch figure of
11	Saint Nicholas which settlers they brought with them to New York, contemporary
12	Santa Claus is as the result of the blending of religious and pagan traditions from
13	many European countries with newer American customs. Such elements as the
14	reindeer, the stockings and the North Pole can round off the modernised legend.
15	Thus, nowadays because Joulupukki of Finland, Papa Noel of French-speaking
16	countries, English Father Christmas and American Santa are very much alike.

Writing: information sheet

▶ **Paper 2, Part 2**

About the exam: In Paper 2, Part 2 you have to write approximately 250 words. You have a choice of four writing tasks. One of these tasks may be writing an information sheet or brochure.

Strategy

Read the instructions very carefully, underlining key words. Plan your answer carefully so that you cover all the things you are asked to do. Write your answer using appropriate lay-out and language for the audience you are writing for. Check your answer carefully for spelling and grammatical errors.

> **Hot tip!**
>
> Don't choose options if you don't have any experience or knowledge of the topic you are asked to write about.

1 Look at this task and the plans two students have written. Which plan (A or B) would produce a good information sheet?

TASK

Your local tourist office has asked you to write an information sheet (about 250 words) telling visitors about three of the most important festivals in your country, region or town. Your information sheet should include the following:

- background information about each festival
- dates when celebrated
- recommendations on how to get the most out of the celebration

---

PLAN A

Heading: Festival fun for everyone!

Introduction
- lots of festivals
- sheet includes some of the best

1 Winter Music Festival
- started 1960
- musicians from all over the world

Dates: Whole of January

Recommendations:
Buy tickets in advance on internet for discounts.
Don't miss: local choirs on last night and open-air opening (both free).

2 Carnival
- celebrated here since 19th century
- used to be called 'Winter festival'

Dates: Varies: February/March

Recommendations:
- pack a disguise
- parades on first night and Shrove Tuesday
- firework displays

3 Country fairs
- traditional
- every village a bit different
- traditional costumes, food and music

Dates: Throughout spring and early summer

Recommendations:
- San Jerónimo: picturesque village
- Parades in the capital
- Country dancing in the market place

PLAN B

Introduction: My favourite festivals and why I would recommend them.

Paragraph 1: Olive harvest festival
Why it is celebrated
When it is celebrated
What makes it different to festivals in other parts of the world

Paragraph 2: Midsummer nights eve
Why it is celebrated
When it is celebrated
What makes it different to similar celebrations in other parts of the world

Paragraph 3: International Women's day
Why it is celebrated
When it is celebrated
How we celebrate it here

Conclusion: Though I like all the festivals, my favourite is the Olive Harvest Festival. Explain why.

2 Now write your answer to the task.

UNIT 3
The root of all evil?

Reading: multiple matching

▶ **Paper 1, Parts 1 and 4**

About the exam: In Paper 1, Part 4 you may be expected to read texts as long as 1,200 words.

Strategy
Once you have read the text, look at each of the questions in turn. Decide which section of the text they might refer to. Scan those sections carefully. Look for 'parallel expressions' (words or phrases that contain the idea of the key words in the questions).

Learner training
Try timing yourself when you read. Reduce the time you allow yourself gradually so that you can complete the task in about 15 to 20 minutes.

1 You are going to read an article about winners of Britain's National Lottery. Before you read, write down a) two things you would do and b) two things you would definitely not do if you won the national lottery in your country. Now skim the article and see if any of the things you listed in a) and b) are mentioned. Give yourself no more than two minutes for this.

2 Look at the questions below. A student has underlined key words and phrases in the first three questions and has also marked the linked sections in the texts. Underline the key words and phrases in the other questions and then scan the text to find the relevant information. Give yourself no more than ten minutes to do this.

3 Now answer the questions. Choose your answers from the list of people on the right. (Note: where more than one answer is required, these may be given in any order.) Allow yourself no more than five minutes for this.

Which lottery winner or winners:		
has not spent any of their winnings on foreign travel?	1 A	
was able to help fellow workers?	2 D	**A** Penny Haigh
says it's important not to be too sensitive?	3 C	
had special skills that made it easier to handle so much money?	4 C A C	**B** Mark Gardiner
feels a relation would have been equally generous in the same situation?	5 A	
wishes they had received better advice?	6 C	**C** Elaine and Derek Thompson
won the respect of a member of their community?	7 B	
have bought properties as an investment?	8 A 9 D	**D** Roger Robar
have tried to help strangers in need?	10 D 11 E	
had some unpleasant reactions from others to their win?	12 B	**E** Doug Woods
continued living in the same area?	13 E	
sees the win as having given them greater financial security?	14 A	

24

OVERNIGHT MILLIONAIRES

Since Britain's National Lottery was launched in 1994 more than six hundred people have become millionaires overnight. For some this new-found wealth has meant nothing but misery, destroying friendships and marriages. For others little has changed. Here are the stories of five lottery millionaires.

A PENNY HAIGH

In March 1996, Penny Haigh, 49, won £1.3 million. She retired two months later and now lives with her husband John in a 17th century house which cost a quarter of a million. But rather than being the pinnacle of their dreams, this is actually just another place on the way for Penny and John. 'We've bought and sold fourteen properties in seven years,' he says. 'We like buying places and doing them up,' she adds. For them, their lottery windfall is much more a useful financial cushion than a ticket to a dream palace.

Penny has made an effort not to let the win affect her behaviour. 'I certainly haven't changed one bit. I don't go on mad spending trips like other Lottery winners. In fact, I still buy all my clothes in charity shops just like I did before I won.' The only thing she wanted to do was to go on the Orient Express. 'We couldn't afford a honeymoon when we got married and I've never been abroad. But my husband won't go.'

After she won, she worked out who she was going to give money to, and how much. Her brother was one of the first to benefit from Penny's win. 'We got used to sharing early on in our family. So I know that if it had been Bunny who won the Lottery, he'd have done the same for me.'

Penny and her husband now spend their time renovating their house. 'We've got to be doing something or we get bored.' Once the renovations are finished, they intend to move on. 'Ideally, I'd like to run a hotel and employ Bunny and his wife Carol as barman and waitress.'

B MARK GARDINER

Mark Gardiner had a half-share in one of the biggest winning tickets so far – £22 million – and swiftly received a dollop of abuse to match. His second wife, who was divorcing him, called him a 'cheating rat'. A 'best friend' revealed he had once saved Mark's life, emphasising that he thoroughly regretted it now. His mother joined in, saying: 'I have a vision of Mark finishing up with a Ferrari going into a brick wall – and I hope it's tomorrow.' Unsurprisingly, within months of winning he claimed the jackpot had ruined his life and that he was a 'prisoner' of his new-found wealth.

According to friends at his local pub, the Royal Standard, Gardiner is a 'normal bloke' who is no more or less worthy than most to benefit from an overnight fortune. Gardiner has spent some of his money taking groups of friends from the pub on luxury holidays but he has also sponsored a football team in his home town, Hastings. He pledged £500,000 over three years to the club, now known as Stamcroft, to improve facilities. Leon Shepperdson, the club chairman, says of Gardiner 'He has put his money where his mouth is. I know plenty of wealthy people who do not help their local area, but that certainly could not be said of him.'

C ELAINE AND DEREK THOMPSON

Elaine and Derek Thompson won £2.7 million in December 1995. With over forty fellow lottery winners the Thompsons have formed a network so that they can swap their often alarming experiences and avoid the pitfalls of instant wealth.

Mrs Thompson, 42, feels that others could benefit from talking to a winner. 'It would have been nice on the night of the win to speak to another winner. We had a winner's adviser but they do not know what it is like to be told you are getting a cheque for £2.7 million. We wanted someone to tell us why we were feeling sick, why we couldn't sleep and all the things flashing in our minds. Ninety per cent of the people I have spoken to feel the same.'

The win for the Thompsons was easier than for most, because Derek was an accountant. Apart from investing in race horses, and taking their family on luxury holidays, the couple have remained very much as before.

She said 'If I meet anyone who is being negative and nervous about the money I say, "There's nothing to be nervous about, spend some time getting used to it."' She also tells them they will have to develop a thick skin and get to know who is genuine and honest.

D ROGER ROBAR

Roger Robar, who now owns his own restaurant, beauty salon and a string of properties, won £5.8 million in June 1996. About fifty strangers asked him for money after his win and he gave to all of them. 'I understand people who have problems so I helped. Maybe I was a bit gullible. I know some of their stories were probably exaggerated or untrue, but I feel people's pain. I couldn't help being moved, especially when the stories were about children.'

Mr Robar's only regret is that the people he helped did not have the courtesy to thank him. 'I am not sorry I gave the money to them, I am only sad they never thanked me. I just wanted them to phone.'

Mr Robar, 49, who was born in the French colony of Martinique, was also very generous to his friends, family and staff. He bought a £250,000 house in Paris for each of his three grown-up daughters, and a holiday home for himself in the French capital. He converted a three-storey building where he used to live into the beauty salon Vindo, for his wife to run. He then bought the restaurant where he used to work as a chef and renamed it 'Roger's'. He kept on all the existing staff but doubled their salaries. For himself, he bought another restaurant in France, a £400,000 house and he spent a further £1.8 million on houses which he rents out.

E DOUG WOODS

Doug Woods collected £2.68 million in September 1995. You might have thought that he would have wanted to get as far away as possible from the flat he rented in Westcliff-on-Sea in Essex. Instead, he went for a walk on the Sunday after his win, 'Saw this place for sale, rang the agents on the Monday, went on holiday to the States and when I got back, the keys were waiting for me.' In fact, he moved no more than 400 yards down the road, into a £66,000 bungalow so unassuming you wouldn't even know it was there.

Doug gets his kicks not from material display, but from giving to charity and from taking family and friends on cruises. He doesn't even drive, though he does enjoy horse racing and has actually sponsored a race meeting, naming one of the races after fellow lottery winners Elaine and Derek Thompson.

As far as Doug is concerned, spending your winnings on a swanky pad is not a very interesting way of using a few million pounds. Not only that, but a luxury house can bring with it the problem of finding yourself living among your former social superiors. 'This is where my friends are,' says Doug Woods. 'This is where I know everyone. What's the point of moving somewhere flash?'

Vocabulary: expressions with *carry*

Look again at the Vocabulary section on expressions with *carry* on p.31 of the *Advanced Gold Coursebook*.

Complete the sentences below with one of the following:

| on | through | your voice | off | much weight |
| out | away | the motion | too far | |

1 She may be a world famous novelist but her opinion certainly doesn't carry .... with me.
2 After they had walked almost 20 kilometres in freezing temperatures they were too exhausted to carry ....
3 What carried him .... the years of poverty was an unflinching belief in his ability as a musician.
4 If you want to become a successful public speaker you need to learn to make .... carry.
5 I thought we would never convince him to back our film project, but somehow we carried it .... and he offered us seven million.
6 There's no need to get carried .... ; we've only won about £30.
7 I thought the debate was going in our favour, but in the end .... wasn't carried.
8 It started off as just a student prank but someone carried it .... and the building caught fire.
9 Why do you keep making threats when we all know you will never carry them .... ?

Grammar check: articles

1 Look again at the rules for article use on p.38 of the *Advanced Gold Coursebook*. Now read this text and for each gap decide if you need to add nothing (the zero article), *a/an* or *the*.

THE FAT ONE

On 11th November 1811 (1) ..&.. Spanish Parliament passed (2) ... law creating Spain's national lottery, one of (3) ... country's oldest. Today ticket sales bring in close to nine billion pesetas (about 350 million pounds). (4) ... lottery lays claim to being (5) ... best in the world for those who buy tickets, with (6) ... seventy per cent of the money they pay finding its way back into their pockets as prize money. (7) ... rest goes to (8) ... government.

(9) ... Christmas Lottery, known as 'El Gordo' (the fat one), has (10) ... largest jackpot. Spaniards spend as much as 272 billion pesetas on (11) ... tickets each year and get over 200 billion of that back in (12) ... prizes. Official lottery shops and bars, restaurants and even small family stores sell tickets for weeks beforehand. The 3,000 peseta 'decimos', as the individual tickets are called, can win (13) ... bearer as much as 300 million pesetas (£2,000,000) tax-free and are frequently split between (14) ... friends and family members, with people spending only (15) ... few hundred pesetas for (16) ... share of (17) ... number.

Much of (18) ... country grinds to (19) ... standstill from 9 o'clock on (20) ... morning of 22nd December as the children of San Ildefonso school in Madrid start to sing out the winning numbers in (21) ... ceremony that is broadcast live on television and radio and which goes on for more than three hours. The organisers claim 'El Gordo' is (22) ... biggest first prize offered in (23) ... national lottery anywhere in the world. Between that and (24) ... other lotteries and games of chance, analysts estimate that each Spaniard spends (25) ... average of 80,000 pesetas (26) ... year on (27) ... gambling, more than (28) ... minimum monthly wage.

26

2 In each of the sentences below there is *one* mistake with the definite, indefinite or zero article. Find the mistakes and correct them.

1 After Sam and Tina won the lottery they went on a luxury cruise in Mediterranean.
2 People are beginning to make lot of money out of the Internet.
3 My sister-in-law works as engineer with a large oil company.
4 What brilliant speech the new finance minister gave at the opening of parliament.
5 Climbing the Mount Everest has become very fashionable among ordinary tourists
6 In the *Newsweek* magazine it said he was one of the ten richest people in the USA.
7 The British have had mixed reactions to introduction of a national lottery.
8 Have a look in the newspaper and tell me what time the new film is on at Odeon.

Speaking

▶ **Paper 5, Part 3**

About the exam: In Paper 5, Part 3 the examiner sets the candidates a problem-solving task which often involves sequencing/ranking/selecting from a number of pictures/written prompts. In this and other parts of the test you are assessed on various aspects of spoken language including INTERACTIVE COMMUNICATION. This includes your ability to initiate and to respond to what the other candidate says.

Strategy
Make sure you express your opinion and ask the other candidate for hers/his.

─ **Hot tip!** ◀
Try to develop the opinions the other candidate expresses rather than simply agreeing or disagreeing.

UNIT 3 The root of all evil

You will hear two different pairs of candidates doing a Part 3 task using the material below.

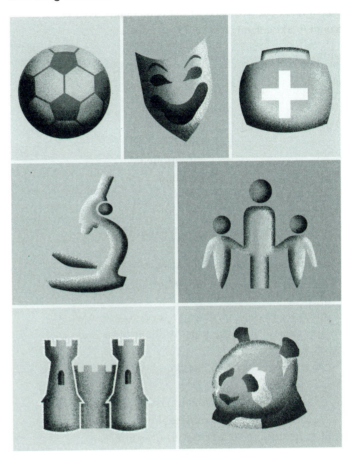

Listen to the candidates and look at the assessor's mark sheet and comments. Decide which candidate received which marks for INTERACTIVE COMMUNICATION. The first pair of candidates you hear are called Nadja and Henrik. The second pair are called Felipe and Tania.

5 Kept discussion going, exchanging turns very naturally and developing what the other candidate had said in previous turn.

5 Worked hard to keep interaction going; initiated and picked up on partner's points but had his work cut out for him.

3 Not enough attempt to elicit partner's opinion; just stated own opinion and refused to budge! No desire or effort to take up any of partner's points.

5 Exchanged opinions and kept discussion going, always developing partner's points. Seemed genuinely interested in what she had to say.

Vocabulary: compound adjectives

1 Match the two parts of the compound adjectives in column A and column B.

Column A
1 level c
2 long g
3 air f
4 tight b
5 mass a
6 so h
7 last j
8 absent i
9 bullet e
10 self d

Column B
a) produced
b) fitting
c) headed
d) made
e) proof
f) conditioned
g) standing
h) called
i) minded
j) minute

2 Use each compound adjective in Exercise 1 to complete one of the sentences below.

1 Tom is one of those .... professor types. He doesn't seem to know what day it is but has the most brilliant ideas and theories.
2 Most hotels in cities like Bangkok are ....
3 Many of the world's wealthiest people are .... millionaires.
4 I'm just going to pop out to do some .... shopping for the party tonight.
5 What do you think of all those .... clothes that are fashionable at the moment?
6 Janet is the sensible one. She's the most .... member of the family.
7 They were disappointed to find the street market full of .... clothing.
8 That .... expert they hired doesn't seem to know much about computers at all.
9 When the Pope visits other countries he drives around in his famous .... 'pope mobile'.
10 Despite their .... friendship, they fell out over a very small amount of money she had lent him.

> **Learner training**
>
> If you see any new compound adjectives when you are reading, record them by noting down the sentence in which they occur. Learn them along with these compound adjectives.

D 3 Use your dictionary to find more compound adjectives with *long*, *tight*, *last*, *self*, *headed*, *made*, *proof* and *minded*.

4 Complete these sentences with one of the following particles: *off*, *up*, *down*, *out*.

1 I wouldn't describe my family as well-..............., but as children we never had to go without.
2 Don't work too hard and let yourself get run-................... . You'll end up getting ill.
3 He was fined for driving too fast in a built-................... area.
4 There was only a broken-................... old wall to protect the secret garden from curious passers-by.
5 Hard-................... shoppers can get some wonderful bargains on electrical goods in the new discount store.
6 You should get rid of that old tracksuit. It's almost completely worn-................... .
7 He gave a one-................... performance at a small jazz club when he was in London.
8 Advertising executives often get burnt-................... after a couple of years on the job.

Grammar plus: verb tenses (1)

IMPORTANT!

Look again at the section on verb tenses in the Grammar Reference and on pp.34–35 of the *Advanced Gold Coursebook*. Look at the conversation between two candidates doing Paper 5, Part 1 and fill in the gaps with a verb in an appropriate tense.

Ewa: Where are you from?
Esther: From Albacete in Spain but (1) .... (live) in London for the last six months. What about you?
Ewa: I'm from Lublin in Poland but (2) .... (live) in London too at the moment. (3) .... (visit) London before you came to live here?
Esther: No. This is my first time away from home, actually. I (4) .... (really enjoy) it. How long (5) .... (plan) to stay here?
Ewa: Until (6) .... (perfect) my English! No, (7) .... (only joke). I (8) .... (think) of taking the Proficiency exam next year, though.
Esther: Wow! So, how long (9) .... (live) here?

28

UNIT 3 The root of all evil?

Ewa: Well, by the end of this month
(10) .... (be) here for
exactly two years.

Esther: That's a long time. (11) ....
(miss) your family terribly?

Ewa: I would be but they (12) ....
(always phone) me and
(13) .... (send) me letters
and e-mail messages so it
(14) .... (be) too bad so far.
Oh, and of course several of them
(15) .... (be) here to visit me.
(16) .... (be) very homesick?

Esther: Yes, but (17) .... (go)
back to Spain for Christmas. I
(18) .... (really look forward)
to it.

Ewa: You must be.

Writing: formal and informal letters

▶ **Paper 2, Part 1**

Look at part of the question for a Paper 2, Part 1 task and the letter a candidate has written.

> ... and asking for advice on potential investments. Then write a letter (100 words) to an old school friend who you know is in financial trouble telling her/him about your lottery win, offering her/him help and arranging to meet up.

The candidate's letter is too long and too formal. Rewrite the letter in an appropriately informal style using layout, openings and closings appropriate to a letter to a friend.

---

2 Haywain Lane
Findon
Sussex

Gianfranco Duranti,
22 Sussex Terrace,
Brighton
Sussex

22nd February, 2000

Dear Mr Duranti,

I have recently been informed of the fact that I have won first prize in the National Lottery. It is difficult to fully appreciate such a remarkable occurrence. Nevertheless, I feel certain that I will, in the course of time, grow more accustomed to it.

I am aware that you have experienced some financial difficulty recently, particularly with regard to the repayments on your mortgage. I am, therefore, enclosing a cheque for £200,000, which I hope you will be willing to accept. I believe this was the amount owing on the mortgage.

I intend to visit Brighton in the near future and wonder if it would be possible for us to see each other there. Might I suggest that we meet at the King's Head at eight o'clock on the evening of Friday 3rd March? Should that be a convenient time for you, would you telephone me to confirm the arrangement? You should not be too concerned if you are unavailable on that evening. I feel certain that there will come a time when we can meet.

I look forward to hearing from you.

Yours sincerely,

Carolina Hernández

Grammar check: relative clauses/pronouns

1 Read the article and answer these questions:
1. What was the currency in Australia before 1966?
2. What was the currency after 1966?
3. What do people remember most about the introduction of the new currency?

2 Read the text again and fill in the gaps using *who*, *whose*, *which* or *that*.

OUT GO THE POUNDS; IN COME THE CENTS

On the 14th of February 1966 Australians said goodbye to the currency denominations (1) … they had known since the European settlement of Australia in 1788. Naturally enough when the British established what was then a penal colony, they used the currency denominations of their homeland, (2) … were pounds, shillings and pence. From as early as 1901, when Australia gained independence from Britain, there had been discussion about the introduction of decimal currency, (3) … has considerable advantages over non-decimal systems. Nevertheless it was more than half a century before it was introduced. The new notes and coins, (4) … names had been the subject of quite heated debate, were roughly parallel to the old denominations. A dollar was the same colour and size as ten shillings, the note (5) … had an equivalent value in the old system. The two-dollar note was greenish in colour like the pound note, (6) … place it had taken. The only completely new coins (7) … were introduced at this stage were the one- and two-cent coins, though many of the old coins, such as the penny, the halfpenny and the threepence, ceased to be valid currency. Others, like the sixpence, the shilling and the two shilling coin, (8) … were the same size respectively as the new five, ten and twenty cent coins, initially mingled with the new currency but were gradually withdrawn from circulation. Australian school children, (9) … had struggled with complicated sums done in the old currency, breathed a sigh of relief on that day because arithmetic suddenly became much easier. The government had put a lot of effort into educating older people as well as children about decimal currency. Perhaps what people remember best is a little song, played constantly on radio and TV, in (10) … they were told 'be prepared folks when the coins begin to mix on the 14th of February 1966'.

3 Combine these sentences with a relative pronoun to form a single sentence.

1. He consulted his bank manager. The bank manager told him it would be unwise to take out a loan.
2. Australian dollars and cents were introduced in 1966. They are completely different from the US notes and coins.
3. Even young children can open bank accounts. They often maintain them for the rest of their lives.
4. Banks carry out extensive market research. The market research tends to show that students are attracted by special offers and free gifts.
5. Mortgages are offered by most banks. Mortgages are special loans for the purchase of property.
6. There were several similarities between the old and new Australian currencies. One of them was the size of some of the coins.
7. I always try to deal with one particular bank teller. He is always very friendly and helpful.
8. One day I had to do my banking with a new teller. I had never spoken to her before.

UNIT 3   The root of all evil?

English in Use: gapped text

▶ **Paper 3, Part 6**

About the exam: In Paper 3, Part 6 you read a text from which a number of phrases or sentences have been removed. You choose from a list of phrases and sentences those which best fill the gaps in the text.

Strategy

- Read the text all the way through to get the general idea.
- Read the text again and think of ways of filling each gap by reading what comes before and after.
- Look at the alternatives and choose the most appropriate.
- Read the text all the way through with the alternatives in place and make sure that it makes sense.

— **Hot tip!** ◀—

Pay special attention to linking words such as *however, in order to, first, according to.*

1 Read the text below and decide if the writer is
a) in favour of gambling, b) against gambling or c) neutral.

2 Read the text again and decide which of the alternatives best fills each gap.

INVESTING OR GAMBLING?

Putting money on horse races is a better bet than investing in the stock market, according to a report (0) . The report's authors have evaluated some of the most popular forms of gambling, including government bonds, shares, the National Lottery and horse racing, and found (1) ... . 'The attitude that gambling is bad and investment is good is very perverse as many investments are speculative gambling,' said Jonquil Lowe, co-author of the report.

Experts found (2) ... and attribute this to the fact that the National Lottery has made it more respectable. The latest figures show (3) ... , a much higher proportion of the population than in the 1980s. The report compared types of gambling according to the size of the maximum win relative to the stake, the chances of winning, the potential loss and the chances of gambling again.

Horse racing and government bonds were in fact given the best overall rating for value for money. They were followed by investing in smaller companies and the National Lottery. The casino games of roulette and black jack were rated as the worst value for money because of the fact (4) ... . Penny Haigh won the National Lottery in March 1996. She made a total investment of £216, at £2 per week, (5) ... . Nevertheless, according to Tim Cockerill, an independent financial advisor, it is inevitable (6) ... . 'Even investing your money in high-risk small companies is better than putting it on the horses or the National Lottery,' said Mr Cockerill. Dr Emanuel Moran, a consultant psychiatrist, who specialises in gambling, agreed. 'Gambling is a form of entertainment and should not be seen as an investment,' he said.

A that the stock market does not always give the best value for money
B that two-thirds of British adults gamble every week
C that she never expected to win
D that the gap between the two is very narrow indeed
E that gambling in Britain has increased since 1994
F that turned into a win of £1,325,202
G that the odds are stacked against the gambler
H that it is not attracting as many people as it did initially
I that in the long run the gambler will lose

J that was published this week

31

UNIT 4

The universal migraine

Grammar check: gerund v. infinitive

Look at the letter a young man wrote to an advice column and the reply he received. Put the verbs in brackets into the correct form (gerund or infinitive). In some cases either the gerund or the infinitive is possible.

Write to Uncle Max

Dear Max,

I've decided (1) ... (write) to you because I've failed (2) ... (come up with) a solution of my own to what is rapidly becoming a serious problem. I'm a successful, good looking, healthy, intelligent and likeable guy in my late twenties, but I regret (3) ... (say) I haven't been able (4) ... (find) a permanent girlfriend ... or even an impermanent one!

It's no good (5) ... (tell) me I should try (6) ... (meet) more girls. That's the whole problem. I've been living here for six months and I haven't succeeded in (7) ... (get to know) more than five women I've genuinely had anything in common with. My best friend suggests (8) ... (take up) a hobby of some kind or (9) ... (join) a club. I suppose I wouldn't mind (10) ... (learn) more about photography or (11) ... (take up) a new sport, but I really don't have much time during the week and come Saturday night, I'm on my own again. Several friends have offered (12) ... (introduce) me to eligible women, but none of them turned out (13) ... (be) what I'd call 'my type' and I've realised I prefer (14) ... (meet) people on my own terms. To make matters worse I've never grown even vaguely accustomed to (15) ... (live) alone. What would you advise me (16) ... (do)?

Yours,

Lonely of London

Dear Lonely of London,

I'm sure you won't deny (17) ... (be) just a tiny bit choosy. You admit to (18) ... (meet) a number of women since moving to London, five of whom you 'genuinely had something in common with' but, even so, you seem convinced that only meeting more women will enable you (19) ... (find) the girlfriend of your dreams. Friends have given you all sorts of excellent advice that you don't even seem to consider (20) ... (follow). I don't understand how you can expect (21) ... (meet) more women if you refuse to make any effort. I can't help (22) ... (think) that much of the problem is of your own creation. Why not try (23) ... (get) in touch with one of the women your friends have been kind enough to introduce you to? If she'll agree (24) ... (go out with) you, you may well find that she's much more your type than you first thought. Don't put off (25) ... (call). Do it today! Stop (26) ... (fool) yourself. If you don't act now, you may be forced (27) ... (spend) the rest of your life alone.

All the best,

Uncle Max

UNIT 4 **The universal migraine**

simile - puirmone

Vocabulary: similes

1 Study the Vocabulary section on similes on p.43 of the *Advanced Gold Coursebook* and then choose the alternative that best completes these sentences.

1 After the only friends Maria had at the college left to study abroad, she felt ... .
   A like a bull in a china shop
   B as light as a feather
   C like a fish out of water
2 What put you in such a foul mood? You're ... !
   A like a red rag to a bull
   B like a bear with a sore head
   C as strong as an ox
3 Whoever it was who phoned him must have given him a terrible fright. He went ... when he answered the phone.
   A as cool as a cucumber   B as white as a sheet   C as quick as a flash

2 Replace the underlined phrases in these sentences with one of the alternatives that you did not use in Exercise 1. Make all other necessary changes.

EXAMPLE *Every time the teacher asked a question, <u>with great speed</u> Pamela would put up her hand even if she didn't know the answer.*
*Every time the teacher asked a question, **as quick as a flash** Pamela would put up her hand even if she didn't know the answer.*

1 He was really nervous before the wedding but on the day he <u>showed no sign of nerves</u>. *as cool as a cucumber*
2 Simon is <u>very insensitive</u> sometimes. He asked Helen about Jeff and everyone knows they've just broken up. *like a bull in a china shop*
3 You should have seen William lift that heavy box. He doesn't look it, but he really is <u>physically very powerful</u>. *as strong as an ox*
4 He gave her a cashmere shawl that <u>weighed very little</u> but kept her wonderfully warm. *like a log*
5 Mentioning marriage while Sheila's around <u>makes her very angry</u>. *like a red rag to a bull*

Reading: multiple matching

▶ **Paper 1, Parts 1 and 4**

About the exam: The text or texts in Paper 1, Part 4 may be spread over two pages which you fold out. There are between 12 and 22 multiple-matching questions.

> *Strategy*
> Because there is a lot to read in Part 4 and because the relevant information is scattered throughout the texts, it is very important to have the whole text or all the texts in front of you so that you can scan them and look for the answers.
> Follow this procedure:
> • fold out the page so that you can see all the texts.
> • skim them to get a general idea of the content.
> • read the prompts or questions and highlight key words.
> • take each prompt in turn and decide which section or sections of the texts they might refer to.
> • scan those sections and see if they contain words or phrases that express the idea of the key words in the prompt.
> • check your answers.

▶ **Hot tip!** ◀

Each section of the text will be used as an answer at least once. If there is a section you haven't used, check your answers again.

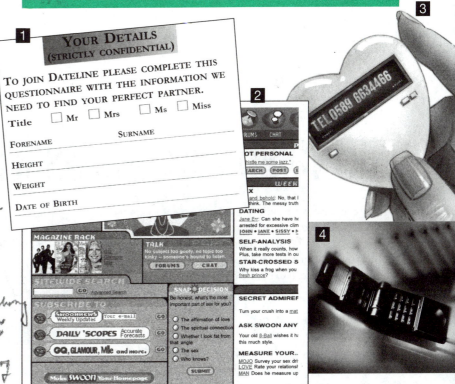

1 Match each item in the picture above to one of the sections in the text about dating services on pp.34–35.

33

2 For each question, scan the texts to find the relevant information. Choose your answers from the list of dating services on the right. Where more than one answer is required, these may be given in any order.

According to the article, which dating service:		
is the oldest?	1 ...	
does not assume all users are looking for a partner?	2 ...	
may bring its creator substantial profits?	3 ...	
is a spoken version of an earlier concept that people had come to dislike?	4 ...	**A** Dating agencies: Dateline International
may change its registrations procedure?	5 ...	
is rather old-fashioned in its approach?	6 ...	**B** Voicemail Personal Advertisements: Advanced Telecom Services Personals
provides a source of income for two organisations?	7 ...	
may succeed because the British now feel more positive about those who are unattached?	8 ...	
ensures that others do not know who you are until you want them to?	9 ...	**C** Dating websites: www.swoon.com
may not be suitable for users in the UK?	10 ...	
involves sending a postal application?	11 ...	
can only be used outside?	12 ...	**D** Dating devices: Smart Heart
has been copied only in its country of origin?	13 ...	
costs users nothing?	14 ...	
has made advertising for a partner seem an attractive and fashionable thing to do?	15 ...	
does not offer users an unlimited number of potential partners?	16 ...	

LOOKING FOR MR OR MS RIGHT?

In the UK there are at least eight million single people between the ages of eighteen and sixty-four. If you are one of them and are not too happy about it perhaps you should try a dating service. Rada Petrovic tells you what's on offer.

A   DATING AGENCIES: DATELINE INTERNATIONAL

Dateline International UK, the country's first national introductions agency, was launched in 1966. Dateline claim to have successfully matched thousands of couples since then and still boast thousands of members nationwide who are regularly informed of potential partners. They emphasise that since they are the longest established agency potential customers can rely on their integrity in preserving privacy and offering good value for money. £150 buys you a year's membership and six initial dates. They cater for people who are seeking 'friendship, love, marriage, or just want to get out and meet some new people'.

To join you fill in a rather traditional questionnaire where you tick boxes in answer to questions about your hobbies, likes and dislikes. For example, the following are the possible 'interests' Dateline customers might have: listening to music, reading, watching TV, watching sport, listening to the radio, being with children, cooking/entertaining, DIY/crafts, gardening and animals'. These are not really anyone under fifty's thing!

Dateline is now moving into the 21st century and have a website on which you can fill in a questionnaire to find out how 'mature' and 'self-aware' you are, input partner preferences (non-smoker, over/under a certain age etc.) and search a database. However, to join you still have to go the tiresome pen and paper route. Marketing director Peter Bennett says that this is largely for security reasons but that they are not ruling out introducing an online service in the future.

UNIT 4 **The universal migraine**

3 Find words or phrases in the text which mean the same as those in a)–i) below. In each case the section of the text in which the words or phrases occur is indicated in brackets.

a) dismissing without considering carefully (A)
b) outer appearance (B)
c) users of products or services (B)
d) sad condition or situation (B)
e) until this time (C)
f) cost a lot of money (C)
g) make a lot of money suddenly (D)
h) someone's special idea (D)
i) pound(s) (D)

4 Five of the words and phrases you found in the texts in Exercise 3 are informal. Use your dictionary to find out which ones.

Learner training

If you look up vocabulary in your dictionary, always make a note of whether or not the word or expression is formal or informal.

B VOICEMAIL PERSONAL ADVERTISEMENTS: ADVANCED TELECOM SERVICES

Up until recently, the only alternative to joining a regional or national dating agency was to place an ad in a 'lonely hearts' column – personal advertisements in a newspaper inviting respondents to write to a box number. The phrase 'lonely hearts', which only completely disappeared in the early 1990s, was heavily stigmatised.

Lonely hearts are still around, but they now come in the guise of voicemail personal advertisements. They work by tapping the market at no cost to the advertiser. The single person – the advertiser – places an ad in a paper for free, and interested punters call up a premium rate number, hear more information and leave a message. Charge bands range from 25p to £1.50 per minute. More and longer messages mean more revenue for the service provider, a proportion of which goes into a publisher's classified ads revenue.

The three companies that provide telephone-based dating services for all the British national and regional papers are all American. Every national paper except the Daily Mail now carries voicemail personals. Cosmopolitan and Esquire – two leading national magazines that target readers in their twenties – have launched voicemail personals too.

'Previously, Cosmopolitan and Esquire wouldn't have touched personal ads, they were beneath them,' says Cindy Asplande of Advanced Telecom Services. 'But these days personals look much more professional in print.' The answer also lies in the recent change in British cultural attitudes towards being single. Nowadays, we all look a little more indulgently – affectionately, even – at the plight of the poor professional single person.

C DATING WEBSITES: www.swoon.com

Swoon is a dating website, based in the USA, that offers a free personals service. It currently holds 100,000 people on its database – that is, advertisers who have posted an online personal – and that figure is constantly growing.

Look at the site (www.swoon.com) and it's easy to understand why Swoon works. Advertisers fill in an online form which is tailor-made for the modern single. While Dateline asks clients coyly whether they like 'pop, rock, jazz or folk', Swoon tells you to list what's in your CD player. You can respond via e-mail to as many ads as you like, or wait for responses to drop into your mailbox.

With its clever design, and editorial tone, Swoon does the hitherto impossible – it makes lonely hearts cool. 'We're a cool site editorially and artistically. And it really is for the users,' says editor-in-chief Melissa Weiner. 'Unlike other dating sites, you can search the database without having to register. We don't force people to place ads. And we're free.'

So far, emulators have been confined to the United States, where the bulk of dating services users reside – and have a pretty good chance of meeting other users in their area. While web dating in theory has no geographical boundaries, long-distance virtual relationships rarely succeed. Nick, 29, an advertising sales executive from London, dated Susie, a 24-year-old postgraduate student in Alabama, for six months. 'After endless e-mails and phone calls and three transatlantic trips I decided I really, really liked her, but didn't actually fancy her. End of story. It did leave a hole in my pocket, and it's not something I'd do again.'

D DATING DEVICES: SMART HEART

Rolf Olsson is an unlikely contender to bring about a technological revolution in the dating industry. After all, he is a 71-year-old grandfather. But you have to give it to Rolf. This septuagenarian has – excuse the pun – his finger well-placed on the button of modern dating. He is also possibly about to make a killing of the most lucrative kind in what is a rapidly expanding industry.

Rolf is an inventor and his baby is the Smart Heart. This is an electronic dating device which will go on sale this month in the UK for about £50. For your fifty quid, you are guaranteed as many dating hits as chance will send you.

The Smart Heart works like a singles' radar, storing data and sending out signals to other devices in the area. You input the criteria of your perfect partner such as age, interests, profession, education, and assign each quality a level of importance. You also specify what type of relationship you're looking for, e.g. long-term or short fling. The device doesn't work inside so you need to get onto the streets, turn it on and hope that someone single and in possession of a Smart Heart matches your criteria. The Smart Heart vibrates and a phone number flashes on your screen.

Of course, the success of the Smart Heart as a dating service is based entirely on whether enough people will buy it – essentially, on whether it becomes a cult.

Grammar plus: modal verbs (2)

Study the Grammar Plus section on modal verbs on p.48 and the Grammar Reference (p.194) in the *Advanced Gold Coursebook*.

1 Choose the modal verb that best fills each of the gaps in this conversation.

A: I wish she hadn't just gone off like that.
B: Yes, I think she (1) **A must B should** have told you she'd met someone else.
A: I don't even know how she met him. She hardly ever went out on her own.
B: Even so, she (2) **A might B can** have met him at college.
A: Yes, I suppose so. I've been spending most of my time alone since she left, you know.
B: That's no good. You (3) **A should B need** try to go out with friends at least once a week.
A: You're probably right. The problem is most of our friends were mutual friends.
B: But you (4) **A must B should** have *some* friends that you knew before you met her.
A: Well, yes. I suppose there are a few, but they all live outside London.
B: Surely, you (5) **A must B can** have made some new friends since moving to London.
A: Yes, but only through work. I never seem to meet anyone *outside* work.
B: Well, I think you (6) **A must B ought to** take up a sport of some kind.
A: Actually, I've been thinking about registering with a dating service but I don't want to spend a lot of money.
B: Why do you say that? I've heard that you (7) **A mustn't B don't have** to spend any money at all to join one of those internet services like 'Swoon'.
A: But I don't like the idea of millions of people knowing my personal details.
B: They won't! The dating service (8) **A should B has to** keep your identity secret.
A: Another problem is that all these services are international and I (9) **A can B might** fall in love with someone who lives too far away.
B: Then specify that you only want to meet people in your area when you fill in the form or write your advert.
A: What if the people who answer my ad don't like me once we've got to know each other?
B: Don't be silly! You (10) **A can't B mightn't** expect everyone to fall in love with you, you know.

2 The writer of this love letter has selected the wrong modal verb in eight places. Read through the letter, find the mistakes and correct them. The first mistake has been corrected for you as an example.

Dear Rodney,

~~You mustn't~~ can't imagine how much I love you. You are never out of my thoughts. I simply must see you again. Please, please, please write back. I probably mustn't let you see how desperate I am to hear from you, but I am and nothing may possibly change my mind about how much I love you. I suppose as time goes by I can begin to love you more calmly but nothing might possibly stop me wanting to be with you. I sent you another letter last week. You must have received it by now. I can't understand why you haven't replied. I suppose it might have surprised you to hear how madly in love with you I am but there's no need to worry. We really may not be apart like this — and we won't be.

Perhaps you think I must move to Scotland to live with you rather than your moving down here. Rodney, darling, you only should say the word and I'll come to you.

Your Allison

P.S. I've sent you a little present!

3 Here is Rodney's reply to Allison's letter. Fill in the gaps in the letter using one of the following modal verbs.

| can | might | must | should | need |

Dear Allison,
I have just opened your second letter. The first one still hasn't arrived. I think it (1) … have got lost in the post. They've also just delivered your 'little present'. You (2) … not have spent so much money on such an expensive gift. It's absolutely ridiculous. (In fact, you (3) … not have bothered as I already have a Porsche!) I (4) … not possibly accept it, of course, and have asked them to return it to you.
You (5) … try to be reasonable, Allison. You (6) … not possibly be as much in love with me as you claim to be. You don't know me at all and (7) … not possibly have any idea what I'm like. If you got to know me, you (8) … even find you didn't like me at all. I (9) … be quite irritating sometimes, I promise you.
I'm afraid I (10) … ask you not to write to me again. This (11) … seem harsh but I know that's the way it (12) … be.
Regards,
Rodney
P.S. You (13) … not acknowledge receipt of this letter.

Speaking

▶ **Paper 5, Part 2**

About the exam: In Paper 5, Part 2 each candidate talks about a set of theme-related photographs. You may need to speculate about relationships, locations or events and to interpret what is happening.

Strategy
Use modal verbs and other speculative language.

— **Hot tip!** ◀

You are not expected to *know* where, when or under what circumstances the photographs were taken. Use clues to speculate about the time, setting or location. Even if you are wrong, you won't lose marks.

1 Listen to two candidates talking about the photographs below. Which candidate uses speculative language well? Elena or Markus?

2 Write a description of the set of photographs the unsuccessful candidate talked about using the language of speculation.

UNIT 4 The universal migraine

37

Vocabulary: noun collocations (with *of*)

Study the Vocabulary section on noun collocations (with *of*) on p.51 of the *Advanced Gold Coursebook*. Now read this review of a television programme and choose between the alternatives to complete each gap. The first one (0) has been done for you.

The Truth about Love

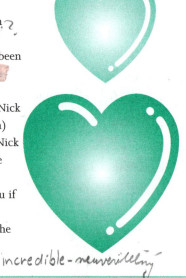

This week we celebrated Valentine's Day … or rather (0) ..C. romantics and those of us who are a bit soft in the head did! The fourteenth of February always gives everyone who's anyone a chance to cast a few pearls of (1) … before their fellow sufferers about the nature of 'the universal migraine' – love. Francis Farnsworth is a case in point. I'm sure the poor old fellow has a heart of (2) … but he really does talk a (3) … of rubbish sometimes! His appearance last night on BBC 1's 'Let's Talk It Over' was no exception. He started off by having what I will politely call a (4) … of opinion with Tania Di Monte, author of 'Tell me the Truth about Love'. Ms Di Monte always expresses the most extraordinary views without any apparent (5) … of contradiction. Last night she was boldly setting out her rules for a perfect relationship when poor old Farnsworth accidentally called her Tina. Tina is of course the name of her ex-husband Darren's second wife and we all know that any mention of him – or her – is like (6) … to Tania. Farnsworth kept apologising and saying that it had been a (7) … of the tongue brought about by a momentary (8) … of concentration, but it took all presenter Greg Lazarre's skills to calm our Tania down again. Francis then started calling her 'darling', which only succeeded in making her even more furious. '(9) … of endearment,' he stammered as she glared at him. She had been vehemently denying that there was even a (10) … of truth in rumours about her forthcoming engagement to football star Nick Pérez. Nevertheless, I'm sure it is only a(n) (11) … of time before we see Tania and Nick on the cover of 'Hi There!' celebrating 'the wedding of the century'. If marrying someone like Tania is what happens to you if you're incredibly successful, as Pérez undoubtedly is, I shudder to think what the (12) … of failure might be!

0	A insufferable	B untreatable	C incurable	D unrecoverable
1	A knowledge	B wisdom	C intelligence	D sense
2	A gold	B silver	C brass	D steel
3	A mound	B load	C pile	D stack
4	A disagreement	B conflict	C contrast	D difference
5	A worry	B anxiety	C concern	D fear
6	A a bull in a china shop	B the bull by the horns	C a red rag to a bull	D a bull market
7	A mistake	B slip	C error	D lapse
8	A lapse	B error	C mistake	D slip
9	A Expression	B Idiom	C Term	D Phrase
10	A grain	B fragment	C particle	D pellet
11	A issue	B question	C problem	D topic
12	A payment	B expense	C price	D sum

38

UNIT 5

Where will it end?

Speaking

▶ **Paper 5, Parts 3 and 4**

About the exam: In Paper 5 parts 1 and 3 you speak to the other candidate. In Part 4 the examiner interacts with you and the other candidate, asking you questions related to the theme in Part 3.

Strategy

In Part 3 it is important to talk to the other candidate – *not* the examiners. You should try to behave as if the examiners were not there. In Part 4, you should respond to the examiner's questions *and* the other candidate's comments.

▶ Hot tip! ◀

It is very important to take the task in Part 3 seriously and to use it as an opportunity to show the vocabulary and structures you know.

1 Look at this Paper 5, Part 3 task.

TASK

Here are some ideas for a possible television documentary series called 'Future Perfect?' devoted to changes and developments over the next century. The programme is intended to attract an audience in their teens and early twenties. Talk to your partner about the ideas and decide which ones you think would make the best themes for the programme and why.

2 Here is a transcript of part of what Guillermo said while he was doing this task. Try to imagine what Gloria said in response and then listen to the recording to see how close you were.

Guillermo:	OK. Shall we start?
Gloria:	(1) ...
Guillermo:	Yes, I do. Or rather I think they'd all make *OK* programmes ... . Well, maybe not 'the aging population'. I don't think that's a very attractive theme. I mean, when you're young it's kind of difficult to even imagine getting older. It's like 'What do I know about being old? I'm only 18'.
Gloria:	(2) ...
Guillermo:	Yes, I suppose you've got a point but I'd personally rather see a programme on entertainment or exciting stuff like what sports are going to be like in the future ...

39

3 Listen again and note down the phrases Gloria uses to check that she has understood what Guillermo has said.

 4 Look at these questions for Paper 5, Part 4 and listen to an example of a Part 4 discussion.

1 Tick the question with which the examiner opens the discussion.
   a) Which do you think young people enjoy watching more: documentaries or soap operas?
   b) Is television's main role to inform or to entertain?
   c) What changes do you both hope will take place over this century?
   d) Is there anything you hope will not happen?
   e) How can people prepare for the changes that will take place during their lifetimes?
   f) What are the main problems that will confront your country this century?

2 Write down the expresions Gloria and Guillermo use to add to and develop each other's comments.

5 Choose one other question from Exercise 4 and discuss it with a partner.

Grammar check: conditionals

1 Study the Grammar check on conditionals in *Advanced Gold Coursebook* p.58 and complete this text with an appropriate form of the verb in brackets.

2 Which of the sentences you have just completed is:
a) about something that is always true?
b) about something that is possible?
c) about something that is not true in the present and unlikely or impossible in the future?
d) about something that is imaginary in the past?

Writing: review

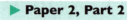 **Paper 2, Part 2**

About the exam: In Part 2 of Paper 2, you may have the option of writing a review. You could be asked to review any of the following: films, television programmes, books (fiction and non-fiction), exhibitions, concerts or other performances (dance, opera etc.).

You will generally be asked to review from a particular perspective e.g. why the film, book etc. would/would not be interesting for people of your own age. You may be asked to compare and contrast two performances, films etc. or even to compare two different things (e.g. a book with a film).

Strategy
Make sure your review includes the following elements in this order:
- background information.
- a *brief* account of the plot of the film, book or play or a *brief* description of the performance or exhibition.
- critical comment (either positive or negative) about what you saw or read.
- your personal opinion and recommendation.

Learner training
Read as many film reviews as you can, particularly those in English (the Internet is an excellent source). Analyse the elements they include. When you see a film write a short review in English afterwards.

SLEEPING IS GOOD FOR YOU

One thing anyone in the medical sciences will tell you is that if human beings and most other mammals don't get enough sleep, they (1) *will become* ill and can even die. It doesn't take long at all for the effects of a lack of sleep to be felt. If you have ever flown from one side of the world to the other or stayed up all night studying, you (2) … (know) just how badly even a minor disruption to our sleep patterns can affect us. Haven't we all gone along to exams or job interviews after a sleepless night and said to ourselves 'If I (3) … (have) a decent night's sleep, I would have performed so much better.'? If you (4) … (keep) a person awake for more than 72 hours they begin to have hallucinations and beyond that their physical and mental health deteriorates further.

But it is not just a problem of physical exhaustion. Even if we (5) … (be) able to lie down in a comfortable bed and rest, if we can't sleep, we (6) … (feel) tired the next day. What is less certain is why this should be so. Clearly if we (7) … (not spend) a third of our lives sleeping, we could accomplish much more. Sleep scientists study those fortunate people who, for whatever reason, need substantially smaller amounts of sleep than others. If they were able to unlock the secret of those who can get by on a couple of hours sleep a night, the rest of us (8) … (benefit) greatly, not least because we (9) … (not feel) so anxious, if, for some reason, we were unable to sleep from time to time.

1 Look at the review below of the film *Bicentennial Man*. The elements of the review have been jumbled. Put them in the right order.

A Despite the impressions that one might have after seeing the opening sequence *Bicentennial Man* is not a children's film. It's an epic for the entire family, exploring such themes as segregation and social prejudice. It is a profoundly moving tale which hopes to touch every audience member on a very personal level. It certainly succeeded with this cinema-goer. Perhaps it will with you too.

B The film begins awkwardly, struggling through a period of Andrew's life when he takes his first steps and performs his first mundane tasks. While this is certainly not excruciatingly tedious I was glad that the film began to pick up steam as we moved through the two hundred years. The character of Andrew is a rather disappointing piece that doesn't ask for any of the trademark flamboyance of the man who performed in such classics as Mrs. Doubtfire and Patch Adams. More noteworthy are Williams' co-stars Neill, Platt and Davidtz.

C Two hundred years is the length of Andrew Martin's life. Andrew (played by Robin Williams) is in fact a robot built and powered up for the first time in 2005 to function as a household servant for the Martin family. During the next few years, the Martins begin to notice characteristics which would set Andrew apart from all other robots: creativity, compassion and a desire for social contact. With their help Andrew begins to learn what it is to be human; but he also discovers that human society is reluctant to accept a robot as one of its number.

He employs a robot mechanic named Rupert Burns (Oliver Platt) to make him a more human facade and begins a subtle but powerful romance with Portia, the great-granddaughter (Embeth Davidtz) of his original owner (Sam Neill).

D Translating books to the screen is always difficult. To begin with fitting the average seventy-year life span of a human into two hours or less presents a hurdle, but directors of film versions of Isaac Asimov's tales face the even greater challenge of fitting hundreds and thousands of years into that same running time. In the case of *Bicentennial Man* this process of adaptation is hugely impressive. As the film's title suggests, what was involved was squeezing two hundred years into a movie of only 130 minutes in length.

2 Study the adverb–adjective collocations in *Advanced Gold Coursebook* Unit 5, p.57. Find three adverb–adjective collocations in the film review above. Then complete these sentences from reviews with a possible adverb or adjective.

1 The director of 'Redshift', William Holmes, has already had a highly .... career as a novelist.
2 Simon Barker looked .... ridiculous in red tights and a pink leotard.
3 On the whole I found 'Chaos at the College' .... disappointing.

3 Write a review in response to the following task. Read the strategy box again before you start writing.

TASK
You have been asked to write a **review** for your college's website of a film you have seen or of a book you have read. You should say why you feel the film or book is likely to be particularly worth seeing or reading for students of English. Write your **review** (250 words).

41

Reading: gapped text

▶ **Paper 1, Part 2**

About the exam: In Paper 1, Part 2 you will read a text from which six or seven paragraphs have been removed and placed after the text. You must decide from where in the text the paragraphs have been removed. There is only *one* correct answer in each case. There is *one* extra paragraph which does *not* belong in any of the gaps.

Strategy

1. Read the main text through to get a general idea of the structure and content. Pay attention to the following:
   - the information and ideas before and after each gap.
   - linking and reference words e.g. *Nevertheless*, *This concept*.
2. Read the extracted paragraphs and see if any of them obviously fit the gaps.
3. Go through the main text again. Stop at each gap and check each of the extracted paragraphs. Look for grammar and vocabulary links.
4. Read the complete text in sequence. Make sure that your answers make sense.

◀ Hot tip! ▶

Make sure you spend sufficient time checking your answers in this part of Paper 1. Remember! There is only *one* correct answer for each gap.

---

1 You are going to read a text about the possibility of holidays in space. Before you read write down two things that might stop these holidays becoming a reality. Now read the text and the jumbled paragraphs to see if any of your ideas were mentioned.

2 Look at the main text and the extracted paragraphs and underline any vocabulary or grammatical links between them. The first one has been done for you. Then decide which of the paragraphs A–H fit into the numbered gaps and read the complete text in sequence to make sure it makes sense.

A   Despite the low profile of these visits, public interest remains high. Surveys show that 60% of North Americans are interested in travelling in space and in Japan 80% of those over 40 said they wanted to visit space at least once in their lives.

B   But unlike exotic destinations on Earth space already has mass appeal thanks to dashing astronauts and glamorous missions like the Apollo lunar landings. What's more, this appeal is culturally broad-based. In a survey by the Japanese Rocket Society, 60% of Japanese respondents said they would be interested in some type of space travel. A similar survey in the United States also indicated significant interest among Americans.

C   'The notion of space walking from an oxygen-rich resort is rather like going scuba diving,' said Wolff. 'You put on a suit and enter another dimension.' Visitors could also experience space gardening using water rather than soil, and it has been suggested that surgery could be better applied in low or zero gravity. Many believe that weightlessness may hold or even reverse aging: an unbelievable concept for the health resort industry.

D   The weird part is that the low orbit space resort will only be 200 miles from earth. It is estimated that visitors could get there in just 90 minutes, which, incidentally, is how long it takes to circle the globe in an orbiting craft.

E   This makes sense as the most expensive part of establishing a space resort is getting things up there in the first place. The fuel tanks will be linked in a ring which will rotate to create a degree of artificial gravity. At the centre visitors will experience zero gravity, presumably the biggest thrill since bungee jumping.

F   It might be quite comfortable once you get there but booking a holiday in space will not be all that simple. Potential visitors to the space resort will go through an orientation in ground-based theme hotels and resorts that will simulate the conditions beforehand.

G   Here in the UK, travel agents Thomas Cook began taking names for 'Lunar Tours' as far back as 1956 in the event that commercial space travel ever materialised. With 10,000 names on the list by November 1996, they closed the database. Since then Wildwings, an independent travel agency, have been taking deposits from punters eager for a place in the stars.

H   However, Buzz Aldrin, the second man to walk on the moon, believes space tourism should not be restricted to the very rich. He has a concept of an international lottery system which will generate funds and also guarantee space trips for ordinary people – that is if you can afford £50 per lottery ticket.

42

UNIT 5 Where will it end?

YOUR FLIGHT INTO LOW EARTH ORBIT IS NOW BOARDING ...

Imagine it. New Year's Eve 2017. You're contemplating a great year ahead with an extra special holiday. Do you choose Tasmania, Zanzibar or Alaska perhaps? Well, they're all rather dull. How about a jaunt to earth's lower orbit and that way you get to see the whole world in one trip?

It may sound far-fetched, but there are plenty of companies out there already actively probing commercial space travel. Two American tour operators are already taking reservations for your flight into space. Passengers will travel to an altitude of 62 miles with a few minutes of weightlessness thrown in. Estimated departure date: 2002. The ticket: a mere $100,000.

1

Yet even if you can get tourists to book up well in advance, there's nowhere to stay. It's no wonder that the challenge of designing a resort in space is the next big thing. Wimberly Allison Tong & Goo (WAT&G), a firm of international hospitality and leisure architects based in Hawaii, have already started drawing up plans. Vice-president Howard Wolff explains, 'We are working on a concept of recycling future space shuttle external fuel tanks into a resort which will be a cross between a theme park and a cruise ship. These tanks are currently burnt up on return to earth. We will salvage them and convert them.'

2

'The reason we want a resort with both low gravity and zero gravity is to make sure we offer the feeling of weightlessness as an attraction and yet guard against space sickness, which 50% of astronauts experience,' said Wolff. 'It also makes sense to offer some of the creature comforts of earth such as showers and toilets, not to mention a night's rest without having to be strapped down.'

3

There's still the transport problem to resolve as well. The development of space resort transport is taking two paths. The first is a single reusable craft which takes off like a shuttle. The second is in two phases. The first takes off like a normal aeroplane. At a second stage a rocket would propel it out of the earth's atmosphere.

4

And now it gets even more weird. 'If you circle the earth every 90 minutes, you have daylight and night every 45 minutes,' said Wolff. 'The plan is to have bedrooms without windows, first because they would be extremely expensive and secondly because seeing the days and nights flashing before their eyes is bound to exacerbate space sickness.'

That might not sound very appealing, but if we adapt what we like to do on earth to the space context, the implications are spell-binding as everything takes on an extra dimension. Games like football, played on a two dimensional pitch on earth, suddenly become three dimensional. Taking space walks is another possibility, followed by visits to space stations like Mir or the International Space Station, due for completion in 2003.

5

But who's putting up the cash? NASA say they don't want to be involved with space tourism and the British National Space Centre are not interested either, and say that they would never send a human into space if they could send a robot instead. It seems that the companies putting time and money into research will have to rely on luxury hotel chains to commission their resorts. Initially only five-star tourists seem destined to go on space holidays.

6

Apart from astronauts, cosmonauts and scientists, three people have in fact already taken a package tour of space, though the details have not been widely publicised. British woman Helen Sherman spent nine days on Mir while two Japanese businessmen paid £5 million to join a Russian space trip in 1997.

7

Perhaps this common interest shows that man has been pursuing the wrong objectives with space technology. Rather than send a space elite reaching for other worlds, a more rational approach would be to concentrate on cheapening the process of getting more people into orbit.

Grammar plus: conditionals (advanced features)

1 Study the Grammar Plus section of the *Advanced Gold Coursebook* Unit 5, p.62 and the Grammar Reference section on conditionals (p.192). One of each of the pairs of sentences below is an example of one of the following uses of conditionals. Match the sentences to the uses. Which:

A is more formal?
B emphasises that something is a chance possibility?
C is a more polite form?
D makes an event seem more hypothetical?
E makes a request more polite?

1 a) Had she realised her research would have be used in this way, she would never have published it.
   b) If she had realised her research would be used in this way, she would never have published it.
2 a) If you happen to pass the theatre, can you book some tickets for next week's concert?
   b) If you pass the theatre, can you book some tickets for next week's concert?
3 a) Supposing you won the lottery, would you give up working?
   b) If you won the lottery, would you give up working?
4 a) If you were to live to be 200, life would probably still hold some surprises.
   b) If you lived to be 200, life would probably still hold some surprises.
5 a) If you'll just hold the line for a moment, I'll put you through to the laboratory.
   b) If you just hold the line for a moment, I'll put you through to the laboratory.

2 Match the clauses in A to the clauses in B to form sentences.

A
a) **Had she known** she was going to live that long,
b) **Supposing you had** the chance to have yourself cloned,
c) **If** space travel **were to** become less expensive,
d) **Imagine you had** smok**ed** until you were 117,
e) **If you will** be so kind as to just take a seat,
f) **If you happen to** be going to London any time in the next few months,
g) **If** her condition **should** change in any way,

B
1 please be so kind as to notify me immediately.
2 would you do it?
3 could you possibly get me a copy of 'Galileo's Daughter'?
4 the doctor will be with you in a moment.
5 would you consider booking a holiday on a space resort?
6 would you bother to give up?
7 she would certainly not have retired so early.

3 Use the structures in bold from Exercises 1 and 2 to modify the meaning of these sentences according to the instructions in brackets.

1 If I told you I was thinking of leaving my job, what would you say? (more hypothetical)
2 If scientists had realised the damage their discovery could do, they would almost certainly have suppressed the information. (more formal)
3 If you take the time to read the instructions, you will see that the machine should never be immersed in water. (more polite)
4 If you pass a chemist's while you're out, could you buy me a bottle of aspirin? (more polite)
5 If you won first prize in a lottery, would you move to Monte Carlo? (more hypothetical)
6 If you require further information, do not hesitate to contact me. (more polite)

UNIT 5 **Where will it end?**

Vocabulary: science and medicine

Use a form of the word printed at the end of each line to fill the numbered gaps in this text.

BREAKTHROUGHS OR DISASTERS?

Of all the (1) ... breakthroughs of the late twentieth century, undoubtedly the one that proved most controversial was the (2) ... of Dolly the sheep in Scotland in 1997. Twenty years had gone by since the first successful 'in vitro' (3) ... and transfer at the (4) ... stage that led to the birth of 'Baby Louise'. Despite the benefits that (5) ... engineering might offer, many people had doubts about the (6) ... of humans by other than natural means and the potential dangers of (7) ... individuals learning the techniques and applying them for profit or other ends. (8) ... had received similar reactions when they first succeeded in splitting the atom. People feared that this (9) ... would lead to the creation of nuclear weapons that would (10) ... humanity. They were not wrong. The Second World War ended with the use of these terrible weapons of mass (11) ... .

science
clone
fertile
embryo
gene
reproduce
ethics
physics
develop
threat
destroy

Vocabulary: collocation (body)

1 Study the Vocabulary section of *Advanced Gold Coursebook* on collocation (body) (p.63). Connect the words on the right to the words on the left.

All but one of these collocations include a possessive adjective (*his, her, my* etc.). Which collocation is the odd one out?

a) hold
b) drum
c) shrug
d) wrinkle
e) crack
f) purse
g) clench
h) twist
i) pull
j) raise
k) shake
l) lick

1 eyebrows
2 fingers
3 lips
4 breath
5 head
6 shoulders
7 nose
8 lips
9 knuckles
10 muscle
11 fist
12 ankle

2 Use the collocations to fill in the gaps in these sentences.

1 Sometimes .... can help you calm down when you feel angry.
2 I wish you'd stop .... on the table like that. I'll be ready in a minute.
3 She asked him why he had broken the window and he just ....
4 I don't think the cat likes that new cat food. He just .... and walked away from the bowl when I put it out for him.
5 When they were told the tragic news they just .... in disbelief.
6 The sound of you .... makes me feel quite sick. I do wish you wouldn't do it.
7 She never says anything when I tell her I'm going to be late home but I know she doesn't like it because she .... and gives me a really filthy look.
8 The angry driver .... and shook it at the pedestrian who had stepped out in front of his car.
9 Ouch! I think I've .... in my leg!
10 If you wear those platform soles you're bound to fall and ....
11 The only thing she ever did to show disagreement was to .... when he expressed a particularly bizarre opinion about something.
12 Everyone was .... and asking for a second helping of Toby's famous vegetarian lasagne.

45

English in Use: error correction (spelling and punctuation)

▶ **Paper 3, Part 3**

About the exam: In one of the two alternative tasks in Paper 3, Part 3 you are asked to identify spelling and punctuation errors in a short text.

> **Strategy**
>
> Read the text through to get the general idea. Read the text again sentence by sentence. Look for the following PUNCTUATION ERRORS:
> *Lack* of:
> - capital letters • commas • full stops • apostrophes • brackets
>
> Look at each word in turn and look for the following SPELLING ERRORS:
> - silent letters that have been omitted e.g. ~~det~~ – de**b**t
> - spelling of suffixes and prefixes e.g. respons~~able~~ – responsibl**e**, ~~des~~advantage – disadvantage
> - homophones e.g. She ~~nose~~ – knows.
> - doubling of consonants e.g. o~~cas~~sion – occa**ss**ion

Hot tip!

As in the other type of error correction exercise, there are usually no more than five correct lines. If you have not found errors in at least ten lines, check again the lines in which you have not found errors.

In the text below the following errors occur:
- omitted letters × 2
- misspelled prefixes or suffixes × 4
- wrong homophone × 2
- mistakes with commas × 2
- mistakes with apostrophes × 1

Find the mistakes and correct them. There are examples at 0, 00 and 000 that have been done for you.

LIVING TO BE 125

0 ✓	The human organism is made up of an estimated 100,000
00 **,**	genes/ all of which will have been completely described
000 *c*	by the year 2005, if not before. By that time, a/cording to
1	the predictions we will not only be able to find the genes
2	that heel the sick, but those that make us ill in the first place.
3	We will have invented new drugs to cure diseases such as
4	Alzheimer's or cancer and vaccines to protect us from AIDS
5	and malaria. Scientists may have even found a way to grow
6	organs for transplants. In 1900, the average Europeans life
7	expectancy was fifty. By 2050, it will not be unnusual to live
8	to be at least ninty. One way our lives might be extended is
9	through the theraputic use of genes to protect us from disease
10	and strengthen our resistence against the ravages of time.
11	Geneticists have already established the location of the gene
12	responsable for keeping time in each cell and helping us know
13	weather it is morning or night. The next step will be to find the
14	gene that determines the rate, at which we grow old. We will
15	think of aging not as inevitable but as a situation that we can control.

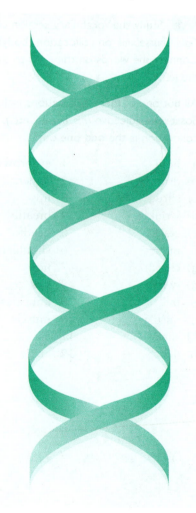

46

UNIT 6 The sporting life

Grammar plus: futures (advanced features)

1 Match the advanced features used to express the future in A to their meanings in B.

A
1 The building is due to be demolished next year.
2 Students wishing to take part in the swimming carnival are to put their names on the list outside the changing rooms by next Wednesday.
3 I'm on the point of saying something to the club president about the state of the courts.
4 You'd better phone her. I'm pretty sure she won't have been told that she's been chosen for the team.
5 By the end of this month the builders will have finished the work they're doing on the pool.
6 Will you be using the badminton court between eleven and twelve tomorrow?
7 By the end of this decade the top players will be earning even more than they do today.

B
a) expresses an assumption
b) makes a polite enquiry
c) says something will be complete by a particular time in the future
d) says something will be in progress in the future
e) refers to the next moment
f) indicates a previously scheduled time
g) indicates a formal arrangement

2 Read this conversation below between two college students. For each gap put the verb in the brackets into one of the future forms from Exercise 1. You will need to use each of these future forms at least once.

Sandrine: Incredible, isn't it?
Sebastian: What?
Sandrine: Oh, of course you (1) ... (**hear**).
Sebastian: Heard what?
Sandrine: The principal says we're not allowed to use the sports hall for the end-of-year disco.
Sebastian: You must be joking!
Sandrine: No, I'm not, unfortunately. He says they (2) ... (**have**) the floor re-varnished the following week and that they need to get it ready over the weekend for the workmen to come in.
Sebastian: And I suppose we (3) ... (**reprint**) all the posters and invitations saying that 'due to unforeseen circumstances it (4) ... (**be**) held on the football pitch'.
Sandrine: That's right! How did you know?
Sebastian: Oh, it's just so typical of him. He (5) ... (**demand**) we wear uniforms next!
Sandrine: Just let him try! Thank heavens he (6) ... (**retire**) next year.
Sebastian: Just think! He (7) ... (**rule**) this college with his iron fist for five whole years by then. Actually, I heard a rumour the other day that he (8) ... (**resign**) over that argument he had with Elena Pérez.
Sandrine: Oh, that (9) ... (**get**) everyone in administration really excited, I bet. I wonder if both of them (10) ... (**come**) to the disco.

3 Choose between the two given alternatives to complete each sentence.

a) 'Will Susi be coming/Will Susi have come to volleyball practice next week?' the coach asked the girl's mother politely.
b) Wilson is picking up the javelin and is on the point of attempting/will be attempting to break his own world record.
c) By the year 2015 experts predict women will have beaten/will be beating men in some sports on a regular basis.
d) Sports shoes with black or coloured soles will not have been worn/are not to be worn inside the gym at any time. They mark the floor.
e) Hurry up! The match is about to start/is due to start in five minutes.
f) Don't tell me the result! I know we will be thrashed/will have been thrashed yet again.
g) The referee is due to/is about to blow his whistle to indicate the start.
h) By the end of the season our team will have scored/will be scoring more goals than anyone else in the second division.

Reading: multiple matching

▶ **Paper 1, Parts 1 and 4**

About the exam: The questions are not presented in the same order as the information in the text(s). You may find the answer to a question in any position or in any of the texts.

> **Strategy**
>
> Look at a question and scan each text to find the relevant information. Try starting from different positions in the text(s).

┌─ **Hot tip!** ◀─
│
│ You do not need to understand the
│ meaning of every word in the text(s).
│ Pausing to worry about unfamiliar
│ words will slow down your reading
│ speed too much.
└─

1 You are going to read a magazine article about long-distance water sports. One of these places is NOT mentioned in the article. Which one: New Zealand, Australia, Colorado, San Francisco, Florida, Portugal, London, Hawaii, the Canary Islands, Guadalupe, Russia, the Azores, Brittany?

2 For each question, scan the texts to find the relevant information. Choose your answers from the list of athletes on the right. Note that where more than one answer is required, these may be given in any order.

WHICH OF THE PEOPLE:		
was completely alone?	1 ...	
wore special protective clothing?	2 ...	
did not consider giving up?	3 ...	
developed an intense dislike of the environment?	4 ...	
found the environment helped them keep going?	5 ...	**A** Ben Lecomte
achieved something many others had failed to do?	6 ...	
may not have broken a record?	7 ...	
believed there was a real possibility that they would die?	8 ...	**B** Lynne Cox
had been told that they might encounter sharks?	9 ...	
did not rest?	10 ...	
used no modern technical devices?	11 ...	
probably covered two times the distance between the start and finish?	12 ...	**C** Tori Murden
dedicated what they did to the memory of a relative?	13 ...	
found cold a major obstacle?	14 ...	
had tried to do the same thing before?	15 ...	**D** Steve Smith
will make a financial contribution to medicine?	16 ...	
realised they had made a mistake in the very early stages of their attempt?	17 ...	
frequently found what they were doing extremely dull?	18 ...	
almost gave up at one point?	19 ...	
ignored medical advice?	20 ...	

48

JUST YOU AND THE OCEAN

Taking on the loneliness of crossing a stretch of ocean 'under our own steam' is something few of us contemplate attempting. Here are the stories of four extraordinary individuals who are the exception to the rule.

A   Ben Lecomte

After overcoming sharks, internal demons and an arm injury, a 31-year-old French-born American became, on 25th September 1998, the first man to 'swim' the North Atlantic.

Ben Lecomte staggered ashore near Quiberon in Brittany after swimming 3,736 miles from Cape Cod in Massachusetts over a period of ten weeks. His spokeswoman, Colleen Turner, was among a large group of friends who greeted him. 'He said he is very happy to feel sand between his toes but his first words were "never again",' she said.

Lecomte's swim included a 500-mile detour in the Azores, after an emotional crisis in which he lost the will to continue. His claim to have set a new long distance swimming record was open to question. He spent seven days ashore in the Azores and he passed some of the Atlantic crossing, between swimming sessions, drifting on currents in his support boat. He undertook the swim as a tribute to his father, who died of cancer in 1991, and expects to raise £50,000 for cancer research.

Lecomte swam for six or eight hours each day, in two-hour sessions. He wore a giant 'monofin' flipper on both legs and was protected from sharks by a force-field of electro-magnetic signals emitted from his support yacht.

Almost at the end of his swim Lecomte said that although France was getting closer, he was 'so tired' and still had to wear two wetsuits because of the cold water. He had been rising at 6 a.m. and swimming an average of four miles an hour. At one point, he was followed by a great white shark. He said he didn't know exactly how big it was but he could see it moving back and forth about 30 feet below him.

B   Lynne Cox

At 9.30 a.m. on August 7, 1987, Lynne Cox jumped feet first from a rock on the shore of Little Diomede island into the frigid Arctic Ocean and set out for Big Diomede. Between the two tiny islands lies the international dateline that bisects the channel that divides them and marks the boundary line between the United States and Russia.

Although the islands are only 2.4 miles apart, Cox would be forced by the strong currents to swim nearly twice as far. The water temperature in the strait would vary from 1°C to 6°C. She was warned about the presence of walruses and sharks but refused to use a shark cage, wear a wetsuit or coat her body in lanolin grease.

She had arranged only to be accompanied by two canoes. One boat contained five journalists and the other three doctors including an expert on the effect of cold on the human body, who had provided Cox with a thermo-sensitive capsule containing a tiny transmitter. It was essential that her inner body temperature never drop below 33.8°C. She swallowed the capsule before the swim and every twenty minutes while she was in the ocean she rolled on to her back and one of the doctors pointed a radio receiver at her stomach in order to register a digital reading.

Fifty yards from shore the cliffs of Big Diomede loomed above Cox. The closest point of land was a rock directly ahead of her, but a welcoming committee was waiting to receive her half a mile away on a snow bank. Cox knew that to get that extra half mile would mean swimming against a current, with three degree water racing north to the Chukchi Sea. The doctors told her to land but she refused. She explained later, 'Touching a rock rather than someone's hand would have meant so much less. I had to keep going.'

C   Tori Murden

Having braved hurricanes and bouts of despair 36-year-old Tori Murden paddled to the shore of the island of Guadalupe in December, 1999 and became the first woman to row across the Atlantic alone. As she docked her boat to complete her 3,000-mile odyssey some 81 days, seven hours and 31 minutes after leaving the Canary Islands near the coast of Africa, Murden said, 'Next time, the Concorde.'

It was her second attempt at a transatlantic passage that had eluded many other athletes, and it nearly ended in disaster because of Hurricane Lenny. Lenny's centre passed within five miles of Murden, whipping up 20-foot waves that upended her 23-foot boat and hurled her into the sea. Using her only connection to the world – a satellite telephone – Murden warned friends that 'if the worst hasn't passed, I'm out of here'. It was a far cry from an earlier stage when she had believed she might have a chance of breaking the transatlantic record of 73 days, set in 1970. On September 30, Murden rowed an astounding 95 miles. Whale and dolphin sightings, calm mornings and signs of land – birds and insects – served to inspire the rower.

She ate energy bars and freeze-dried meals and drank water from a desalinating pump, powered by solar panels that also charged the batteries of her computer, the phone and the lights. At night, she closed the hatches, tied down her oars and slept on a hammock-like cloth, waking occasionally to check the boat's position. By late in the day, she often had to fight boredom. 'It is very slow, tedious work,' she said at one point.

D   Steve Smith

One half of a British partnership attempting to make the first human-powered circumnavigation of the globe has given up halfway through. Steve Smith, 32, who conceived the 29,000-mile Pedal for the Planet expedition seven years ago, jumped ship in Hawaii, claiming that he had created a monster he could no longer control. 'For me the expedition was always intended as an attempt to live close to the earth, but by day two, the harsh realities hit: seasickness, chronic fatigue and no variety of colour, sound or smell. The deep ocean is a lifeless desert.' But despite Smith's disillusionment, his partner, 31-year-old Jason Lewis, is determined to continue with his friend's dream and raise money for the Council for Education in World Citizenship.

The attempt began in the mid 1990s when Smith discovered that no one had ever circumnavigated the globe entirely by human power. After several years of planning, he and Lewis finished construction of their 26-foot wooden pedal boat. They started out by mountain bike from Greenwich Observatory in London in July 1994, using the pedal boat to cross the Channel before continuing to Portugal by mountain bike. They then spent four months crossing the Atlantic. After landing in Florida, they headed for San Francisco, Smith going by mountain bike, Lewis by rollerblades. But in Colorado, Lewis was hit by a car, breaking both legs. It was three years before they could continue their journey, leaving the Golden Gate Bridge in September, 1998.

They intended to reach Australia by the Millennium, but by the time they got to Hawaii, Smith had suffered enough. Lewis, meanwhile was pedalling furiously on the 2,200-mile next leg of the journey. Even if he makes it to Australia, Lewis will still have to kayak through the Indonesian islands and cycle through Asia and Europe before finally crossing the Channel, this time by man-powered airship.

Grammar check: modifiers and intensifiers

Study the Grammar Check section on modifiers and intensifiers in the *Advanced Gold Coursebook* p.74. Read this text about running marathons. Choose the most appropriate word to fill in each gap from the two options given below.

WHY RUN 26.2 MILES?

It is a(n) (1) ... life-changing event that requires 37,000 steps, hundreds of miles of training and a(n) (2) ... strong will. It can be physically and emotionally draining and is almost always (3) ... humbling. Why would anyone choose (4) ... willingly to run a marathon?

'A marathon is a 26.2-mile test. You have to be (5) ... committed to finish the race. It's not a team sport. Nobody picks up those legs and puts them down for you,' says Bill Wenmark, director of the American Lung Association Runners' Club. 'A marathon is definitely a notch above almost any other distance run,' he continued. 'There's an appeal and the mystique of trying to tackle that great a challenge.'

The mystique dates to 490 BC when a soldier ran from the Plain of Marathon to Athens to announce the news of a Greek victory over the invading Persians. He was (6) ... exhausted and dropped dead when he got to Athens. It was this event that inspired the Olympic Officials to include a 25-mile race from Marathon to Athens in the 1896 Olympics. The present distance originated in England in 1908 because King Edward VII was (7) ... determined to see the start of the race from his home, Windsor Castle. The distance from Windsor Castle to London is 26 miles, 385 yards.

Many distance runners are (8) ... mesmerised by the mystique of the historic Boston Marathon. John Naslund, a 46-year-old stockbroker, is no exception. He became (9) ... obsessed with marathon running, competing in Boston and another 130 marathons. 'I guess I was pretty single-minded about running. I'd run one marathon and then couldn't wait to run the next. I've never been (10) ... concerned about winning though. What matters to me is finishing.'

1	A rather	B absolutely	6 A very	B completely
2	A very	B quite	7 A absolutely	B pretty
3	A pretty	B absolutely	8 A completely	B terribly
4	A terribly	B completely	9 A totally	B very
5	A totally	B rather	10 A terribly	B rather

UNIT 6 The sporting life

English in Use: word formation

▶ **Paper 3, Part 4**

About the exam: There are 15 items in the word formation task in Paper 3. The most common transformations are: noun to adjective/adverb, verb to noun, verb to adjective/adverb, noun to verb. There is always at least one item that involves the use of a prefix (*un-, dis-, il/im* etc.)

Strategy

Read the text straight though once to get an idea of meaning. Read it again and decide what part of speech is needed in each gap. Always check that the word you have formed is not only grammatically appropriate but also makes sense in the context. If it doesn't, you may need to add a prefix.

Hot tip!

Check your spelling once you have formed the word. The most common spelling mistakes are:
- doubling consonants when you add a prefix
  (e.g. *dis + approve* = one 's' only)
- omitting the consonant at the end of the prefix
  (e.g. *un + necessarily* = two 'n's)
- failing to double a consonant when you have added an ending (e.g. *occurrence*)
- leaving 'e' in after you have added an ending
  (e.g. *advis**e**able* ✗ *advisable* ✓)

LEARNING TO SURF

Anyone who has ever (1) .... stood up on a surfboard and carved through the water will not deny that it is an (2) .... experience. Gaining (3) .... of the technique is not easy, though. It is certainly worth paying for some qualified (4) .... before you venture into the waves. You should also get (5) .... on what kind of board to buy. The (6) .... of the board is a particularly crucial (7) .... Inevitably, you will be a bit (8) .... at first but after you've caught your first wave, your (9) .... will improve. A few more waves, plus the necessary practice to improve your paddling (10) ...., and you will be beginning to derive the kind of (11) .... from this ancient sport that causes (12) .... normal people to organise their lives around it. Of course, the perfect wave can be (13) .... but weather should never be a (14) .... The enormous (15) .... of modern wetsuits available will keep you warm and dry whatever the weather.

SUCCESS
FORGET
MASTER
COACH
ADVISE
LONG
DECIDE
SHAKE
CONFIDENT
ABLE
ENJOY
OTHER
ELUDE
DETER
VARY

51

Vocabulary: language of gender

1 Study this vocabulary section in the *Advanced Gold Coursebook* p.74 and fill in the gaps in these sentences with one of the following expressions with *man*. You may need to change the expression in some cases to fit grammatically into the sentence.

a) a man of the people
b) man an office (verb)
c) be your own man
d) every man for himself
e) man in the street
f) man (noun)
g) a man of my word
h) as one man

1 I'm sorry, but I can't lend you my notes at the moment. It's *every man for himself* at exam time, you know.
2 The centre *man an office* around the clock by friendly, well-trained medical personnel.
3 The crowd jumped to their feet and cheered *as one man*.
4 I'm *a man of my word*. I said I'd pay for you to go to the States if you passed your exams and I will.
5 He's one of those politicians who likes to think of himself as *a man of the people*. He's always going round shaking people's hands and kissing babies.
6 You should always try to *be your own man* and not let others persuade you to do things you believe are wrong.
7 The average *man in the street* is probably not particularly bothered about whether girls get to play football or not.
8 *Man*, while longing for peace, has always been at war.

2 Replace the expressions with *man* with non-sexist expressions.

3 Find words in this wordsearch grid for:

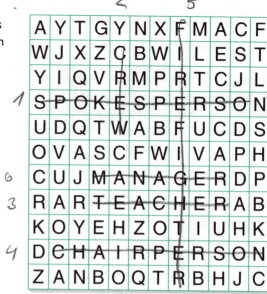

1 a person who is in charge of a meeting
2 people who look after the comfort of passengers while they are on a flight
3 a person who teaches in a primary or secondary school
4 a person chosen to speak officially for a group
5 a person who puts out fires
6 a person who manages a business or other activity

Writing

▶ **Paper 2, Part 1**

About the exam: In Paper 2, Part 1 the task often includes a brochure, leaflet or letter and notes that have been made on it. You incorporate this information into your answer. You are expected to use your own words and to avoid repeating the same wording as the task input.

Strategy
Spend some time when you plan your answer thinking of other ways to express the ideas included in the task.

◀ **Hot tip!** ▶

Make sure you have written the required number of words! Work out how many words you normally get to a line and count the lines of your draft. You may lose marks for writing less than the required number of words – and for writing a lot more.

Look at this task and the answer a student wrote. The student has not followed the instructions in a number of important ways. She has also used a lot of the same words as there are in the input. Decide what is wrong with the student's answer and then write an answer of your own that follows the instructions accurately and uses different wording.

TASK

You recently joined a local gym. You paid for a year's membership but now a month later you are very disappointed with the facilities and have decided to write to the director to ask for your money back. Read the original brochure from the gym (and the notes you wrote on it) and part of an e-mail message from a friend who you told about joining the gym. Then using this information:

1. write a letter (200 words) to the Director of 'Fighting Fit' telling her why you are so dissatisfied and want your money back.
2. write an e-mail message (50 words) to your friend, telling her what you have decided to do.

---

subject: hi

Hi,

Great to hear from you and glad to know you had a good Christmas.

By the way, you know that gym you said you'd joined? I'm thinking of joining it too. Can you send me the details? Happy New Year!

Love,
Sara

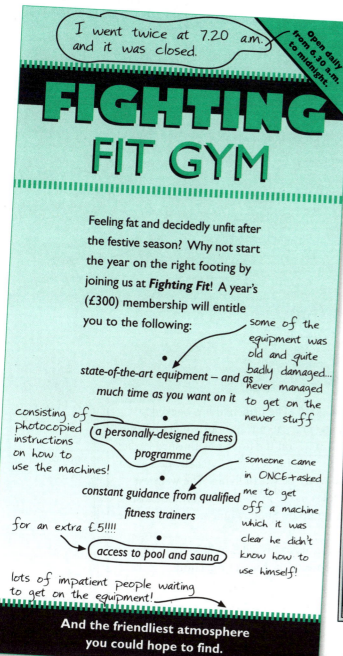

Dear Sir,

I am writing to complain about your gym, which I joined immediately after Christmas. I am sorry to have to tell you that I am extremely dissatisfied with the facilities.

Firstly, you say in your brochure that the membership fee is £300, but I had to pay almost £500. Why was that? Secondly, it says that you have state-of-the-art equipment, but most of it was very old and badly damaged. I never managed to get on any of the newer machines. Finally, the pool was filthy and the sauna was always closed when I went there. Furthermore, the personal trainers were all very impatient and unfriendly.

I look forward to hearing from you in the near future,

Yours sincerely,

Sonia Delgado

Sonia Delgado

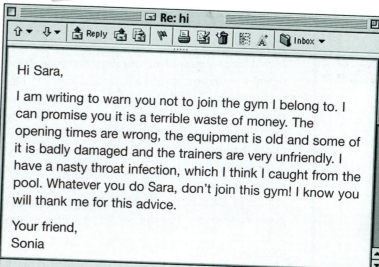

Hi Sara,

I am writing to warn you not to join the gym I belong to. I can promise you it is a terrible waste of money. The opening times are wrong, the equipment is old and some of it is badly damaged and the trainers are very unfriendly. I have a nasty throat infection, which I think I caught from the pool. Whatever you do Sara, don't join this gym! I know you will thank me for this advice.

Your friend,
Sonia

English in Use: register transfer

▶ **Paper 3, Part 5**

About the exam: In Paper 3, Part 5 you are required to read two texts and transfer information from one to the other. The second text will have gaps and will be written in a different 'register' from the first. You must complete each gap with no more than two words. Do NOT use words from the first text.

Strategy

1. Read the complete text once before you start attempting to complete the gaps.
2. Make sure you understand the meaning of each sentence including gaps.
3. Refer to the equivalent part of the first text to check the exact meaning of the missing part.
4. Decide on the part of speech of the missing word(s).
5. Complete the gap paying careful attention to the form and spelling of the words you insert.

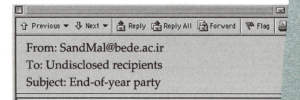

Check your answers to make absolutely sure you have not included any words from the first text.

SAINT BEDE'S COLLEGE founded 1935

Principal's Office
Saint Bede's College
Waterford

Sandrine Malone
President of the Students' Union
Box 236
Union House
Saint Bede's College
Waterford

24th May 2003

Dear Ms Malone,

I am writing to let you know that I have been able to reconsider my decision about the use of the sports hall for the annual summer party and discotheque.

As you know, I understood that the hall would be unavailable because of the need for long overdue maintenance work on the floor to be undertaken. Fortunately, this has been completed well ahead of schedule and the hall is already open for use by sports hall members.

To prevent damage to the facilities and inconvenience to users, however, I must ask you to impose the following rules on those attending and organising the party:

1 no footwear with black or coloured soles to be worn inside the gym area
2 no smoking
3 all clearing up to be completed by Sunday lunchtime
4 all rubbish to be deposited in skips at campus gates

I look forward to having the opportunity of presenting you and the other committee members to my wife at the party.

Yours sincerely,

John Cross

Principal

From: SandMal@bede.ac.ir
To: Undisclosed recipients
Subject: End-of-year party

Hi All,

Incredible as it may seem, our demonstration did some good. The principal has backed down! I've (0) *just* opened a letter that says he's changed (1) … about the sports hall and that we can use it after all. Apparently, the work they were (2) … on the floor was finished earlier than (3) … . In fact, he says that people are already (4) … again. Anyway, typically he's given me a list of rules that everyone (5) … follow or my life won't be worth living. The weirdest one is that we are (6) … to wear shoes with coloured soles in the gym. Predictably, he's also (7) … a total ban on smoking. We have to (8) … clearing up by Sunday lunchtime and all the rubbish has to (9) … in the skips near the gates.

Horror of horrors, he says he's looking forward to (10) … us to his wife, so he's obviously planning to come. You can bet I'll be giving his shoes a pretty thorough inspection!

Take care,
Sandrine

54

UNIT 7 The ties that bind

Speaking: weak forms

Listen to the recording and mark the weak forms in these sentences.

EXAMPLE *My sister would <u>have</u> loved <u>to</u> be able <u>to</u> come <u>to the</u> wedding.*

1 I didn't know your father came from Greece.
2 How long have your family been living in Canada?
3 Do you think of yourself as Greek or Canadian?
4 Have you got any older brothers and sisters?
5 What does your sister do?
6 Has your sister-in-law finished university?
7 How many children do your sister-in-law and brother have?
8 Do you think they'll have any more?
9 How old are the children?

Vocabulary: word + prepositions (1)

Study the Vocabulary section on word + prepositions in the *Advanced Gold Coursebook* p.85. Now look at the sentences below. In eight of them an incorrect preposition has been used. Find the incorrect prepositions and replace them with appropriate prepositions.

1 One of the reasons many musicians get frustrated is that they are always striving at perfection.
2 Because of that, they are never entirely satisfied for their performances.
3 In some cases the musicians' teachers have been very demanding and this has had an influence in their development.
4 Even when they get excellent reviews they are not convinced by them and always believe they could have played better.
5 How well musicians cope with the stress of a career as a performer depends at how well they can control feelings of self-doubt.
6 According with some experts, extreme cases of stage fright are more common among student musicians.
7 Withdrawal of approval by a respected teacher can represent a major crisis for young musicians.
8 There has been a marked reduction on the number of jobs in orchestras in the last few years.
9 Failure to find paid work can lead on a loss of motivation for the musician.
10 Young musicians usually have considerable respect to conductors and senior members of the orchestra.

Grammar check: hypothetical meaning

1 Study the section on hypothetical meaning on p.86 of the *Advanced Gold Coursebook*. Complete each of the following sentences in a meaningful way by choosing one of the options given.

1 I know Adela wishes she *has/would have/could have* another baby, but the doctor says it might not be possible.
2 If only I *hadn't got/wouldn't have got/didn't get* so angry with Patrick last time we met.
3 I'd rather we *wait/waited/had waited* before telling Billy he's going to have a little brother.
4 I wish you *would visit/would have visited/had visited* your grandmother a little more often now that she's so frail.
5 If only Grandpa *would be/has been/were* alive to see this.
6 Don't you sometimes wish you and Dad *would not get/did not get/had not got* married when you were so young?
7 I really wish I *would go/could go/went* to Australia for my nephew's wedding.
8 It's high time you children *start/will start/started* helping your mother around the house a bit more.
9 I wish I *did/would/will* not live so far away from the rest of my family.
10 Suppose you *have had/had had/would have had* triplets instead of twins. Do you think you would have been able to manage?

2 Complete these sentences in your own words.

1 I know the older members of my family wish the younger ones ....
2 If I had the choice, I'd rather my family ....
3 I really wish I ....
4 If only my family ....
5 It's high time young people in my country ....
6 Suppose .... ? Would people be happier?

55

Reading: multiple choice

▶ Paper 1, Part 3

About the exam: In Paper 1, Part 3 you answer between five and seven multiple-choice questions after reading a text. The questions follow the order of the text. The last question is often about the text as a whole and asks you about the attitude or opinion of the writer, the reader or someone mentioned in the text.

Strategy

After reading the whole text through to get a general idea of what it is about, concentrate on each of the questions in turn. Read the parts of the text that each question refers to very carefully, paying particular attention to attitudes and opinions. These are often expressed through modal verbs (*should, may, might, would* etc.). In the final question make sure you know whose attitude you are being asked about.

─ Hot tip! ◀ ─
There is only ever ONE possible answer

1 Look at the photograph and the title of the text. Think of three possible connections between the title and the photograph. Read the text to see if any of your connections were mentioned.

A FAMILY TRAGEDY

Today, Cecile Dionne looks much like any other suburban grandmother, but she and her four identical sisters were once the most celebrated[a] children on the face of the planet. They were known to the world as the Dionne Quintuplets.

5 25-year-old Elzire Dionne, the wife of a proud and struggling French-Canadian farmer named Oliva, and already the mother of five children, gave birth to the quintuplets in May, 1934. Identical sisters developed from a single egg, they were born two months premature in the
10 family home in rural Ontario. No one expected the five tiny infants to survive, least of all the country doctor who helped deliver them. [1]But when Annette, Emilie, Yvonne, Cecile and Marie did – the first quintuplets ever to do so – they quickly became a sensation.

15 Within days of their birth, their father sold a promoter the rights to exhibit his daughters. He was to keep 23 per cent of admission fees. Stung by the resultant public outcry[b], the Ontario government stepped in. The girls were taken away from their parents and placed under the care of
20 a board of guardians excluding both Oliva and Elzire Dionne. 'Their parents were viewed as nothing more than a nuisance,' says John Nihmey, co-author of a book about the quints.

It was not long, however, before the guardians, too,
25 began to exploit them. The Ontario authorities built a nine-room nursery on Oliva's farm right across the road from the family home, later expanding it into a bizarre facility nicknamed 'Quintland'. It included a horseshoe-shaped observatory, where crowds peered[c] through screened glass
30 windows while the little girls played. The quints soon developed into a major tourist attraction, drawing as many as 10,000 visitors a month. They sparked[d] a boom in the local economy, rescuing the nearby city of North Bay and the neighbouring town of Callander from possible
35 bankruptcy.

The quints, too, should have earned a fortune, certainly enough to last them the rest of their lives. They were on the covers of magazines. They appeared in films and on radio. They endorsed[e] a host of products. But there was a huge
40 catch: the people who looked after the quints also spent a lot of the money that the girls earned.

Still, by the time they were seven years old in 1941, $1 million had accumulated in a trust account held for the girls until they turned 21 in 1955. [2]Emilie never did. She
45 died in 1954, at the age of 20, in a Quebec convent, the victim of the epilepsy that began to plague her soon after the quints were finally reunited with their parents and siblings (three more were born after them) when they were nine. Around that time, the parents won back custody
50 of the girls and greater access to the trust fund fed by their earnings. When the four surviving sisters reached their 21st

birthday, the trust had <u>dwindled</u>[f] to $800,000. About $50,000 went towards construction of the three-storey, yellow brick mansion that was built to accommodate the reunited family.

Cecile has <u>decidedly</u>[g] mixed feelings about her parents. In John Nihmey's book and a subsequent television drama her mother is portrayed as consumed by love for the five little girls. That is not the way Cecile remembers her. 'I didn't even really know my mother. She was always too busy. But I suppose there were too many for her to love. After all, she already had seven other kids by the time we went back to the big house.' If there is a <u>glimmer</u>[h] of sympathy in Cecile's attitude to her mother, [3]there is little for her father. 'He was a difficult man to know,' she says. 'We never did manage to communicate.'

Despite the bleak picture that Cecile paints of the principal characters in her life, at the same time she does not remember her early years as being unpleasant. She admits there were <u>harrowing</u>[i] moments, such as those when the quints' nurses locked them in broom closets or tied their wrists to their beds. [4]But at the same time, the early years were, on balance, good ones for the quints. 'The best part of our lives was in the beginning,' she says. 'When we were young, we were treated like princesses.'

The difficult moments came later, after the Dionnes were reunited. There were two distinct entities in the family. On the one hand, there were the five little girls who had finally returned home. [5]On the other, there were brothers and sisters who had watched them develop from afar, both proud and envious at the same time.

It was not an easy situation. Cecile remembers it well. 'We lived separate lives,' she says. [6]'But there was always so much tension in our relationships, always so many quarrels. Our brothers and sisters, even our parents, always <u>clung</u>[j] to the idea that we were the cause of their misery, their unhappiness.'

2 Read the text and answer these questions.

1 The Dionne sisters became so famous because they were the only quintuplets:
  A who had lived past infancy.
  B who were not born in a hospital.
  C whose mother had already had children.
  D who nearly died at birth.

2 Why did the Ontario government take the girls away from their parents?
  A They thought their parents would cause problems.
  B They thought their father was exploiting them.
  C They responded to people's reactions to the quints' situation.
  D They wanted to make money out of the girls.

3 What happened when the quints were nine?
  A Their mother had triplets.
  B They gained more control over their finances.
  C They earned $1 million dollars.
  D They went back to live with the rest of the family.

4 How does Cecile feel about her parents?
  A She feels sorry for them both for having had such a large family.
  B She appreciates the difficulty of her mother's situation.
  C She wishes she had been able to talk to her father.
  D She feels they were not properly portrayed in a book and TV programme.

5 What is Cecile's lasting impression of the quints' early years at Quintland?
  A The nurses were cruel to them.
  B The other quints missed their parents.
  C People made a lot of fuss of them.
  D They had very little privacy.

6 Why was life more difficult when the quints moved back to live with their family?
  A The family were divided over what to do with the quints' earnings.
  B The other Dionne children felt ambivalent about them.
  C The girls couldn't spend as much time together as they had before.
  D They made the rest of the family miserable by quarrelling all the time.

7 How does the writer of the article react to Cecile's account of her childhood?
  A She is not convinced by it.
  B She accepts it as fact.
  C She thinks Cecile is concealing the truth.
  D She thinks Cecile is exaggerating.

Look at the context in which the words below occur in the text 'A Family Tragedy' on pp.56–57 and match them to the explanations 1–10 which follow.

a) celebrated (l. 3)
b) outcry (l. 18)
c) peered (l. 29)
d) sparked (l. 32)
e) endorsed (l. 39)
f) dwindled (l. 52)
g) decidedly (l. 57)
h) glimmer (l. 68)
i) harrowing (l. 78)
j) clung (l. 100)

1 without doubt, clearly
2 express approval or support
3 well-known, famous
4 a small uncertain sign
5 refuse to let go
6 become steadily fewer or smaller
7 distressing
8 a public expression of anger
9 be the cause of
10 look very carefully or hard

Grammar plus: substitution and ellipsis

1 Study the section on substitution and ellipsis on p.84 of the *Advanced Gold Coursebook* and the Grammar Reference pp.196–197. What has been left out or replaced in the highlighted sentences in the text 'A Family Tragedy' on pp.56–57?

2 Read this text about falling birthrates. Use substitution and ellipsis to reduce the number of words and improve the style of the text.

WILL THE CRADLE ROCK?

It is a fact of modern life that in Europe and the USA people are having fewer children than their parents and grandparents did. In the States the current birth rate is 2.1 children per woman. In Europe the average rate is 1.5 children per woman: Spain has the lowest rate at 1.24 children per woman. Italy is not far behind Spain, and Germany and Greece follow Italy with a birth rate of 1.35. So the birth rate is falling, but why is the birthrate falling? In a recent poll, many people said that they wanted to have more children but they believed that they could not afford to have more children. When they were asked how many children they intended to have some people said that they intended to have one child though the majority of people said that they intended to have two children. A few people said that they intended to have four children or more than four children. Of course some people who want to have children are unable to have children or unable to have more children

UNIT 7 **The ties that bind**

3 Look at these mini-dialogues and decide which, if any, of the responses is NOT possible.

1   A: Do you think Tony will ever speak to his brother again?
    B: a) He might.
       b) He might do.
       c) He might do it.
       d) He might not.

2   A: Are you and Simon going to have any more children?
    B: a) We hope we will.
       b) We hope so.
       c) We hope we are.
       d) We hope we are going.

3   A: Would your little boy like an icecream?
    B: a) No, thank you. He's just had.
       b) No, thank you. He's just had one.
       c) No, thank you. I don't think he should.
       d) No, thank you. He doesn't want.

4   A: Were you thinking of coming into the office tomorrow?
    B: a) No, but I can do.
       b) No, but I can.
       c) No, but I can be.
       d) No, but I can be thinking.

5   A: Which of your sisters is it that works as a social worker?
    B: a) The eldest
       b) The eldest one.
       c) None of them do.
       d) None.

after they have had a first child. One woman who was interviewed by the researchers said she would like to have more children but she was worried about not having enough money to pay for their education. When she was asked if she would have more children if she inherited a million dollars, she said that she thought she would have more children, but she wasn't sure. A young man said that his parents and grandparents had produced a lot of children because they had been farmers and children were a benefit on a farm. In the city, however, they are not a benefit. He had therefore decided that he did not want to have a family, though his wife was very keen to have a family. Another man with no children said his wife did want to have a family but that he didn't want to have a family. Why didn't he want to have a family? Because his parents had been divorced and he didn't want to inflict this on his children.

59

English in Use: multiple-choice cloze

▶ **Paper 3, Part 1**

About the exam: In Paper 3, Part 1 you choose which of four alternatives best fills gaps in a text.

Strategy

1. Read the title to get an idea of the kind of text you are going to read.
2. Read the text through quickly to get a general idea of what it is about.
   - Read it again paying attention to the words before and after each gap.
   - Try to fill the gaps without looking at the alternatives.
   - Look at the alternatives and choose the one that fits best.
3. Read the text through again to see if it sounds natural. Make any changes you think are necessary.
4. Transfer your answers to the answer sheet

▶ Hot tip! ◀

Fill in the actual words as well as circling the letter on the *question paper*. This will make it easier to read the text through when you are checking your answers. NOTE only put the letters on the answersheet.

1 Look at the title of this text.
Do you expect it to be:

a) the story of how someone researched their family tree?
b) advice on researching a family tree?

Read the text through once quickly to see if you were right.

2 For questions 1–15 read the text below and then decide which word best fits each space.

HOW TO RESEARCH YOUR FAMILY TREE

Creating a family tree can be an absorbing and rewarding pastime, and who knows where it might (1) ... ? You might discover you have royal (2) ... , a hereditary title and a coat of arms, a forgotten legacy or even an infamous mass murderer in the family. You'll be creating a(n) (3) ... and valuable resource to share and a fascinating insight into your own life and times for future (4) ... . Before you begin, ask around to see if any of the (5) ... research has already been done. Most families have at least one (6) ... historian whose records may be able to get you off to a good (7) ... . Older family members can give you a first-hand (8) ... of recent family history, though remember to (9) ... some tact and always be sensitive to any skeletons and scandals that you may uncover. Official documents such as old birth, marriage and death certificates are an invaluable (10) ... and family photo albums can provide a(n) (11) ... of information. Postcards and letters also often contain useful historical snippets and even (12) ... photographs of places and buildings can provide additional (13) ... of exploration. Start with an Internet search of your family name. You may come (14) ... a family home page providing a link to long-lost relations or overseas (15) ... of the family.

	A	B	C	D
1	guide	follow	**lead**	direct
2	**ancestry**	lineage	pedigree	descent
3	sole	**unique**	only	single
4	offspring	**generations**	ages	progeny
5	inaugural	beginning	introductory	**initial**
6	**amateur**	beginner	apprentice	unskilled
7	beginning	initiation	**start**	**outset**
8	way	access	**account**	entrance
9	**exercise**	have	apply	practice
10	fount	origin	root	**source**
11	**wealth**	abundance	profusion	richness
12	indistinguishable	**obscure**	unknown	nameless
13	courses	passages	avenues	**ways**
14	around	to	**across**	through
15	**branches**	portions	sections	parts

60

Vocabulary: commonly confused words

For each question 1–16 choose between the two options given to complete the text appropriately.

'I wish you wouldn't behave so
(1) *childlike/childishly*. I'm really beginning to
(2) *lose/loose* patience with you. I think you'd better go to your room and spend an hour
(3) *alone/lonely* thinking really (4) *hard/hardly* about how Grandma must have felt when you threw her present into the (5) *canal/channel* as if it were completely (6) *priceless/worthless*! It was (7) *especially/specially* cruel when you know how fond of you she is. And then to (8) *imply/infer* that she had got it for free when she went to Switzerland on holiday last year. Well, that really was the limit. I know it had (9) *"Memory/ Souvenir* of Basle" on the packet but I'm sure she bought it. Even if she didn't it's the
(10) *principal/principle* of the thing that bothers me. When I was a little girl getting really lovely
(11) *stationery/stationary* like that was a thrill. I used to spend hours (12) *practicing/practising* my best writing before I was prepared to use so much as a sheet! Your father and I have always done our best to (13) *ensure/insure* that you children never wanted for anything and just look what it's done for us. You're all spoilt, ungrateful and rude! And don't you dare (14) *rise/raise* your voice when you speak to me! I'm absolutely furious with you! I think (15) *laying/lying* down for a while might have a calming (16) *affect/effect* on both of us, actually!'

Writing: leaflet

▶ **Paper 2, Part 2**

About the exam: In Paper 2, Part 2 you may have the option of writing the text of a leaflet.

> *Strategy*
> Pay particular attention to the audience to whom the leaflet is directed and its purpose. This will help you choose an appropriate style and register. Use leaflet layout i.e. section headings and bullet points. Time yourself. Try to complete the task in an hour.

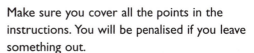

Make sure you cover all the points in the instructions. You will be penalised if you leave something out.

1 Look at this task and underline key words and phrases.

> **TASK**
> The Student Counselling Service at your college has asked you to prepare **a leaflet** (250 words) on how students can improve their relationships with their parents and brothers and sisters. The leaflet will be given to students who use the Counselling Service in the weeks leading up to the summer holidays. You should explain why problems occur in the first place, why they can be particularly acute during holiday periods and how people can learn to cope with problems like these. Write your **leaflet**.

2 Consider the following points:

- What is the minimum number of sections your leaflet can have?
- What headings will you use for each of your sections?
- What points will you use under each heading?
- Will you use a) an informal register b) a more formal academic register?

3 Write a draft of your leaflet. Check it carefully for spelling and grammatical mistakes.

UNIT 7 **The ties that bind**

UNIT 8 As luck would have it

Reading: multiple choice

▶ **Paper 1, Part 3**

About the exam: In Paper 1, Part 3 you answer between five and seven multiple-choice questions after reading a text.

Strategy

1 Read the whole text through once quickly to get an idea of the main areas referred to.
2 Read each question and locate the part(s) of the text which relate(s) to it.
3 Read the relevant part(s) of the text carefully and underline key words and phrases.
4 Consider the possible options for each question carefully. The incorrect options will be wrong for different reasons:
   • they are not referred to in the text, but may be true.
   • they contradict what is in the text.
   • they are partially (but not completely) true.
   • they are irrelevant to the question.
5 Select the correct option.

▶ Hot tip! ◀

Even if you are uncertain NEVER leave a question unanswered.

1 Read the following newspaper article and then answer the questions 1–7.

SUPERSTITIONS EVERYWHERE

Was it poor visibility or superstition that made Manchester United's players abandon their grey strip for away games in the middle of a Premiership match in 1996? 'The players couldn't pick each other out,' manager Alex Ferguson told reporters at the time. 'It was nothing to do with superstition. They said it was difficult to see their team mates at a distance.' But his protest failed to mention that on the five occasions the grey strip had been worn, the team had failed to win.

Dr Richard Wiseman, a psychologist at Hertfordshire University, says United's players may have <u>succumbed</u> to the power of superstition without even realising it. 'I might argue that the players may have unconsciously noticed that when they do certain things, one of which might well involve the wearing of red shirts, they are successful.' He draws a parallel with research into stock market speculators. Like gamblers they swore that certain days were lucky for them. Eventually it was shown that the successful market speculators were unconsciously <u>picking up on</u> numerous indicators and were shadowing market trends but were unable to explain how they did it. 'Superstition plays a part whenever people are not certain what it is they do to achieve a good performance and people who have to perform to order are particularly vulnerable. It is as if the imagination steps into the gap in the dialogue between the conscious and the unconscious mind.'

Many superstitions have deep roots in the past according to Moira Tatem, who helped edit the 1,500 entries in the Oxford Dictionary of Superstitions. 'People today observe superstitions without knowing why and they'd probably be surprised to discover their origins. The idea that mail vans are lucky is a good example. Children often say they are and Sir Winston Churchill, the British Prime Minister during World War 2, was said to have touched a mail van for luck whenever he saw one in the street. The reason for this superstition resides in the ancient belief that Kings and Queens had the ability to cure by touch. Monarchs, naturally enough, grew fed up with being constantly touched and at some point started trailing ribbons with gold medals or coins out of the door of their coaches when travelling and people touched them instead. Mail vans carry the

UNIT 8 **As luck would have it**

1 According to their manager, Alex Ferguson, Manchester United decided to change out of their grey shirts because:
  A they had lost every time they had worn them.
  B the colour was not bright enough.
  C it was difficult for the other team to see them.
  D a psychologist told them they might play better without them.

2 Dr Wiseman says Manchester United players and stock market speculators are similar in that:
  A both groups can identify the factors that contribute to improving performance.
  B both groups attribute their success to wearing particular items of clothing.
  C neither group can understand why they do well on some occasions and not on others.
  D both groups believe that certain days of the week are lucky for them.

3 According to Moira Tatem, what would most British people say if you asked them why touching a mail van is considered lucky?
  A 'A famous politician used to do it too.'
  B 'The vans are lucky but I don't know why.'
  C 'Being touched by a monarch can cure disease.'
  D 'The royal coat of arms is on the side of the vans.'

4 Which older superstitions have been preserved?
  A Those that still seem meaningful.
  B Those connected with life in the city.
  C Those connected with life in the countryside.
  D Those that are created and held by individuals.

5 How does going without food affect some string players?
  A It makes them feel too tired and hungry to play well.
  B It helps them play with more assurance.
  C It makes no difference to the way they perform.
  D It ensures that they perform brilliantly.

6 Why doesn't Ralph Kirshbaum keep the superstitious practices of other musicians?
  A He can't be bothered with them.
  B He has his own complicated rituals.
  C He doesn't think they always help.
  D He is not superstitious.

7 What attitude does the author of the article have to superstitions?
  A He thinks they are harmful.
  B He thinks they are inevitable
  C He thinks they can be nonsensical.
  D He thinks they can be beneficial.

Crown symbol on the side and touching the van is a direct throwback to that earlier belief.'
  While some ancient superstitious beliefs and practices have been maintained, others have died out. This is because those practices with a connection to farming and a life spent in close proximity to nature no longer make much sense now that so many of us live in cities. Nevertheless, we continue to develop our own sometimes very private and personal superstitions. Many people carry or wear lucky objects although they may not in fact think of them as such. It only becomes obvious that the object forms a part of a superstitious belief when the person is unable to wear or carry it and feels uncomfortable as a result.
  Experts agree that these individual superstitious practices can be an effective means of managing stress and reducing anxiety. The self-fulfilling nature of superstitions is what can help. The belief that something brings you good luck can make you feel calmer, and as a result, able to perform more effectively. International cello soloist Ralph Kirshbaum says musicians are a good example of the effectiveness of these very particular rituals. 'I know string players who won't wash their hands on the day of a recital and others who avoid eating for eight hours prior to a performance. They can then play with confidence.'
  But this self-fulfilling aspect of superstitions can also work against you. This is why Kirshbaum prefers to confront the superstitious practices of other musicians. 'If you're in a situation where you can't avoid eating or forget and wash your hands, you then feel that you'll play badly. And you often do, simply because you feel so anxious. I wash my hands and have broken the taboo about eating. My only vice is to insist that people leave and give me two minutes complete silence in the dressing room before I go on.'
  Superstitions can become even more harmful when they develop into phobias or obsessions, often characterised by elaborate collections of rituals. 'It's not a problem if I carry a lucky object of some kind,' says psychologist Robert Kohlenberg of the University of Washington. 'But if I don't have it with me and I get terribly upset and turn the house upside down looking for it, that's a bad thing.'

2 Use the underlined words and expressions from the text to complete these sentences. Sometimes you need to change the form of the word or expression.

1 I've .... but I can't find my car keys anywhere.
2 I suppose it was one of those .... prophecies. I thought something terrible was going to happen and it did.
3 The cabin crew will move through the aircraft immediately .... departure to check that all hand luggage has been correctly stowed.
4 She finally .... to the temptation to eat the last two chocolates in the box.
5 I didn't .... the fact that she was upset, though she did seem a little quieter than usual.
6 A lot of today's fashions are a .... to the 1970s.

63

Grammar plus: verb patterns (2)

Study the Grammar Reference and the section on verb patterns (2) on p.94 of the *Advanced Gold Coursebook*.

1 The verbs in bold in the sentences below are followed by one of the patterns in the box. Decide in each case which it is and correct the sentence accordingly.

- the *-ing* form
- the infinitive form with *to*
- an object and the infinitive form without *to*
- either the infinitive form with *to* or the *-ing* form with little or no difference in meaning

EXAMPLE 1 *Superstition plays a part whenever people are not certain what it is they do **to achieve** a good performance and people who have to perform to order are particularly vulnerable.*

1 Superstition plays a part whenever people are not certain what it is they do **achieve** a good performance and people who have to perform to order are particularly vulnerable.
2 Monarchs, naturally enough, grew fed up with being constantly touched and at some point started **trail** ribbons with gold medals or coins out of the door of their coaches when travelling and people touched them instead.
3 Nevertheless, we continue **develop** our own – sometimes very private and personal – superstitions.
4 The belief that something brings you good luck can **make** you feel calmer, and as a result, able to perform more effectively.
5 I know string players who won't wash their hands on the day of a recital and others who avoid **eat** for eight hours prior to a performance.
6 This is why Kirshbaum prefers **confront** the superstitious practices of other musicians.

Learner training

The *Longman Active Study Dictionary*, the *Longman Dictionary of Contemporary English*, the *Longman Language Activator* and the *Longman Essential Activator* provide information about verb patterns. Firstly, they tell you whether a verb is transitive or intransitive (see verb patterns 1 in Unit 1). Secondly, they tell you what pattern follows the verb. When you learn a new verb use your dictionary to check what verb patterns it is followed by, record these with examples in your vocabulary notebooks and make up more examples of your own.

2 In eleven of the sentences below a verb has been followed by the wrong pattern. Find these sentences and correct them.

1 I detest be kept waiting.
2 He encouraged me apply for a promotion.
3 She is threatening reveal everything to the press.
4 Although he seemed familiar, we couldn't remember meet before.
5 Even though we don't remember their origins, many superstitions continue have considerable influence.
6 I think I will always regret not celebrate the end of the millennium.
7 I wouldn't risk go out in this weather if I were you.
8 Something made me stop before I walked into the room.
9 Many people have attempted explain coincidence.
10 You neglected inform me that there would be a delay with the delivery.
11 I was already at the checkout when I realised I'd forgotten get any bread.
12 There are people who don't dare to go outside on a Friday the 13th.
13 He could see the wall in front of him but somehow he couldn't avoid hit it.
14 The psychologist helped her overcome her fear of open spaces.

3 Complete these sentences in your own words using an appropriate verb pattern.

1 I sometimes regret ... .
2 My parents would let ... when I was 12.
3 My secondary school teachers encouraged ... . Many of us took their advice.
4 I don't think I would ever dare ... .
5 I sometimes miss ... . It's something I used to do a lot when I was younger.
6 I have always detested ... .
7 I expect ... until I retire.
8 Something I know I should try ... is ... .
9 But what I hope to avoid ... is ... .
10 I've always been very grateful to ... . S/he helped ... .

UNIT 8 As luck would have it

Vocabulary: synonyms

Study the Vocabulary section on synonyms on p.95 of the *Advanced Gold Coursebook*.

Match the words a–c (or b) to the definitions 1–3 (or 2).

1 a) boost
   b) increase
   c) maximise

   1 become larger in amount, number or degree
   2 increase something to the greatest possible size
   3 increase something; improve

2 a) far-fetched
   b) unlikely
   c) inconceivable

   1 not probable or expected
   2 difficult to believe
   3 difficult or impossible to believe

3 a) typically
   b) generally
   c) normally

   1 usually; by most people; considering something as a whole
   2 usually; showing the usual signs or qualities of a particular group
   3 in the usual or expected way; usually

4 a) countless
   b) numerous

   1 very many
   2 many

5 a) concidence
   b) luck
   c) chance

   1 something that brings you good or bad fortune, as if by chance
   2 the force that seems to make things hqppen without cause or reason; possibility
   3 a combination of events, happening by chance, which are often surprising

Listening: multiple matching

▶ Paper 4, Part 4

About the exam: In Paper 4, Part 4 you listen to five short extracts linked by topic but recorded by different speakers. You hear the whole recording twice. You either answer multiple-choice questions about each of the speakers or do two multiple-matching tasks. In the multiple-matching tasks you match the extracts with five words or phrases (**A–H**). In each task there are always three other words or phrases you do not need to use.

> **Strategy**
>
> Read the questions carefully. The first time you hear the recording concentrate on task one. As you match a word or phrase to an extract cross it out on your question paper. The second time you listen focus on task two. On your question paper cross out the words or phrases you have matched to the extracts.

 Listen to the following five extracts about different people's dreams.

TASK ONE

For questions **1–5**, match the extracts as you hear them with the topics **A–H**.

A an unusual learning experience   1 _____
B a false recollection
C a prophesy of reconciliation   2 _____
D a recollection of past lives
E a visit from a ghost   3 _____
F an experience of a disaster   4 _____
G a premonition of a death
H a lucky escape   5 _____

TASK TWO

For questions **6–10** match the extracts as you hear them with what the speaker says about dream **A–H**.

A S/he thought they had invented the dream.
B S/he doesn't believe it was a dream.   6 _____
C S/he remembered almost nothing of the dream initially.   7 _____
D S/he was injured in the dream.
E S/he had a dream that helped other people.   8 _____
F S/he incorporated reality into the dream.   9 _____
G S/he forgot her dream for several weeks.   10 _____
H S/he didn't have the dream s/he describes.

65

Grammar check: reported speech

1 Study the section on reported speech on pp.96–97 of the *Advanced Gold Coursebook* and put these sentences into reported speech.

1 'Water freezes at 0°C,' explained the science teacher.
2 'Will you be able to come to the lecture this evening?' Marie asked Clare.
3 'Do you need a lift to the airport tomorrow?' he asked me.
4 'Who did you speak to when you phoned last week?' the woman asked her.
5 'I'm thinking of going to France next summer,' said Christine.
6 'Have you seen the new Keanu Reeves film?' Tim asked Lynnette.
7 'I may have to leave early this afternoon,' Simon explained.
8 'Where's the nearest petrol station?' asked the man.
9 'You should take a few days off,' said the doctor.
10 'What time will you be back?' my mother is always asking me.

2 Rewrite the following sentences in reported speech using one of the reporting verbs in the box

| promise remind warn apologise admit |
| suggest promise deny agree accuse |

1 'I'll take you out to dinner on your birthday this year without fail,' her boyfriend told her.
2 'It wasn't me who broke the vase,' said the girl.
3 'Yes, it's true. I have been spending a lot of time with Andrew,' said Sarah.
4 'Why don't you take out a subscription to an English magazine?' his teacher asked him.
5 'You mustn't forget to buy your husband a present for your wedding anniversary,' her personal assistant told her.
6 'Sitting in the sun will make your head cold worse, you know,' the woman told her husband.
7 'I know you've been seeing someone else all the time we've been together,' said John to Sarah.
8 'All right. I'll cook the dinner for a change,' said Jane.
9 'I'm really sorry I spoke to you all so rudely yesterday,' the head of department told them.

Vocabulary: word formation (prefixes)

1 Study the Vocabulary section on word formation (prefixes) on p.97 of the *Advanced Gold Coursebook*. Read the paragraph below. In each sentence the word or word stem in bold needs the addition of a prefix to give meaning to the sentence.

AN AMBITIOUS PROJECT

I have decided to write my -**biography**! Now, you may think at 25 that I am too -**mature** to embark upon such an ambitious project but I think age is completely -**relevant**. Anyway, I'm sure that my literary abilities will allow me to -**come** that hurdle only too easily. It will be written in the form of a -**logue** in which I tell the world about some of the -**believably** interesting events in my life so far. I also intend to clear up some very common and totally -**logical** -**conceptions** about the supernatural and finally convince people that all those -**intellectuals** at universities have got it all wrong. Being my friend, I know you'll buy a copy when I finish it. It would be extremely -**loyal** not to do so, after all.

---

2 In each sentence below one word needs the addition of a prefix to give meaning to the sentence. Identify the words which need prefixes and add them.

1 He never phones his friends or goes out any more: he's becoming really social.
2 With 600 billion people, population has reached crisis proportions.
3 Don't you think it was a little responsible to leave a six-year-old alone in the house?
4 There are too many mistakes in this composition: I'm afraid you'll have to write it.
5 He added a script to his letter to say that he had received her cheque.
6 She kept trying to involve him in the conversation but he just gave syllabic responses to her questions.
7 I think I must have done the steaks: they're very tough.
8 Drugs are legal in almost every country on earth.

UNIT 8 As luck would have it

English in Use: multiple-choice cloze

▶ **Paper 3, Part 1**

About the exam: Paper 3, Part 3 tests your knowledge of fixed phrases and collocation. These can include word + preposition combinations, phrasal verbs and idioms.

Strategy

Read the whole text through concentrating on meaning first. Don't look at the alternatives. Decide what you would put in the gap. Then look at the alternatives and find the one that fits your meaning best.

Learner training

When you learn vocabulary, record and learn collocations e.g. *poor* visibility, *fail* to mention, uphold *a tradition* rather than individual words.

AN ANCIENT CURSE EXPLAINED

The archaeologist Howard Carter died in Egypt only five months after uncovering the tomb of King Tutankhamen in the Upper Valley of the Nile. Twenty-five others (0) *A.* in the project also died within a year of the excavation of the tomb. Newspapers at the time (1) ... the deaths to the 'Mummy's Curse' after a journalist (2) ... to have found a hieroglyphic inscription at the entrance to the tomb. The writer Sir Arthur Conan Doyle, (3) ... of the famous fictional detective Sherlock Holmes, also advanced the story, insisting that a 'pharaoh's curse' was (4) ... for the deaths. Doctors have long speculated that they (5) ... victim to some sort of bacteria, but now Dr. Nicola Di Paolo, a kidney disease expert and (6) ... archaeologist, has obtained the first clinical proof of the (7) ... growth of a (8) ... toxic microscopic fungus. 'In tombs which have been closed for centuries, air and damp may penetrate minute cracks in the walls, (9) ... the growth of poisonous moulds,' Di Paolo said recently. He speculated that an explorer who entered a tomb that had been closed for centuries without using a mask must have inhaled dust full of toxins from the mould. (10) ... , he said, researchers handling the mummy and other (11) ... found in Tutankhamen's tomb could have breathed in the toxic mould. While small (12) ... are thought to be (13) ... , Di Paolo said (14) ... exposure could be fatal, causing (15) ... degeneration of the kidneys and liver.

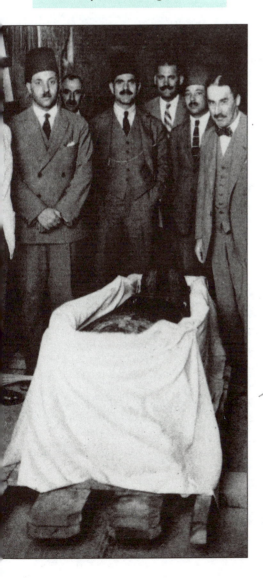

0	A involved	B hired	C concerned	D employed
1	A blamed	B associated	C attributed	D implicated
2	A said	B insisted	C held	D claimed
3	A creator	B designer	C discoverer	D mastermind
4	A guilty	B responsible	C culpable	D reprehensible
5	A fell	B felt	C became	D came
6	A beginner	B apprentice	C amateur	D unprofessional
7	A quick	B fast	C swift	D rapid
8	A highly	B rarely	C absolutely	D rather
9	A letting	B permitting	C admitting	D leaving
10	A Similarly	B Likely	C Exactly	D Identically
11	A matters	B objects	C commodities	D goods
12	A measures	B masses	C quantities	D numbers
13	A innocent	B inoffensive	C pardoned	D harmless
14	A long-standing	B long-range	C long-term	D long-distance
15	A severe	B grave	C dangerous	D perilous

Writing: competition entry

▶ **Paper 2, Part 2**

About the exam: In Paper 2, Part 2 you may have the option of writing a competition entry. This could be an article, a description, a review, a story etc.

Strategy
Use interesting vocabulary and language structures to keep the reader's attention.

Hot tip!
NEVER memorise a piece of writing to use as an answer to a Paper 2 task. It is extremely unlikely that what you have memorised will be suitable.

Look at this task and the answer a student wrote.

TASK
**COMPETITION!
DOES GOOD FORTUNE SMILE OR FROWN UPON YOU?**

Write and tell us about an occasion on which you have been extremely lucky … or unlucky. We're offering a prize for the three most interesting, well-written stories. The first-prize-winning entry will be included in the November edition of the college magazine.

1 Look at the answer below carefully.

1 Find words or phrases in the text that mean:
a) walked unsteadily
b) very wet
c) very surprised
d) break
e) sharp
f) without thinking that something might be wrong
g) very dark
h) made a dull sound by hitting
i) were ignored
j) without any good result
k) went quickly

2 What structure does the student use to mark the point where things start to go wrong?

3 How does the student build up to that point?

4 How does the student use punctuation to create interest at the beginning and ending of the story?

2 Now write your answer to the task using interesting vocabulary and creating suspense.

I've never been superstitious – or rather I hadn't been until the 13th January, 2000.

That day, I woke at 6.30 and stumbled into the bathroom. While I was in there I heard a horrible groaning noise coming from the hall. I ran out, dripping wet, and was stunned to see the hall mirror fall to the floor and shatter into hundreds of jagged pieces. Nevertheless, I swept up the broken glass, dressed and left for work without really giving it a second thought.

I had a nine o'clock meeting with some very important clients. I'd spent weeks making a detailed model of the new building we had designed for them. When I got to their head office, I got into the lift to go up to the top floor boardroom. No sooner had the doors closed than I realised something was horribly wrong. The lift wasn't moving and it was pitch black inside. I shouted and thumped on the door but my cries for help fell on deaf ears. I looked at my watch and it was five past nine. I was going to be late for my meeting. I continued shouting and thumping to no avail for another hour. At exactly ten thirty the lights came on and the lift started moving. I rushed into the boardroom just in time to hear our clients congratulating our competitors on winning the contract.

I didn't lose my job, but I certainly didn't get the promotion I had been promised either. Sometimes I think I should just have stayed in bed that day and, I must admit, I do sometimes wonder about the date … and that mirror.

UNIT 9
Where there's a will ...

Vocabulary: expressions with *make/get/keep/gain/resolve*

1 Study the Vocabulary section on expressions with *make/get/keep/gain/resolve* on p.107 of the *Advanced Gold Coursebook*.

2 Read this text about how an elite football coach motivates his players and fill in the gaps by choosing between the alternatives A, B, C and D.

3 Fill in the gaps in these sentences with *do* or *make*.

1 If you don't have anything to ...., why don't you give your father a hand in the kitchen?
2 He had a minor accident on the way to work. Fortunately, he didn't .... much damage to the other car.
3 I wonder if I could .... a suggestion? Wouldn't it be a better idea to buy a new photocopier?
4 I'm sure the interior designer will .... a fantastic job on the living room. It will look completely different.
5 I didn't feel up to going to the party so I decided to phone and .... an excuse.
6 It took me weeks to .... all the arrangements for my holiday and then I realised there was no one to look after my cats.
7 She decided she would have to .... more of an effort to learn Polish.
8 You would .... everyone a favour if you were to agree to be Head of Department.
9 Would you be able to .... use of this sofa bed? It's really too big for my living room.
10 Why don't you take a few weeks off? It would .... you the world of good!
11 If you .... the beds, I'll .... the dishes.

A top coach for a top team

How can a contemporary football coach expect to (1) ... any real impression on the very wealthy young men in elite football teams like Manchester United? The problem is how to motivate people who have often become used to being treated like kings. Manchester United coach Steve McClaren looked for solutions in sports where coaches had already managed to (2) ... a similar problem and that meant the US sports in which multi-million-dollar contracts have been commonplace for many years. Here's what he had to say. 'I still read the books of eminent American football and baseball coaches. What they give you is an insight into dealing with millionaire athletes. It's a matter of trying to instill selflessness. You have to (3) ... them feel "it's 'we' rather than 'me' that matters." With the team I coached before it was mainly a question of analysing the opposition and how best to operate against them, so as to (4) ... an advantage in the match itself. With Manchester it's a matter of focusing 99 per cent on our players. To an extent, competition helps. But you still need to reassure people and resolve their (5) ... about themselves and their place in the club. Once the training session is over what really (6) ... a difference is taking a personal interest in the players. Good, strong management helps too. I always (7) ... my word. The players know that. If there is any tendency to lose motivation, they know there are plenty of others dying to (8) ... that promotion from the reserves. The coach's best friend is the bench. At the end of the day, it's the only way you can (9) ... control over them. Because they all want to play. Sometimes they ask me: "Where the hell do I go from here?" It's a good question since many great players do (10) ... into trouble when they move on from an elite club. Some do go into coaching, though. The trouble is a lot of players now don't want to start at the bottom. They want an assistant manager's job at least. They don't want to work with kids or the reserves. But you only (11) ... experience through working your way up through the ranks. That's what I (12) ... to do when I was younger and look where I am today.'

1	**A** get	**B** achieve	**C** do	**D** make
2	**A** resolve	**B** solution	**C** absolve	**D** dissolve
3	**A** get	**B** have	**C** do	**D** make
4	**A** win	**B** gain	**C** achieve	**D** get
5	**A** debts	**B** doubts	**C** debits	**D** deficits
6	**A** gets	**B** has	**C** does	**D** makes
7	**A** keep	**B** retain	**C** maintain	**D** hold
8	**A** have	**B** take	**C** get	**D** make
9	**A** take	**B** obtain	**C** gain	**D** acquire
10	**A** get	**B** hit	**C** fall	**D** arrive
11	**A** have	**B** gain	**C** win	**D** achieve
12	**A** solved	**B** absolved	**C** resolved	**D** dissolved

Listening: multiple matching

▶ **Paper 4, Part 4**

About the exam: In Paper 4, Part 4 you will listen to a series of five short extracts of about 30 seconds each. You will hear the five extracts twice. The speakers will all be talking about a similar topic. You will either have a multiple-matching task or a multiple-choice task.

Strategy

Before you listen:
1 Read task one and task two before you listen for the first time.
2 Predict any key vocabulary you might expect to hear.

As you listen for the first time:
3 Focus mainly on task one.
4 Make a note of any key words or phrases you hear.
5 Cross off any prompts you are sure you have matched correctly. Put a question mark next to any you are not sure about.

As you listen for the second time:
6 Focus mainly on task two.
7 Listen particularly carefully to the extracts you are not sure about.

Hot tip!

Don't leave a question unanswered. It is better to guess than to leave a blank. Marks are NEVER deducted for wrong answers.

TASK ONE

You will hear different people talking about New Year's Resolutions they have made. For questions 1–5, match the extracts as you hear them with the resolutions **A–H**.

A stop drinking alcohol   1 _____
B give to charity
C use public transport more often 2 _____
D lose weight
E get a better job   3 _____
F get a driver's licence
G stop smoking   4 _____
H keep in touch with someone
                                   5 _____

TASK TWO

For questions **6–10**, match the extracts as you hear them with **A–H** below. Which speaker

A can't understand why others have found it so difficult?
B feels to blame for what happened?   6 _____
C found his/her attitude had changed?   7 _____
D felt s/he was setting a bad example?   8 _____
E believes her/his job contributed to the problem?   9 _____
F agreed with someone else that a change was necessary?   10 _____
G is reacting against other people's behaviour?
H does not believe s/he will succeed?

Grammar plus: emphasis (1)

1 Study the sections on emphasis in the *Advanced Gold Coursebook* p.108 and *Grammar reference* p.192.

2 Match the beginnings a)–h) to the endings 1–8 to form complete sentences.

a) She loved the job but she could barely get by on what she earned so, what she did
b) I don't really want anything to eat; what I'd really like
c) I know he's supposed to be brilliant but what really gets on my nerves
d) She got back at midnight after a ten-hour flight and couldn't find her keys. What had happened
e) He sometimes practised for eight hours without a break. What made him so motivated
f) It all sounds wonderful but what I'd like to know
g) Paula's incredibly patient, generous and loyal but what I value most about her
h) You're obviously tired and over-anxious. What I think you should do

1 is where we're going to get the money to do it.
2 was that she had left them in the drawer of the bedside table in the hotel.
3 is a nice cup of tea.
4 was the fact that his parents hadn't let him play when he was a child.
5 is her ability to laugh at herself.

70

6 is take a couple of weeks holiday
7 was to finally pluck up enough courage to ask him for a promotion.
8 is the way he always behaves as if whatever we decide to do was his idea.

3 Complete these sentences in your own words.

1 What the world needs now ...
2 What would almost certainly help me improve my English ...
3 What makes young people today different from their parents ...
4 What I will be doing in five years' time ...
5 What makes ... so fantastic ...

4 Add appropriate beginnings to these endings.

1 ... was that he decided to give up playing football altogether.
2 ... is a good night's sleep.
3 ... are people who park their cars on the pavement.
4 ... is what his motive was for doing such a terrible thing.
5 ... are his bravery and compassion.

Speaking: comparing and contrasting

▶ **Paper 5, Part 2**

About the exam: In Paper 5, Part 2 you may be asked to compare and contrast two or more photographs. You will also be asked to comment on a specific aspect of the photographs. For example you might be asked which photograph you find more appealing.

> **Strategy**
>
> Make a comment on one of the photographs and then make a comment on the other saying why it is different from or similar to the first photograph. Alternate between making comments about one photograph and then the other.

Hot tip!

Do not interrupt the other candidate while they are talking about the photographs. Pay careful attention to what they say as you will be asked to comment at the end.

UNIT 9 **Where there's a will ...**

 1 Listen to two examples of Part 2 of Paper 5. You will hear first Ingrid and then Adam talking about the pictures below. One of them was given very good marks for 'discourse management' (= 'the ability to express ideas and opinions in coherent connected speech'), the other did not do as well. Who received the higher grade?

2 Listen again and note the language the better candidate uses to compare and contrast the photographs.

71

Vocabulary: leisure activities

1 Study the Vocabulary section on leisure activities in the *Advanced Gold Coursebook* p.110.

2 Find words for the following in this wordsearch grid.

a) a leather seat made to fit over the back of an animal, especially a horse
b) the words of a song, especially a modern, popular song
c) a short description of the contents of a book written on the cover or on an advertisement
d) leather bands put on a horse's head to control its movements
e) large rubber shoes like the limbs of certain sea animals worn when swimming under water
f) a practice session for a play or concert
g) a tube with a mouthpiece allowing a swimmer under water to breathe
h) a three-legged support e.g. for a camera
i) a rubber garment worn by underwater swimmers, surfers etc.
j) a person who directs the playing of a group of musicians
k) a piece of glass or other transparent material which makes a beam of light passing through it bend, spread out, become narrower, change direction etc.

C	O	N	D	U	C	T	O	R	E	B
A	L	E	N	S	N	O	R	K	E	L
D	C	W	E	N	S	E	T	R	D	U
T	W	B	K	S	D	T	E	G	B	R
R	E	H	E	A	R	S	A	L	R	B
I	T	P	U	D	X	A	F	Y	I	K
P	S	B	A	D	Y	D	F	R	D	F
O	U	Z	L	L	E	N	S	I	L	T
D	I	G	M	E	C	I	U	C	E	H
A	T	T	I	J	M	N	M	S	T	D
O	D	F	L	I	P	P	E	R	S	E

3 Use the words you found in the grid to complete these sentences. Some of the words need to be changed grammatically to fit the sentences.

1 He's got three cameras, I don't know how many ...., a .... and countless albums of his photographs but no dark room.
2 A man emerged from the water wearing a huge pair of ...., a .... and a mask.
3 At the first ...., the .... always expects choir members to be able to sight read the score of a new work.
4 As soon as Trigger sees me coming wearing my crash helmet and carrying his .... and .... he runs off.
5 I can't stop humming the tune but the .... are pretty meaningless really.
6 The .... on the back of the paperback edition of her latest novel called her 'the greatest living British novelist'.

UNIT 9   Where

Grammar check: verb tenses (2)

Study the section on tenses on p.111 of the *Advanced Gold Coursebook*. Read the text below and then decide for each gap which of the three alternatives A, B or C would be possible.

'No Smoking Day' Research Studies

Teenagers are a vital weapon in the battle to stop people smoking, according to research published to coincide with 'No Smoking Day'. The study shows that at any given point in time more than 75 per cent of teenagers (1) … to persuade their parents to quit. Even youngsters who (2) … to smoking themselves say they have nagged their parents to give up. The survey of 11- to 15-year-olds (3) … that children and teenagers (4) … smoking as rebellious and trendy any more. They (5) … more concerned about the effects of their parents' habit on their own health. Smokers with children (6) … also more likely to want to quit and to have tried to give up. The researchers who carried out the study (7) … that almost three-quarters of 10,000 asthmatic youngsters who (8) … in the survey (9) … other people's cigarette smoke had made their condition worse. Of those, 31 per cent (10) … with someone who (11) … at some stage. Two further studies (12) … to mounting evidence that genes (13) … an important role in nicotine addiction. People taking part in the survey who had started smoking at 16 or younger and who (14) … repeatedly to successfully kick the habit share a common genetic make-up. But genes hardly (15) … the full story. In about 25 per cent of identical twin pairs only one twin (16) … , though they (17) … the same genes. Clearly, environment and willpower (18) … a role as well. Last year, two million people (19) … in 'No Smoking Day' with an estimated 40,000 giving up for good. Over the past 10 years an estimated half a million people (20) … helped to stop smoking by the venture.

1	**A** are trying	**B** tried	**C** were trying
2	**A** are admitting	**B** admit	**C** have admitted
3	**A** had suggested	**B** suggests	**C** is suggesting
4	**A** have not seen	**B** do not see	**C** did not see
5	**A** are	**B** were	**C** have been
6	**A** are	**B** were	**C** have been
7	**A** are finding	**B** have found	**C** found
8	**A** took part	**B** take part	**C** were taking part
9	**A** are believing	**B** believe	**C** believed
10	**A** were living	**B** live	**C** are living
11	**A** smokes	**B** was smoking	**C** had smoked
12	**A** are adding	**B** have added	**C** added
13	**A** are playing	**B** had played	**C** play
14	**A** had failed	**B** are failing	**C** fail
15	**A** tell	**B** are telling	**C** told
16	**A** is smoking	**B** was smoking	**C** smokes
17	**A** shared	**B** have shared	**C** share
18	**A** have played	**B** play	**C** are playing
19	**A** took part	**B** had taken part	**C** have taken part
20	**A** were	**B** have been	**C** had been

73

English in Use: error correction (spelling and punctuation)

▶ **Paper 3, Part 3**

Hot tip!
Check all nouns ending in 's' to make sure that they are not possessives requiring an apostrophe.

About the exam: In Paper 3, Part 3 you have to check a text of about 15 lines for errors. There are always three lines at the beginning that are examples numbered **0, 00** and **000** (one that is correct, one with a spelling error and one with a punctuation error). There is usually an unnumbered line or part of a line at the end of the text that you don't need to correct.

Strategy
1. Read the text through to get the general idea.
2. Read the text again sentence by sentence. Look for the following punctuation errors.
   Lack of:
   - capital letters
   - commas
   - full stops
   - apostrophes
   - brackets
3. Look at each word in turn and look for the following SPELLING ERRORS:
   - silent letters that have been omitted e.g. ~~det~~ ➔ debt
   - spelling of suffixes and prefixes e.g. respons~~able~~ ➔ responsible, ~~des~~advantage ➔ disadvantage
   - homophones e.g. She ~~nose~~ ➔ knows.
   - doubling of consonants e.g. o~~c~~assion ➔ occasion

In most lines of the following text there is a punctuation or spelling error. For each of the numbered lines write the correctly spelled word(s) or show the correct punctuation in the spaces on the answer box. Some lines are correct. Indicate these lines with a (✓) in the box. The exercise begins with three examples (0), (00) and (000).

THE PROMISES WE MAKE OURSELVES

0	As the clock strikes midnight on 31st December many of us make
00	New Years resolutions. Recent surveys have shown that only 20
000	per cent of the people, who make them really stick to them. So why
1	do we resolve to continue to resolve? It seems that almost all cultures
2	have a special day in which people have the oportunity to change
3	themselves, subtracting from their knew and improved selves a few
4	flaws and credit-card bills. These festivals are all times in wich
5	people look back at the past and resolve to be healthier wealthier
6	and wiser in the year ahead. Western societys tradition of making
7	resolutions dates back to ancient Rome, when people pledged to
8	improve themselves as part of paying hommage to the two-faced
9	god Janus who, like mortals on the cusp of a New Year, had
10	the ability to look in two directions at the same time. Too of the most
11	popular New Year's resolutions are to loose weight and to give up
12	smoking. Next in popularity come doing more exercise and 'psychological
13	resolutions' such as being more confident or ambicious. So how can you
14	make sure you don't break your resolutions? Experts say the key is to keep
15	the list short and to identify the especific steps you will need to take to reach your goals.

0	✓
00	Year's
000	people who
1	
2	✓
3	
4	
5	
6	
7	
8	
9	
10	
11	
12	
13	
14	
15	

74

UNIT 9 **Where there's a will ...**

Writing: report

▶ **Paper 2, Part 1**

About the exam: You may be asked to write a report either in Part 1 or as an option in Part 2. In Part 1 report-writing tasks you may be given the results of a survey to report on.

> *Strategy*
> Use clear layout with section headings and numbered points.

── **Hot tip!** ◀──

Plan your report so as to ensure coverage of all aspects of the task. If you leave something out you will lose marks.

1 Look at this task and the answer a student has written. Pay attention to the ✓ the examiner has put next to interesting vocabulary and sophisticated structures as well as the errors s/he has underlined. Then look at the band which the examiner has put this answer into – Band 3.

> **TASK**
> Your college magazine undertook a survey to find out whether students at your college make and keep New Year's Resolutions. You have agreed to write a 250-word report on the results of the survey for the college magazine saying why you think students responded as they did. Write your **report**.

New Year's Resolutions: A Survey

1 Did you make New Year's Resolutions this year
   Yes = 74 No = 26

2 If you answered 'yes' to question one, what New Year's resolutions did you make?
   A Get more exercise   (41)
   B Give up smoking   (33)
   C Save money   (28)
   D Lose weight   (25)
   E Find a (better) job   (15)
   F Make new friends   (12)
   G Get on better with family   (9)
   H Be more self-confident   (6)
   I Other   (7)

3 If you answered 'yes' to question one, now that we are at the end of the year, to what extent would you say you kept your New Year's Resolutions?
   A not at all   (33)
   B in a limited way for a short time   (20)
   C completely for a short time   (7)
   D in a limited way for the whole year   (10)
   E completely for the whole year   (4)

4 Do you plan to make resolutions next New Year?
   A Yes   (57)
   B No   (30)
   C Undecided   (13)

75

Promises Promises!

We've just finished the survey on New Year's Resolutions and I must say the results were _considerably_ amazing.

It surprised me most the fact that so many students make resolutions – three quarters of you, in fact – but almost nobody keeps them. _Being_ more precise, most people keep them for a while or to some extent, but a staggering 33 out of 74 don't _keep_ at all.

Anyway, what resolutions are the most popular ones? Top of the poll were getting more exercise and giving up smoking, but since _hardly nobody_ keeps their promises it's not surprising that we're _a so unhealthy lot_. Saving money and losing weight were next. _It occurred me_ that one way of killing two birds with one stone would be to stop eating in the student canteen! A small _amount_ of very sensible people had resolved to find a job, make new friends and get on better _with_ their family. Last but not least were _few_ timid individuals who were hoping to be more _confidence_ throughout 2001. _In the end_, there were some odd resolutions that were only mentioned by one or two people.

Another surprise was that _despite that we have so few success in_ doing what we said we were going to do, many of us are planning to make New Year's Resolutions again this year. I suppose that just goes to show that we're a well-intentioned bunch after all.

> **Examiner's note:** Not enough on reasons for student responses

Band 3 ✓ — Either a) task reasonably achieved, accuracy of language satisfactory and adequate range of vocabulary and range of structures or b) an ambitious attempt at the task, causing a number of non-impeding errors but a good range of vocabulary and structure demonstrated. There may be minor omissions but content clearly organised. Would achieve the required effect on target reader. Presentation – Right tone for a college magazine, but more like an article than a report.

2 Rewrite the student's answer. Improve it by responding to the examiner's comment written on the student's answer and correcting the errors that s/he has underlined in the report.

UNIT 10 The trials of technology

Vocabulary: computers

Study the Vocabulary section on computers on p.118 of the *Advanced Gold Coursebook*.

1 Match the definitions in column A to the words and phrases in column B.

A

a) remove a file from the computer's memory
b) be connected to a computer or telecommunications system
c) a list of instructions that must be given to a computer in order to make it perform operations
d) transfer a file from one computer to another
e) cause the system to fail so that data are lost
f) a company that provides individuals or other companies with access to the Internet
g) a person who illegally gains access to and sometimes tampers with a computer system
h) a device usually consisting of a keyboard and a screen by which you can give instructions to a computer and get instructions from it
i) the set of keys on a machine such as a computer

B

1 an Internet Service Provider
2 to <u>download</u> a file
3 to be <u>online</u>
4 to <u>delete</u> a file
5 to <u>crash</u> a system
6 a (computer) <u>hacker</u>
7 a keyboard
8 a <u>software</u> program
9 a terminal

2 Now use the words to complete this text. You need to use some of them more than once. You may need to change the grammatical form. There is one word you do not need to use.

The other day I was trying to (1) .... a file from the Internet. It was taking absolutely ages and just when it was nearly finished something happened that (2) .... the system. I must have pressed every key on the (3) .... but nothing I did seemed to make any difference. Finally, I had to switch the computer off. When I had switched it on again I couldn't get back (4) .... to continue (5) .... the file. In the end I decided to phone my (6) .... Apparently, a (7) .... had been tampering with their system that same afternoon. Fortunately, not much damage had been done but some of their (8) .... programs had been (9) .... That was why I had been having so much trouble.

Grammar plus: *it* as preparatory subject/object

1 Study the sections on *it* as preparatory subject in the *Advanced Gold Coursebook* on p.118 and Grammar reference pp.193–194. Rewrite these sentences using *it* as preparatory subject.

EXAMPLE That relations between employees and management have deteriorated to such an extent is sad. ➡ *It is sad that relations between employees and management have deteriorated to such an extent.*

1 That the Internet is plagued by hackers, virus writers and hoaxers is a pity.
2 To make back-ups of all your files is vital.
3 How dependent people have become on computers is surprising.
4 That you must have deleted an important file seems obvious.
5 To choose a good Internet Service Provider can be difficult.
6 For people to warn each other about dangerous computer viruses is important.
7 That you should not tell other people your password is stated in the regulations.

2 The following sentences are incorrect. Insert *it* as preparatory object in the appropriate place in each one.

1 The new computer made easier for her to finish the project.
2 He made clear that she was not going to get the promotion.
3 I find surprising that there are still plenty of people who have never used a computer.

77

4 The constant power failures made difficult to use a computer.
5 Most people consider unwise to download files from suspicious websites.

3 Look at the following sentences. Three of them are correct. In the other seven, you need to insert *it*. Correct the incorrect sentences.

1 I love going to the theatre to see a really top-class performance.
2 I can't stand when people keep me waiting.
3 I found very odd that he didn't even phone to say he wouldn't be coming.
4 I don't think you should have made so obvious that you didn't like what she was wearing.
5 I wish you wouldn't always leave up to me to make the travel arrangements.
6 Let me put to you that you were not at home with your wife on the night of 23rd September, but in Joe's Bar.
7 Our neighbours are making impossible for us to sleep at night.
8 The very wet weather made our holidays a misery.
9 Would you consider an insult if someone pretended not to see you in the street?
10 I realised she didn't really like him very much.

Speaking

▶ **Paper 5, Part 2**

About the exam: In Paper 5, Part 2 you may be asked to talk about two or three of a set of four or five photographs. The other candidate listens and then responds briefly.

> **Strategy**
> If you do not know what something in a photograph is or what it is called in English use the language of approximation. (See the *Advanced Gold Coursebook* p.120, Speaking.)

═ Hot tip! ◄

In tasks in which you share the same set of photographs it is particularly important to listen to what the other candidate says as you may be asked which photographs s/he talked about.

1 Listen to a candidate doing Part 2 of Paper 5. Which of the five photographs does she describe and in what order?

2 Listen again and tick the phrases that Renate uses.

As far as I can work out, it's some kind of ...
I'm not exactly sure but it seems to have a sort of button thing ...
I could be wrong, but ...
I can just about make out ...

3 Now you talk about the photographs Renate did not describe, saying why the people might be using the computers.

78

UNIT 10 **The trials of technology**

Listening: note-taking

▶ **Paper 4, Part 1**

About the exam: In Paper 4, Part 1 your ability to understand specific information is tested. You hear one person making an announcement, giving a radio broadcast, leaving a telephone message or delivering a speech, talk or lecture. You complete between eight and ten note-taking questions.

Strategy
Before the recording is played, study the notes. Try to predict what kind of information (date, number etc.) you need to listen for.

— Hot tip! —

You will only need to fill in one to three words, a number or a date in each gap. Do not write more than this.

Listen to this lecture given by James Fearing, a psychologist specialising in computer game obsessions, and complete the notes.

COMPUTER GAME OBSESSIONS: Dr James Fearing

Advantages of computer games
- entertaining
- develop concentration
- develop (1) .... skills.

Reasons for addictions to computer games and Internet chat lines
- avoidance of marital and financial problems.
- improved self-esteem through online (2) ....

Computer addicts:
- are unable to stop despite (3) ....
- are (4) .... about time spent using computer
- adopt defensive attitude about computer use
- experience adrenaline rush when connecting to Internet
- feel guilty after long periods of use
- show irritability if (5) ....
- have computer game (6) ....

Treatment
- computer use stopped abruptly
- user learns to set increasing (7) .... on game playing
- admission to clinic for recommended period of (8) ....

English in Use: open cloze

▶ Paper 3, Part 2

About the exam: Paper 3 English In Use, Part 2 is an open cloze of approximately 200 words containing 15 gaps. One word is required to fill each gap. The emphasis is on grammatical words.

Strategy

1. Read the title and complete text quickly to get the general idea of it.
2. Go through the text again and make a note of the answers you are confident about.
3. For the remaining gaps look carefully at the surrounding context. Decide on the part of speech of the missing word. Remember, the missing words are usually small 'grammatical' words e.g. prepositions, auxiliaries and articles.
4. Read the complete text again to make sure that all your answers make sense in context.

◀ **Hot tip!** ▶

In some cases there is more than one possibility for a gap. Even if you can think of more than one word that is correct in terms of grammar and meaning only put one word on the answer sheet.

1 Read the title of this text. Do you expect it to be:

- a humorous article on the problems people have with e-mail?
- a serious article on what kinds of conventions exist in relation to e-mail?

2 Now read the article to see if you were right.

3 Read the article again and fill each gap with one word.

 Send & Receive Reply Reply to All

THE ETIQUETTE OF E-MAIL

 New

 Forward

 Address

 Flag

 Find

 Print

 Delete

Just as telephones created new ways of communicating, e-mail is introducing conventions of its own. E-mail is just text, and (1) ... else. There (2) ... no hand-writing to show personality or perfumed stationery to make the recipient aware that it is a love letter. The speed of the service and the ability to quote a message easily and respond (3) ... it line by line give the feel of a conversation. However, the process of sitting in front of a computer writing and editing a message for spelling or grammatical errors (4) ... many letter-like qualities. E-mail (5) ... the sender to avoid showing how she feels through things (6) ... tone of voice, facial expressions and body language. It has also (7) ... shown that people are more honest about negative information over e-mail (8) ... over the telephone. In some situations, that can (9) ... good, because you get straight down to business without wasting time on preliminaries. In more volatile situations, however, people often (10) ... e-mail disagreements very much to heart because the fact that they can't hear the other person's voice or see their face (11) ... it more difficult to feel sympathetic towards them. (12) ... problem is that when people try to come to an agreement electronically, they find (13) ... more difficult to pay attention to other people's points of view. In a face-to-face group meeting, people pay attention to the person speaking, and when that person has finished, their very presence in the room remains (14) ... a reminder of their point of view, whereas (15) ... such reminder exists in an e-mail conversation.

80

UNIT 10 **The trials of technology**

Grammar check: making comparisons

One of the words in the box on the right is missing from each of the highlighted comparative and superlative structures in the text below. For each numbered gap choose the correct missing word.

| as | than | the | more | most |

The Pokemon Phenomenon

Last weekend 20,000 children descended on a shopping mall in Detroit for the US launch of (1) ... latest character in a hand-held Japanese computer game called Pokemon. Every day there are fewer and fewer American pre-teens who have not been touched by the (2) ... successful computer game of all time. Nintendo, the game's makers, have taken every known toy craze and combined and refined them into the Pokemon phenomenon. The game is based around 151 collectable Pocket Monsters ('Pokemon' for short) which look as cute on a Game Boy, (3) ... they do on a TV or cinema screen or on the shelves of your local toy shop. There are also collectable balls, books, stickers, clothes, sweets, lunch boxes, key rings and cards. Over $30 million was spent on advertising to launch Pokemon in America, three times (4) ... much as Nintendo has spent on similar games in the past. It has already engulfed Japan, America, Australia, most of Latin America and more recently Britain. Nintendo have spent six years perfecting this craze – three times longer (5) ... any other computer game before it. And so far it has surpassed even the wildest executive's dreams. Twelve million copies of the game have been sold in Japan and two spin-off games are now selling so rapidly they're breaking the records set by the original Pokemon titles. In Japan the film was (6) ... second biggest grossing release of 1998 and the follow-up did even better. In America, Pokemon trading cards are selling so quickly that a black market has emerged on which they sell for four times (7) ... than they do in the shops. Pokemon is (8) ... most contrived and controlled phenomenon ever conceived. There are two versions of the game and each has 139 Pokemon. The central aim is to collect the other twelve Pokemon. You might think that it's then a question of paying out a lot more money for the others. But not so, it's far (9) ... subtle than that. Children are encouraged to trade Pokemon with other players. This social element initially made Pokemon the (10) ... parent-friendly game ever conceived.

Vocabulary: words from other languages

Study the Vocabulary section on words from other languages on p.126 of the *Advanced Gold Coursebook*.

1 Match the definitions below to the words in the box.

| drama confetti origami mammoth marmalade siesta |
| chauffeur duvet kindergarten mattress |

1. the art or skill, originally Japanese, of folding paper to make decorative objects
2. a large bag filled with feathers or man-made material, which is placed inside a washable cover, and is used on a bed instead of a sheet
3. a short sleep after the midday meal as is the custom in many warm countries
4. a person employed to drive a car for someone else
5. an exciting and unusual situation or set of events
6. extremely large, huge
7. small pieces of coloured paper thrown over the bride and groom after a wedding
8. the top part of a bed consisting of a strong cloth cover filled with solid, soft material
9. jam made from citrus fruits, especially oranges
10. a school or class for young children between the ages of two and four

2 Now use the words to fill in the gaps in these sentences.

1. When she was a small child she was driven to .... every morning by a uniformed ....
2. Oh no! You've spilt .... on the .... again. I hope it washes out.
3. I always adored coloured paper when I was a child and spent hours making .... animals or cutting the paper up into tiny pieces to use as ....
4. Almost as soon as he lay down for his .... the uncomfortable .... started to hurt his back.
5. She always turns the most insignificant little incidents into some kind of ....

81

English in Use: gapped text

▶ **Paper 3, Part 6**

For questions 1–6 below, read the following text and then choose from the list A–I given below it the best phrase to fill each of the spaces. Each correct phrase may be used once. Some of the suggested answers do not fit at all. The exercise begins with an example (0).

THE INTERNET'S IMPACT

For some, the advent of television marked the beginning of the end of civilised society. More and more, people have watched TV at the cost of playing cards or board games, or other communal pastimes. Many fear that (0) ..J..

That may be true but, as researchers at Stanford University in the USA are the first to say, further study is needed. In a recent survey they found that (1) ..I.. . What's more, people who go online are likely to watch less television than others.

The study makes two things clear. Contrary to all the fuss in the media, the Internet's popularity is still in its infancy. More than half of US households are not connected yet, but (2) ..E.. .

Workers may be using the Web on the job for such personal ends as checking sports scores but, according to the study, (3) ..A.. . Just 4 per cent of the surveyed Internet users said they had cut back on their working hours since getting connected to the Internet.

But will the Internet make us more isolated socially? While a fourth of the Internet users say they spend less time talking on the telephone with friends and relatives, (4) ..G.. . Since e-mail is free and can be sent and received at any hour of the day, it has many built-in advantages. For some, it has actually revived the highly social art of letter writing. As for spending less time on the telephone, (5) ..D.. .

Few would argue that the Internet has had a profound effect on the lives of many in its first decade of common use. But assessing its long-term impact is difficult. That's why for all the questions they raise, (6) ..E.. . If we don't pay close attention to how we use the Internet, it will change our lives not just for better, but for worse.

A they also use the Internet to work from home
B the continuing boom in mobile phone use makes an overall decrease less and less likely
C they also use it to buy and sell shares on the stock market
D their phone bills are much lower
E studies such as Stanford's are so useful
F the Internet's potential impact on how we live and interact is enormous
G e-mail allows them to stay in touch, regardless of distance
H people will always find the Internet attractive
I the Internet and the use of e-mail have actually increased some forms of human interaction
J the Internet too will further limit social interaction

Writing: article

▶ **Paper 2, Part 1**

About the exam: In Paper 2 you may be asked to write any of the following: articles, contributions to leaflets and brochures, notices, announcements, personal notes and messages, formal and informal letters, reports, reviews, instructions, directions, competition entries, information sheets and memos. In Part 1 you normally have to write two or more of these.

> **Strategy**
> Underline the parts of the task in which you are told what types of text you have to write.

1 Look at the Paper 2, Part 1 task on p.83 and decide whether the following statements are true or false.

1 You have to reply to the principal's memo.
2 You have to write an informal letter.
3 You have to write the same number of words in both the texts you write.
4 You will need to use some of the ideas from the poster.
5 In one of the texts you will need to warn your fellow students about something.
6 You are going to send your friend a copy of something you have written.
7 You can use the same language in your article as your friend has used in the poster.

UNIT 11

TASK

You are the student welfare officer at your college. You have received the attached memo from the college principal on which you have written some notes.

You have decided to write **an article** for the college newspaper encouraging people to behave more sensibly in relation to e-mail and Internet use in the light of the principal's memo. A friend from abroad has sent you a copy of the poster displayed in computer rooms at her college and you intend to use some of the ideas from the poster in your article as well.

You also plan to write to your friend to thank her for the poster and to tell her about the principal's memo as well as enclosing a copy of your article.

- Write **an article** for the college newsletter (150 words).
- Write **a letter** to your friend (100 words).

E-MAIL AND INTERNET: A GUIDE

Before you use the facilities think about the following:

▶ Is my message or the work I want to do on the Internet important?

▶ Are other students waiting to use the computers to finish course work?

'No' to the first question, 'yes' to the second? Then come back later.

Before you send a message think about the following:

▶ Is there anything in my message I would not want others to read?

▶ Will all the people I have copied my message to really want to receive it?

'Yes' to the first question, 'no' to the second? Then don't send the message.

Before you panic about a virus warning think about the following:

▶ Is the person who sent me the message in a position to know about these things?

'No'? Then disregard the message. 'Yes'? Forward the message to the network administrator.

memo

TO: STUDENT WELFARE OFFICER
FROM: COLLEGE PRINCIPAL
SUBJECT: COMPUTER ROOM USE

Are these people all students?

It has come to my attention that a number of students have been using the computer room exclusively for 'recreational purposes'. By this I mean using the connection to the Internet to access sites of a non-academic nature such as online games, chatlines and other leisure-related pages. I have also been informed that many of the e-mail messages sent by students are of an entirely personal nature and have little or nothing to do with their academic work.

warn students that e-mail messages can be read by others e.g. network administrator

As you are already fully aware, internet access was provided so that students could take full advantage of it as an educational resource. There are, of course, many students who do just that and still more who go to the computer room to write their assignments, making use of the word processing software and printers. It is just these people who often wait hours to get onto a machine. — *give them priority*

We have received a number of complaints from staff and students about the situation and unless something is done to improve matters, I see no option but to restrict Internet access in the computer room. *people have complained to Welfare Office too*

2 Now write your answer.

1 Begin by writing plans for both texts, taking into account the audience for the two texts and the information from the task.

2 Write a draft of the two texts, remembering to change any language from the task into your own words

3 Revise your draft to make sure that you have covered all the points in the task and expanded upon them where necessary. Check the style of the two texts to make sure they are appropriate for the audience.

4 Proof read your draft for spelling, grammar and punctuation errors.

Getting away from it all

Listening: sentence completion

▶ **Paper 4, Part 2**

About the exam: In Paper 4, Part 2 you will hear a monologue of approximately two minutes, which you will hear once. It could be a radio broadcast, a lecture, a speech etc. You will have to complete either sentences or notes with missing information (a maximum of three words). There will be 8–10 questions. Each question is worth one mark. You will be tested on your understanding of specific information.

Strategy

You will have 30–45 seconds to look at the question before the recording begins. Read the incomplete sentences and predict what the missing words might be. Listen and make a note of the missing words you hear in the text so that they fit grammatically with the rest of the sentence. There may be more than one way of completing the missing information.

Hot tip!

If you miss a question, try to fill in an answer from memory. This is better than leaving a blank.

You will hear Ben Wood, a travel writer, talking about writing travel books. As you listen complete the sentences for questions 1–10.

Listen carefully as you will hear the recording ONCE only.

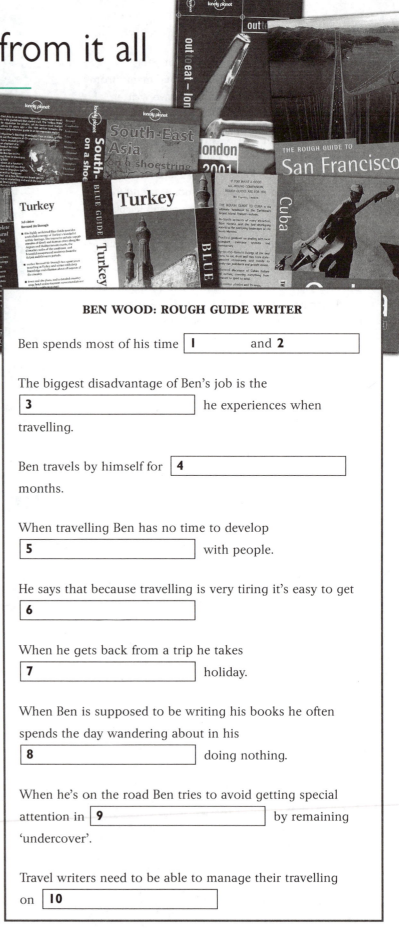

BEN WOOD: ROUGH GUIDE WRITER

Ben spends most of his time **1** _____ and **2** _____

The biggest disadvantage of Ben's job is the **3** _____ he experiences when travelling.

Ben travels by himself for **4** _____ months.

When travelling Ben has no time to develop **5** _____ with people.

He says that because travelling is very tiring it's easy to get **6** _____

When he gets back from a trip he takes **7** _____ holiday.

When Ben is supposed to be writing his books he often spends the day wandering about in his **8** _____ doing nothing.

When he's on the road Ben tries to avoid getting special attention in **9** _____ by remaining 'undercover'.

Travel writers need to be able to manage their travelling on **10** _____

Grammar check: linking words

Study the Grammar check on linking words in the *Advanced Gold Coursebook* p.137.

There are nine mistakes with linking words in the article on the right on tourists and travellers. Read the article and correct the mistakes.

Vocabulary: expressive description

Study the Vocabulary section on expressive description in the *Advanced Gold Coursebook* p.135.

1 Look at the extracts on the right from guidebooks on North West Wales and Tokyo and find words or expressions that mean:

1. covered by trees
2. with a lot of wind
3. difficult to pronounce
4. find by chance
5. without people
6. pleasant
7. hidden
8. isolated area
9. all the way along
10. walking very slowly
11. with trees providing shade
12. goes (but not in a straight line)

2 Now use some of the language to make this description more expressive.

Halfway through the morning we found by chance a path that went through the valley to the village of Saint Bartholomew, hidden just beyond Mount Saint Clare in a place that is very difficult to find. Since it was Sunday morning there were no people in the village square when we first arrived, but when the morning church service finished there was a parade and we found ourselves in the middle of a large crowd. We walked very slowly along village streets with names that are very difficult to pronounce and with picturesque cottages all the way along them. Finally, we found ourselves in a pleasant park with trees providing shade and sat down to eat our picnic lunch.

We might set out on our travels without a fixed itinerary, hotel bookings or a representative to meet us at our destination, but we still run the risk of failing to engage with the local people, of causing offence and even damage because our often superficial attitude to the places we visit.

In the beginning, let's take 'travellers' visiting countries like Vietnam. At the first place, they all dress alike … T-shirts, short skirts or baggy trousers and shoulder-bags. As result they are all virtually indistinguishable from each other. Furthermore, their style of dress is often offensive to local people. Secondly, backpacker travellers like these all tend to stick together. They stay at the same hostels, eat and drink in the same bars and restaurants and even use the same types of transport. In spite of public transport is cheap, many of these travellers prefer to take mini-buses run by private companies and charging twice as much as locals pay for the same journey.

It is often said that these 'travellers' benefit a country more than package tourists. Travellers do spend most of the money they have in the countries they visit. Package tourists, on another hand, have often paid for tours and even hotel accommodation in their country of origin. The main objective, however, of many independent travellers is to spend as little as possible and they therefore [make little] contribution tha[n] tourists who are [obsessed] with prices and bargaining.

At last, travellers often make a negative impact on a place simply because they try so hard to get off the beaten track. It starts with just one or two people but word travels fast and before too long local cultures and even the environment are threatened. Package tourists, in contrast, stick to the planned and authorised itineraries and do less damage so.

Despite they have such a bad reputation I'd rather be a package tourist any day.

The north-west of Wales has steep, wooded valleys, wind-blown moorland, clean air and vast tracts of unspoilt land – reason enough to go. In addition, it boasts tongue-twisting place names, stormy weather, steam trains and music festivals. A highlight of the region is the Snowdonia National Park. It is best explored by putting the map away and getting lost. No matter how well you think you know the area you'll always stumble upon new and interesting things, such as a deserted sandy cove or some idyllic village tucked away in the middle of nowhere.

Takeshita Dori is a pedestrian-only street that's best recognised by its shoulder-to-shoulder crowd on Sunday afternoons. Lined by shops that cater for teenagers, it's packed with young people hunting for bargains in inexpensive clothing, music, jewellery and so on. After inching your way along this narrow lane, you will eventually find yourself on a busy thoroughfare, Meiji Dori. If it's the first or fourth Sunday of the month, turn left (north) onto Meiji Dori, where in a couple minutes on your left you'll see Togo Shrine, popular for its flea market held the first and fourth Sundays of every month, when everything from old chests, dolls, and kimonos are for sale, spread out on a tree-shaded path that meanders around the shrine.

Reading: multiple matching

▶ **Paper 1 Part 4**

About the exam: Part 4 of Paper 1 Reading is a multiple-matching task. You are usually required to read a text of 700–1,200 words. This is often made up of a group of short texts or one continuous text. You will be required to match the questions with the relevant information from the text. There may be more than one correct answer for some questions. You should spend no more than 18 minutes on this task.

Strategy

Look for the specific information that the question asks you to find. Don't be distracted by irrelevant information in the text.

Hot tip!

Make sure you have used each of the items in the list at least once.

1 Discuss with another student what features you would expect a good guide book to have. Then read the article below through once to see how many of the features you thought of are mentioned.

2 Answer questions 1–14 choosing from the list (A–G) on the right below. Some choices may be required more than once.

Of which guide or guides are the following stated?			
The publisher believes one volume in particular will be read by people who may have no intention of visiting the place.	1		
It pays more attention to entertainment and what to buy than providing background information about the country.	2		**A** Blue
They say they can help readers see below the surface of the places they visit.	3	4	**B** Lonely Planet
They are particularly attractive to look at.	5	6	**C** Rough
They began with a single volume that led to the creation of publishing businesses.	7	8	**D** Everyman
It was among the first to be published.	9		
It was written because the author couldn't get the information he wanted.	10		**E** Insight
It tells you where to go both to wash your clothes and get them washed for you.	11		**F** Eyewitness
It provides information about accommodation at both ends of the price scale.	12		**G** Cadogan
It would only have been used by very wealthy people when it was first published.	13		
One of its guides seeks to educate readers about a neglected aspect of a country's culture.	14		

The 'Good Guide' Guide

CHOOSING a guide book is like choosing a new outfit: you want it to serve a practical purpose but, above all, to represent the kind of person you think you are[1]. The tourist as sightseer will plump for a traditional descriptive volume: one from the Blue or Companion series. The young and footloose, carrying only a change of underwear and a thirst for new experience, will go for Lonely Planet or Rough Guides, which claim to get below the superficial impression given by holiday brochures and show the traveller what a country is really like[2].

The new Everyman city guides, by contrast, suit travellers more interested in shopping, eating and night-life than in understanding the country they are visiting. Dorling Kindersley's glossy Eyewitness series, with their alluring use of pictures and design, are for those who want a style accessory as well as a useful tool[3]. Cadogan Guides try to cover all classes of tourist. Insight guides make a feature of their splendid photographs. And beyond the mainstream are guides for travellers with special interests: hikers, amateur archaeologists, lovers of gardens or battlefields, compulsive shoppers …

Until the second half of this century only the rich could afford to go abroad as tourists. The earliest guide books concentrated on instructing their pampered readers how to minimise the disturbances of travel and to cope with the idiosyncrasies of the locals who insisted on getting in the way of the superlative views and begging outside historic buildings[4].

The first uniform series of travel guides were the Handbooks, launched in the 1830s by John Murray, a British publisher. Travel writing was an undiscovered area of literature at the time. In one of the earliest Handbooks, which was about Switzerland, the author set out the guide book writer's creed: 'In order to travel with advantage in a country previously unknown, something more seems necessary than a mere detail of certain lines of road, and an enumeration of towns, villages, mountains, etc.'

A few years later Karl Baedeker launched a rival series, which would become more renowned[5]. He introduced the practice of awarding stars to places of outstanding beauty and interest and his system was later adopted and adapted by others. In 1918, when the first Blue Guide (to London) was published by Macmillan in London and by Hachette in Paris[6], the market for travel writing was still restricted to the upper class. 'London in winter is apt to be depressing to the visitor unless he has adequate social introductions,' it warned. The 16th edition, published this year, takes the modern, gung-ho approach: 'London is an all-year-round tourist and business destination, with an exciting calendar of events.'

A guide book has two main functions: to explain to tourists why they ought to visit a place, then give enough detailed information to render their visit convenient, enjoyable and instructive. No matter how well-written and researched the guide book entry, visitors who arrive at a chateau, museum or temple when it is about to close for lunch have been let down.

The range and detail of its factual information may determine the choice of guide. People needing the times of buses and the opening hours of launderettes buy a Lonely Planet or Rough Guide. If you are looking for a hotel suite in Manhattan for upwards of $1,000 a night, then the Everyman city guide will point you towards it. Yet publishers prefer not to pigeonhole and are at pains to stress the breadth of their appeal. Thus Everyman also embraces New York hotels at less than $150. 'The Rough Guide to the Pyrenees', while singing the praises of a local launderette, the Laverie Foch in Perpignan, also mentions some luxury hotels which will arrange your laundry for you[7]. Rachel Fielding, a founder of the Cadogan Guides, sums up the credo of her series as 'from slum it to splurge'.

Although practical detail is important, the best books balance it with a welter of information on a country's culture, history, politics and people – lumped together in the Rough Guides in a section headed 'Contexts'. Mark Ellingham, their publisher, believes that one purpose of travel is to gain an understanding of a country. Thus the Moroccan guide contains translations of Moroccan stories; and the Bulgarian volume, conceding that 'knowledge of the country's literature is scant', seeks to correct that lack with three pages of poems.

Mr Ellingham explains: 'People may spend a lot of time on trains or buses and our book may be the only thing that they have to read[8]. We even get letters from readers praising the bits about places they never managed to get to.' Rachel Fielding agrees: 'We've just done a Cadogan Guide to Antarctica. Some cruise ships call there but I expect quite a lot of people will buy the book just to read it, not because they are necessarily planning a trip.'

Guide books, especially of the back-packer kind, are a peculiarly personal form of publishing, which explains why some successful modern series began almost accidentally[9]. Tony Wheeler, who is the British founder of Lonely Planet[10], wrote the first book in 1973 in response to questions about the trip he and his wife, Maureen, made from England to Australia by sea, rail and road. There are now nearly 200 titles.

In 1982 Mark Ellingham went to Greece and wrote the first of the Rough Guides. 'The only guides I could find then[11] were those that had plenty about the archaeological sites but nothing about the beaches,' he recalls. He sold the book and the idea for a series to a publisher. Today there are more than 100 Rough Guides and he controls a staff of 40, as well as teams of researchers.

One fault editors have to be alert to is that their authors, anxious to convey the impression of having been everywhere and seen it all, allow a touch of world-weariness to creep in. This is not to say that the best guide books eschew all criticism, but the national slurs of the past are unacceptable today. As travel broadens the mind, so has the nature and extent of modern travel broadened and mellowed the guide books' agenda, encouraging understanding rather than prejudice. No longer tools for survival in a hostile environment, the best of them build bridges between visitors and their hosts. They make the world a smaller and more tolerant place.

Grammar plus: relative clauses

1 Look at the underlined relative clauses in The 'Good Guide' Guide and decide if they are defining or non-defining.

2 In this paragraph there are ten mistakes with the punctuation of relative clauses. Find the mistakes and correct them.

In 1973 which was the year I visited the city for the first time I was completely bewitched by London. My friend Gillian and I found a small hotel just off Holland Park Road. By an amazing coincidence it was the same hotel, in which Gillian's father had stayed five years before – and they remembered him! Near the hotel there were several buses none of which ran particularly regularly in those days. Every morning we would catch one of these buses to Oxford Street and spend hours looking in shop windows at the wonderful things, which two young women on a shoe-string budget could not afford. Gillian also liked to go to Knightsbridge where there were even more expensive shops such as Harvey Nicholls and the famous Harrods. The only things we could afford to buy there were beautiful linen handkerchiefs which we gave to our friends when we got back to Canada. Gillian's older brother who had visited London earlier that year had given us a list of the places, that he had visited. We happily retraced his steps, sometimes stopping for a cup of tea in one of the cafés, which he had recommended.

3 Fill in the gaps in these sentences with a relative pronoun. Sometimes there is more than one possibility.

EXAMPLE *The dog, ... owner was nowhere to be seen, was running frantically back and forth outside the entrance to the hotel.*
*The dog, **whose** owner was nowhere to be seen, was running frantically back and forth outside the entrance to the hotel.*

1 The person to .... I spoke told me to call back on Monday.
2 Tim Markham, ... first travel guide was published earlier this month, will be speaking in the Great Hall on Thursday at 7 p.m.
3 Bus 243, ... takes you to the quaint village of Saint George, leaves the bus station at 7 a.m.
4 The road .... winds its way through the foothills is definitely the more scenic of the two routes.
5 The cathedral, ... foundations were laid in 1156, is still a magnificent sight.
6 Passengers .... have booked accommodation should wait outside the terminal.
7 The staff, many of .... are also students of hotel management, are all extremely competent and friendly.
8 My husband, for .... the trip was an anniversary present, was delighted by the charming street market.

4 Fill in the gaps in these sentences with *what* or *that*.

EXAMPLE *I don't know .... I should do with our cat Felix while we're away.*
*I don't know **what** I should do with our cat Felix while we're away.*

1 We visited all of the places .... the guide book mentioned.
2 The receptionist listened patiently to .... the guest was saying.
3 You can't always rely on .... the holiday brochures tell you about a resort.
4 The photographs .... appeared on page 3 of your brochure are utterly unlike the villa we were unfortunate enough to stay in.
5 There was so much choice we always had trouble deciding .... to do in the evening.
6 Something .... always attracts holiday-makers is good weather.
7 The interpreter translated .... the man was saying into faultless English.

UNIT 11 **Getting away**

English in Use: register transfer

▶ **Paper 3, Part 5**

About the exam: In Paper 3, Part 5 English in Use, you are required to read two texts and transfer information from one to the other. The second text will have gaps in it and will be written in a different register from the first e.g. more formal/informal. You must complete the gaps with no more than two words and NOT use words from the first text.

Strategy

1. Read both texts to get a general idea of what they are about.
2. Read the second text again, sentence by sentence, and make sure you understand the meaning of each sentence which includes a gap.
3. Refer to the equivalent part of the first text to check the exact meaning of the missing part.
4. Underline or highlight the relevant words/phrases in the first text, if necessary.
5. Decide on the part of speech of the missing word(s).
6. Complete the gap, paying careful attention to the form and spelling of the words you insert.
7. Do not use words that appear in the first text.

— **Hot tip!** ◀—

Check for spelling and grammar mistakes in the words that you use to fill each gap.

Read the information on the right from a website about youth hostels. Use the information in it to complete the numbered gaps in the letter below it from a travel agent to a client. Use no more than two words for each gap. The words you need do not occur in the website.

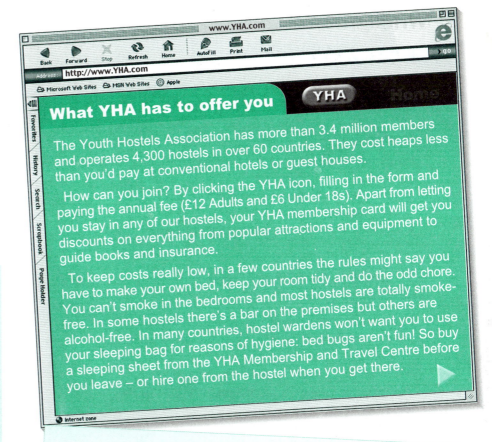

What YHA has to offer you

The Youth Hostels Association has more than 3.4 million members and operates 4,300 hostels in over 60 countries. They cost heaps less than you'd pay at conventional hotels or guest houses.

How can you join? By clicking the YHA icon, filling in the form and paying the annual fee (£12 Adults and £6 Under 18s). Apart from letting you stay in any of our hostels, your YHA membership card will get you discounts on everything from popular attractions and equipment to guide books and insurance.

To keep costs really low, in a few countries the rules might say you have to make your own bed, keep your room tidy and do the odd chore. You can't smoke in the bedrooms and most hostels are totally smoke-free. In some hostels there's a bar on the premises but others are alcohol-free. In many countries, hostel wardens won't want you to use your sleeping bag for reasons of hygiene: bed bugs aren't fun! So buy a sleeping sheet from the YHA Membership and Travel Centre before you leave – or hire one from the hostel when you get there.

Dear Dr Wilson,

In response to your enquiry about budget accommodation, we would recommend the Youth Hostels Association.

There are hostels in over 60 countries offering accommodation that is (1) .... than conventional hotels and guest houses. I would strongly advise you (2) .... a member.

Annual membership for people of eighteen years or (3) .... is £12. This (4) .... to stay in any of the 4,300 hostels worldwide and to obtain discounts on a (5) .... of items, including popular attractions, equipment and insurance.

Please bear in mind that hostel regulations may sometimes (6) .... to make your own bed, tidy your room and do small chores. There is (7) .... on smoking in the bedrooms and in some cases it is (8) .... anywhere in the hostel. While some hostels actually (9) .... alcohol, others do not allow its (10) .... on the premises. Because of the risk of bed bugs and other infestations in some countries, hostel wardens do (11) .... the use of sleeping bags and ask you to use a regulation sleeping sheet instead. These can (12) .... from the YHA Membership and Travel Centre prior to (13) .... or hired on arrival at the hostel.

Please do not hesitate to contact me if you have any further enquiries.

Yours sincerely,

Helen Walters

Helen Walters

ting: brochure

▶ **Paper 2, Part 2**

About the exam: One of the options in Part 2 may involve writing part of a brochure or an information leaflet.

Strategy
Pay particular attention to the following information in the task input:
- what kind of information your brochure entry must include.
- the audience to whom your brochure is directed.

1 Look at the Paper 2, Part 2 tasks below and answer these questions.

1. Which task is directed to a more specific audience?
2. In which task would you be likely to have at least four sections?
3. Which task is concerned with informing the people who will read it as well as encouraging them to visit the place?
4. In which task would you be more likely to mention the seasons or months of the year?
5. In which task do you have a choice of things to write about?
6. In which task are you writing part of a longer text?
7. Which task asks you to write for a particular kind of audience?

TASK A
Your local tourist authority is concerned that too many of the visitors to your town or region come on package tours that they have paid for in their country of origin. They now wish to attract young independent travellers. They are planning a new brochure called 'What's cool in X?'. You have been asked to write a contribution to the brochure. You should include information on cheap places to eat, accommodation, night life and transport.

TASK B
You have been asked to write an information leaflet on either a) places to spend time outdoors in your city or b) walking and picnic spots in your region. You should say what kinds of activities are possible at these places and say if there are any restrictions on access or use of the facilities at different times of year.

2 Now look at this sample answer to one of the tasks above.

1. Which task is being answered here?
2. Does the answer include all the information necessary?
3. Would it have the desired effect on the audience?
4. Is it laid out in an interesting and appropriate way?
5. Has the writer avoided using too much language from the task?
6. If it is supposed to be part of a longer text, is this clear?

This summer you should come to Formentera. It has a lot to offer the young independent traveller like you, even though it also attracts a lot of people who are on package holidays they have paid for in their country of origin.
But we want you to come. Here is some cool information for you.

Cheap places to eat
There are plenty of cheap places to eat on Formentera. In Es Pujols you can get hamburgers and fast food like chips and there are lots of pizzerias with reasonable prices too. Cheaper still would be to buy some food in a supermarket and have a picnic on the beach, but remember to take your rubbish with you when you go!

Accommodation
Formentera has all kinds of accommodation from luxury hotel complexes, villas and country houses to economical apartments and pensions. If you're travelling on a shoestring you will probably want to stay at a pension. You will find many of these in both La Sabina and San Ferran. Camping is not allowed, so don't sleep on the beach.

Transport
To get to Formentera you catch a ferry or a jet foil from Ibiza. This costs about £30 return. On the island you can rent a car, jeep, moped or bicycle to get around. Bicycles are cheapest. There is also a bus but it doesn't run very regularly. Some people hitchhike but there aren't a lot of cars so you can wait a long time for a lift. In the summer there is a lot of traffic so you should be careful on the roads to avoid having an accident.

We hope you come to Formentera. You'll have a great time!

---

3 Make any improvements you think necessary to the sample answer.

4 Write your answer to the other task.

90

UNIT 12 Mind over matter

English in Use: word formation

▶ **Paper 3, Part 4**

About the exam: In Paper 3, Part 4 there are two short texts (no longer than 130 words each) with a total of 15 word-transformation items. The texts are extracts from magazine and newspaper articles, encyclopedia entries, letters etc. The extracts are always taken from two different types of text.

Strategy

Read the texts all the way through to get an idea of what they are about before you start to tackle the word formation items.

Read the text and use the words in the box to the right of the text to form one word that fits in the same numbered space in the text.

Learner training

When *recording vocabulary* it is helpful to include the following information:

- an example of the word in a sentence: *I was particularly intrigued by a story she told me about her grandmother.*
- a definition or explanation of the meaning of the word (this might include a translation equivalent in your language): *ruminate = think carefully about (rumiar)*
- grammatical information about the word: *ruminate about/over. Can also be intransitive* e.g. *He sat ruminating.*
- a phonemic transcription of the word with the stressed syllable marked /ˈruːmɪneɪt/
- various forms of the word e.g.

verb	noun	adjective	adverb
persuade dissuade	persuasion	persuasive	persuasively

THE MYSTERY OF MIRRORS

Mirrors, those (1) ... surfaces which produce an image of objects placed in front of them, are a (2) ... image in Western art. Painters seem to have been fascinated by the (3) ... between the virtual reality which spontaneously appears in a mirror and the one which they artificially create by painting on plaster, paper or canvas. In both cases, the (4) ... sees something which is not where it seems to be. But in contrast to a painted image, which presupposes that the painted surface can be seen, what we see in a mirror requires that the reflective surface is (5) ... . When mirrors are represented in paintings, the situation becomes complicated in a particularly (6) ... way: the virtual reality of the picture includes a second virtual reality in the form of a painted (7) ... .

1 MAGIC
2 RECUR
3 RELATE
4 OBSERVE
5 VISIBLE
6 INTRIGUE
7 REFLECT

91

Reading: gapped text

▶ **Paper 1, Part 2**

About the exam: The main text in Paper 2, Part 1 always contains more words than the paragraphs that have been removed.

Strategy

Always read the main text first. Try to predict what kind of information most logically fills each gap before you look at the paragraphs.

> **Hot tip!**
> Make sure you only use each of the paragraphs once.

1 Read the text once through and give it a title.

2 For questions 1–6 you must choose which of the paragraphs A–G fit into the numbered gaps in the magazine article. There is one extra paragraph, which does not fit in any of the gaps.

3 Match one of the numbered words (1–9) in the main text and the missing paragraphs to the meanings below (A–I).

A surprising
B (not a) bit
C continued to be widespread
D actions needing skill
E increase in strength or amount
F large number of events of the same kind coming together in time
G quick and willing readiness
H a collection
I full of

What babies and toddlers know and when they know it are questions that have long fascinated parents, for whom nearly everything a baby does seems fraught[1] with meaning. They wonder whether that fledgling attempt at speech or that earnest imitation of daddy's funny face means their baby actually understands more than the childcare handbooks say.

1

Scientists now believe that newborns only a few hours old can distinguish the human face. Even these tiny babies seem to prefer looking at pictures of faces with their features in proper alignment. Twelve hours after birth, infants can pick out their mother's voice from other voices, possibly because that's the one they heard most in utero. By 5 months they may be able to add and subtract small numbers in their heads. And at 6 months they are capable of manipulating a computer to get the result they want.

2

Take the question of how well babies remember things. Until recently, the views of Swiss psychologist Jean Piaget prevailed[2]. He believed that until their second birthday babies' senses were too uncoordinated for them to develop memories. That meant they couldn't picture their absent mothers, for example; or if they saw someone hide a toy under a pillow they wouldn't look for it because for them it would no longer exist.

3

And babies' long-term memory, too, is better than conventional wisdom has held. Psychologist Nancy Myers placed a group of 10-month-olds in a dark room with objects that emitted different noises; she then used special cameras to film their individual reactions. Two years later, Dr Myers repeated the experiment, testing the original group as well as a control group who had never been in the room. 'The original group wasn't frightened of the dark room,' reports Dr Myers, 'and they reached for objects with greater alacrity[3]' than those who hadn't seen them before. The reason? Dr Myers says the first group remembered their experiences.

4

A group of 5-month-old babies were shown one Mickey Mouse doll, which was then placed behind

92

a screen; next, they were shown another Mickey Mouse doll, which was placed behind the screen as well. When the screen was removed, it sometimes revealed the correct number of Mickey Mouses – two – and sometimes an incorrect number of dolls, such as one or three. The babies always stared longer at the incorrect numbers. indicating they had expected one doll plus one doll to equal two dolls.

| 5 |

In her study, babies listened to a number of vowel-consonant combinations, such as ooh, ah, baa and ga. When one sound was replaced by a new one, a toy bear in a box was lit up and made to dance. Soon the babies looked towards the bear every time they heard a sound they didn't recognise. Interestingly, babies ignored subtle variations in their native languages (both Swedish and American infants were studied), but registered similar variations in a foreign language as 'new'. They already recognised which sounds they would need for speech in their native tongue.

Can adults enhance[4] a baby's learning? Actually they probably do automatically. Experts believe that grammar and speech are facilitated through 'motherese' ... the high-pitched speech that many of us adopt around infants ... because it holds the baby's interest in a way that adult speech does not.

| 6 |

The best teaching tool is the warm and loving relationship a parent develops with the child. Almost all a baby's learning takes place in the context of relating to another person. Through affectionate give-and-take, babies learn – and the adults who love them learn how amazing their children really are.

A Other new studies show that long before a child says his first word, he hears and understands plenty. Research conducted by speech scientist Patricia Kuhn has shown that an 8-month-old who hears the word 'ball' will look over at a ball in the room. Even 6-month-olds can distinguish between a number of spoken sounds to find those that are meaningful, Dr Kuhn has found.

B Not only is that understanding possible, say researchers, it is likely. The view, dominant for centuries, that babies are capable of only limited intellectual activity has been largely discredited by a spate[5] of recent studies. The new thinking is that infants possess an array[6] of skills far more sophisticated than adults ever dreamed possible.

C It doesn't take formal teaching to develop children's intellectual abilities. 'If you pay attention to their progress through the early stages and can be the kind of parent who changes as they do,' says child psychiatrist Stanley Greenspan, 'you will be promoting a wiser and happier child.' Here's what Dr Greenspan has found works best.

D Perhaps the most startling[7] information about infants' abilities is the new evidence suggesting that they can do simple arithmetic. In her research, Karen Wynn, a psychologist, relied on a well-known phenomenon: infants, like adults, look longer at new or unexpected events than at routine or familiar ones. In this way they reveal what they expect (or know).

E These skills aren't limited to gifted babies; every normal baby has always been naturally capable of surprising intellectual feats[8]. Nowadays adults are better at finding out how to measure what infants can do.

F But most experts take a dim view of formalised courses for infants, particularly those that claim to teach reading and maths. There isn't a shred[9] of independent scientific evidence that these programmes work.

G Yet new research indicates that babies do remember and, given the means, will seek out what they want. In a recent experiment, mothers read their 3- to 6-month-olds a rhyme twice a day for two weeks. The babies were then given a five-minute 'training' session with specially equipped dummies, in which they learned that their sucking actions caused a computer to recite various rhymes. They consistently showed a preference for the familiar rhyme by manipulating the computer to recite it.

Speaking

▶ **Paper 5**

About the exam: Paper 5 takes approximately 15 minutes to do. Usually two candidates are examined together. Sometimes candidates do Paper 5 in groups of three. You are evaluated on the basis of the following criteria:

Grammar and Vocabulary (Accuracy and Appropriacy)
This refers to your ability to use grammatical structures and vocabulary so that you do not need to pause or paraphrase too often. This scale includes verb tenses, hypothetical meaning, modal verbs, verb patterns, articles etc. It also includes the range of vocabulary you know as well as your knowledge of collocation, style and register.

Discourse Management
This refers to your ability to link ideas and language together clearly. This scale includes the use of the language of comparison and contrast, linking words, relative clauses etc. It also includes your ability to keep talking for a minute on your own in Part 2 and your other contributions to the conversations in parts 1, 3 and 4.

Pronunciation (Individual Sounds, Linking, Stress and Intonation)
This refers to all aspects of pronunciation. You are not expected to have an accent like a native speaker of English. As long as what you say and your attitudes and feelings are easy to understand it doesn't matter if your first language influences your accent.

Interactive Communication (Turn-taking, Initiating and Responding)
This refers to your ability to ask and answer questions, make, accept and reject suggestions, offer and ask for opinions etc. Included here is your ability to understand and respond to questions without hesitating for too long and your ability to develop the theme of the conversation with the other candidate(s). REMEMBER: You do not lose marks if you need to ask the examiner to repeat or clarify the instructions before you start the task.

Paper 5	Preparation	Strategy in Exam
Part 1 (3 minutes)	Revise language for talking about: • your region or town • home and family • hobbies/interests • work or studies • reasons for learning English • short-term and long-term future plans	• Ask the other candidate questions as the examiner suggests. • Listen to what the other candidate says and respond with interest to her/his answers as you would if you had met the other candidate in a social situation.
Part 2 (3 to 4 minutes)	Revise the language of: • comparison • contrast • description • speculation	• Listen very carefully to the instructions the examiner gives you and make sure you do all the things s/he asks you to do. • Alternate between making comments about one photograph and then another. • If you do not know what something in a photograph is or what it is called in English use the language of approximation (see p.120 *Advanced Gold Coursebook*). • If it is <u>not</u> your turn to speak for about a minute, listen to what the other candidate says but do not interrupt. You may be asked which photographs s/he talked about. Only give a short response to the examiner's question (about 20 seconds).

UNIT 12 **Mind over matter**

Part 3 (3 to 4 minutes)	Revise the language of: • asking for, giving and responding to opinions • asking for, making, accepting and politely rejecting suggestions • 'fillers' like 'Well, now ...' and 'Let me see ...'	• Talk to the other candidate – *not* the examiner. • Make suggestions and express your opinion but also ask the other candidate what s/he thinks. • Don't let silences occur in your conversation with the other candidate. If you can't think of any more ideas, ask the other candidate if s/he can.
Part 4 (3 to 4 minutes)	Work out what you think about current issues such as the environment, transport, work, travel, ways of life in the past, today and in the future, but don't be tempted to learn set opinions off by heart and then recite them in the exam. You will not sound natural or spontaneous.	• Respond to the exminer's questions *and* the other candidate's comments. • Try to develop the opinions the other candidate expresses rather than simply agreeing or disagreeing.

 Listen to two candidates doing Paper 5 and look at the photos and visual prompts they refer to. Assess each candidate on the categories listed below. Write P (poor), G (good) or E (excellent) in the spaces.

	Grammar and Vocabulary	**Discourse Management**	**Pronunciation**	**Interactive Communication**
Carmen				
Piotr				

Grammar plus: emphasis with inversion

1 Study the sections on emphasis with inversion on p.145 of the *Advanced Gold Coursebook* and Grammar Reference p.193.

2 Use each of the following adverbials and make all the other necessary changes to give greater emphasis to these sentences.

> Never ... Not only ...
> Rarely ... At no time ...
> Hardly ... Only after ...
> No sooner ... Scarcely ...
> Under no circumstances ...

1 I had just sat down to eat my supper when I heard someone knocking at the door.
2 This city has not often been in greater need of cheap public transport than it is today.
3 I had never met such a fascinating and intelligent person as Madeleine.
4 He forgets people's names and he also finds it difficult to remember the words for common objects.
5 You should not let people in under any circumstances if they don't have identification on them.
6 Barely a second after she began to speak someone in the audience shouted 'fire'.
7 She posted the letter and then realised she had forgotten to enclose the cheque.
8 She did not doubt at any time that he would come home.
9 Immediately after she had found her seat on the plane a flight attendant asked her if she would mind moving.

UNIT 12 **Mind over matter**

Listening: note-taking

▶ **Paper 4, Part 2**

About the exam: There is only enough space on the answer sheet to write from one to three words for each question.

> **Strategy**
>
> Do not write more than three words to fill each gap. If the answers include numbers, write these in figures rather than words

> ◀ **Hot tip!** ◀
>
> Remember to check spelling on your answer sheet.

You will hear part of a lecture on dreams. As you listen complete the notes for questions 1–8. Listen very carefully as you will hear the recording ONCE only.

Dreaming sleep

Frequency of occurrence: every
(1) _____

Duration of each period of dreaming sleeps:
(2) _____ (approximately)

Alternative term for dreaming sleep
(3) _____ or REM sleep

Characteristics of the typical dream
- *(4) _____*
- *fade from memory in (5) _____ (approximately)*
- *can last for more than (6) _____*
- *incorporate physical discomfort and (7) _____*

Function of dreaming: provides necessary substitute (8) _____ for the brain

Vocabulary: sound and light

1 Study the Vocabulary section on sound and light on p.149 of the *Advanced Gold Coursebook*.

2 Choose the alternative that best fills each of the gaps in these sentences.

1 The *roar/hiss* of the steam from a coffee machine was a sound the she always associated with her student days and the many happy hours spent chatting with friends.
2 As he scanned the horizon he saw a sudden *sparkle/flash* of bright light.
3 He acted as if he had never set eyes on her before but we all noticed a momentary *flicker/beam* of recognition in his eyes.
4 There was a deafening *crash/bang* as the ceiling of the burning building collapsed.
5 She could hear the *screech/hum* of brakes as the car took the corner sharply.
6 He was mesmerised by the *sparkle/flash* of the diamond necklace in the candle light.
7 He heard a loud *crash/bang* as if a gun had been fired somewhere outside in the street.
8 The *roar/hiss* of a jet flying over made it impossible for them to continue speaking.
9 She could just make out the faint *beam/flicker* of a torch light somewhere at the end of the tunnel.
10 As she was walking back up the stairs she heard the *bang/thud* of a heavy parcel landing on the doormat.
11 At first she thought he was serious and then she saw the telltale *twinkle/glow* in his eyes and she realised that, as usual, her grandfather was only teasing her.
12 The soft contours of the surrounding hills were turned pink by the *glow/beam* of the approaching dawn.
13 As she entered the room the *hiss/hum* of animated conversation rapidly ceased and they all stood and stared.

3 Use your dictionary to find at least one more example of the use of the words in Exercise 2.

> **Learner training**
>
> If you come across these words when you are reading, make a note of the sentences in which they occur.

97

Grammar check: questions

1 Read the article below and decide which of the following statements best summarises the content.

a) The author was cured of nightmares because she learnt something important about herself.
b) The author was cured of nightmares because one of hers came true.

HOW I WAS CURED OF NIGHTMARES

In my late twenties, I was cured of nightmares. This is how it happened. I'd been having a recurring 'bad dream' for years. In the dream, I was making my way up a mountain in a place that looked like Transylvania – certainly vampire country. Night was falling. We – a vague group – stopped at a country inn. I would be given a room off an upper corridor, and go to bed and try to sleep. But
5   moonlit forest branches scrabbled against the window; and eventually claws, too, and the window would crack, and howling demented creatures spring at me – and I'd awake and the terror would last for hours.

Then one night reality caught up with the dream. I went on a touring holiday in Austria with my then husband, my small child and an au pair girl. Night was falling as we took the mountain road
10 out of Innsbruck. To my terror I recognised the road as the one in my dream. With every curve the place became more familiar. Trees bending in over the road, bare slabs of rock gleaming in the moonlight. We stopped at the first inn we came to – thankfully it wasn't at all like the one in the dream. I remember my relief. But then it turned out the inn was full. Staff led us to an annexe – and there the nightmare house stood, in all its gabled steep-roofed detail. Up the familiar stairs with the
15 carved oak banisters, along the upstairs corridor; the white-aproned maid showed us to our two rooms, facing each other. In the room to the right, moonlit branches scrabbled against the pane – the one to the left looked out over the valley, calm, benign and still. I put the au pair girl and my child in the haunted room, and chose the other for myself and my husband. I am not proud of it. I knew the better way, but chose the worse.
20 All passed a quiet night. I even slept, for once dreamlessly. I had survived the night but my relief was short-lived – I spent the next few days in terror waiting for something dreadful to happen. But nothing did.

I never had the dream again. I don't think I've had a nightmare since. There was no way I could pretend any longer that I was so nice and good that evil must come from outside me, not inside
25 me. I realised I was responsible for my own nightmares.

2 Read the article again and make appropriate questions for the answers below.

EXAMPLE 1 *When were you cured of nightmares?*

1   When I was in my late twenties.
2   For years.
3   Like Transylvania.
4   No, I was with a group of people.
5   At the first inn we came to.
6   No, not at all, thankfully.
7   Because the inn was full.
8   The au pair girl and my child.
9   Very well, actually. I didn't even dream.
10 No, I don't. Not since then.

3 Decide if these questions are correct or not. If not, correct the mistake.

1   Shouldn't you have slept in the haunted room?
2   Who did show you to your rooms in the annexe?
3   Did you use to have this nightmare often?
4   About what were you worried?
5   Wasn't the au pair afraid to sleep in the haunted room?
6   Did your husband know why did you choose the room with the view of the valley?
7   Did you ask the au pair whether she had slept well?

98

UNIT 13 An interesting business

Grammar check: passives

Read this article about a man who has turned a hobby into a successful business. Put the verbs in brackets into the correct active or passive forms.

CHAIRMAN OF THE SNOW BOARD

The sport of snowboarding is booming and the person responsible for this is Jake Burton. Burton, the antithesis of a hard-nosed businessman, is the president and founder of what is now a multimillion-dollar corporation. 'I have the best job in the world,' says Burton. 'I ride my board several days a week, the company is making money, the sport is blossoming.'

Though Burton (1) .... (*often call*) the inventor of the snowboard, he (2) .... (*refuse*) to take credit for anything more than improving on somebody else's idea. He (3) .... (*settle*), instead, for the label 'snowboard pioneer'. The first snowboard-like object (4) .... (*produce*) by Sherman Poppen who, in 1965, (5) .... (*bolt*) two skis together for his children to slide on. Poppen (6) .... (*call*) his invention the Snurfer. Jake Burton (7) .... (*give*) a Snurfer when he was 14 years old. 'I (8) .... (*always feel*) there was an opportunity for it to (9) .... (*market*) better,' he says, 'for serious technology to (10) .... (*apply*) to it, so Snurfing could (11) .... (*become*) a legitimate sport instead of a cheap toy.' According to Jake's father, although Jake (12) .... (*not possess*) any innate entrepreneurial spirit, once he had the idea for this board in his head, he (13) .... (*put*) every bit of his energy into it.

Jake Burton's teenage years (14) .... (*mar*) by tragedy: his older brother (15) .... (*kill*) in Vietnam when Burton was 12, and their mother (16) .... (*die*) of leukemia five years later. 'The losses made for two things,' says Burton, 'real independence and an ability to (17) .... (*persevere*).' Both (18) .... (*bring*) into play in December 1977, when, shortly after he (19) .... (*earn*) a degree in economics and (20) .... (*leave*) a small sum in his grandmother's will, he (21) .... (*found*) Burton Snowboards. He was 23.

In the beginning Burton (22) .... (*employ*) as a barman by night and (23) .... (*make*) snowboard prototypes by day. After constructing more than 100 models, he finally had a board he was pleased with. That hurdle overcome, he had to (24) .... (*convince*) people to buy the things. One major stumbling block was the fact that snowboards (25) .... (*ban*) at virtually all ski areas. Finally, after 1983, when restrictions at many ski resorts (26) .... (*loosen*), snowboard sales (27) .... (*climb*). Now 95% of the ski areas in the US (28) .... (*allow*) boarding, as do all ski areas in Europe. An international circuit of snowboard racing and freestyle events (29) .... (*start*) in '86, and the sport (30) .... (*make*) its Olympic debut at the 1998 Winter Games in Nagano, Japan.

Grammar plus: participle clauses

Study the sections on participle clauses on p.158 of the *Advanced Gold Coursebook* and Grammar Reference p.195. Participle clauses can be used to express reason, result or time sequence. They are slightly more formal than clauses beginning with words like *since, so, so that, because, after* and *then*. Thus, they are more often found in written than spoken English.

1 Replace the underlined words in these sentences by using a participle clause.

EXAMPLE *Since she had phoned to say her plane was delayed, she knew her friends would not be worried.* → **Having phoned to say her plane was delayed, she knew her friends would not be worried.**

1 I had finally got a job at Johnson and Barnet, <u>so</u> I was anxious that my first advertising campaign should be effective.
2 He sold all his shares in Burchfield Books <u>because</u> he realised that the company was in trouble.
3 <u>Once</u> the people in the village had gone into debt to traders, they missed out on what they should have been earning.
4 <u>After</u> I had closed the door quietly behind me, I tiptoed into the room.
5 The drilling in the street continued throughout the three-hour exam <u>so that</u> it completely destroyed his concentration.

2 Participle clauses can also be used to combine sentences. Combine the sentences below using participle clauses.

EXAMPLE *More than 2 million people work in the telecommunications industry. This makes it one of the country's most significant employers.* → **More than 2 million people work in the telecommunications industry, making it one of the country's most significant employers.**

1 There are 2.3 million snowboarders in the United States. They represent nearly 20% of the people who visit ski resorts annually.
2 Burton spent the summer of 1978 in Europe. He was testing his boards on Austrian glaciers.
3 Burton Snowboards still dominates the industry. The company sells more than 100,000 snowboards a year in North America.
4 Sometimes key ingredients for a product are not available locally. This makes it necessary to find alternatives.
5 He remembers getting very excited. At the time he was teaching his students in Bangladesh how economic theories provided solutions to problems.
6 Manufacturers throughout the world have patented just about every imaginable car name. This makes it extremely difficult to find a suitable name for a new model.

English in Use: open cloze

▶ Paper 3, Part 2

About the exam: The texts in this part of Paper 3 are approximately 200 words in length. They always have titles. The missing words are usually grammatical words (prepositions, pronouns, auxiliaries etc.).

> **Strategy**
> 1 Read the complete text to get the general idea.
> 2 Go through the text again and make a note of the answers you are confident about.
> 3 For the remaining gaps look carefully at the surrounding context. Decide on the part of speech of the missing word.
> 4 Read the complete text again to make sure that all your answers make sense in context.
> 5 Transfer your answers to the answer sheet.

― Hot tip! ◀

Try reading the text 'aloud' in your head. This may help you to work out some of the answers.

1 For questions 1–15, complete the following article by writing down the missing word. Use only one word for each space. The exercise begins with an example (0).

0	them

UNIT 13 An interesting business

TASTE A WORLD OF DIFFERENCE

Wherever you are in the world, the billboards and supermarket shelves are saturated with the same brand names. But just try tasting (0) *them*. The packaging and product may look identical but the flavour may be far (1) ... familiar. More (2) ... than not even the most famous brand names are specially formulated to appeal to individual national palates. Americans prefer many products, particularly chocolate, to be (3) ... more sugary than Europeans do. Preferences for saltiness and colour differ (4) ... well. Local water and soil will affect the taste of home-grown raw ingredients and some key constituents may not be available, meaning that alternatives (5) ... be found. Sometimes, (6) ... in developing countries, premium grade components are replaced (7) ... lower-quality equivalents. Extremes (8) ... climate will require different additives and preservatives to be used. Chocolate calls (9) ... an alternative recipe in hot countries (10) ... it is to maintain its texture and taste. And multinationals must conform (11) ... national laws and regulations (12) ... additives, flavourings, colourings and artificial low-calorie sweeteners. Local religious sensibilities must also be observed. Even McDonalds, (13) ... proclaims the homogeneity of its Big Macs (14) ... the globe, has to serve lamb (15) ... than beef burgers to its Indian customers.

2 Now transfer your answers to this answer sheet.

1	less
2	often
3	the
4	as
5	could
6	more
7	by
8	in
9	for
10	who
11	that
12	to
13	who
14	around
15	more

Vocabulary: language of business

Study the Vocabulary section on the language of business on p.160 of the *Advanced Gold Coursebook*.

1 Find words in the grid below to match the following definitions.

1. the parts of a company that people can buy and own
2. money that is paid out to investors when a company makes a profit
3. total amount of business a company does measured in money terms
4. unable to pay debts
5. to make workers redundant because there is not enough work (2 words)
6. dismiss someone from their job
7. refuse to work because of a disagreement
8. a period of time away from work or duty
9. work schedule where workers can choose when to begin and end the working day
10. time in which an older person no longer works

F	L	E	X	I	-	T	I	M	E	S
S	L	A	Y	O	F	F	A	T	M	E
D	O	G	B	H	C	R	T	Y	U	S
I	C	P	O	B	B	O	R	S	X	A
V	U	S	L	E	A	V	E	H	O	I
I	T	O	Y	R	N	L	Y	A	D	U
D	U	P	R	S	K	A	E	R	Y	S
E	R	E	T	I	R	E	M	E	N	T
N	N	P	J	B	U	K	N	S	R	R
D	O	J	K	P	P	O	U	B	F	I
I	V	P	I	H	T	M	S	A	C	K
S	E	C	O	U	N	G	H	V	F	E
A	R	D	J	K	Y	T	R	B	V	W

101

2 Use words from the grid to complete this text.

It looks like the writing is really on the wall for Rambler. The board informed (1) .... holders at a meeting on Tuesday night that yet again they would be unable to pay a dividend. (2) .... is down 5% on last year and it seems inevitable that some 10,000 workers at their Morwell plant will be (3) .... The long and very acrimonious strike last spring over pay and conditions certainly didn't help matters, though no one can deny that it was completely justified. Management's unwillingness to even discuss the implementation of (4) .... and repeated violations of the law in relation to maternity (5) .... understandably provoked the workforce. The very real possibility of Rambler going (6) .... also spells doom for its executives. Chief Executive Officer, Blair Paton Smythe, has already been (7) .... while Sir George Manning has 'chosen to take early (8) ....', according to a spokesperson – very early, I might say, since he's only 50!

Vocabulary: phrasal verbs with *up/down*

1 Study the Vocabulary section on phrasal verbs with *up/down* on p.164 of the *Advanced Gold Coursebook*.

2 Put in the missing word in each of the following sentences. In some cases two positions are possible.

1 I missed some classes at the beginning of the course and it took me ages to catch with the others.
2 Trying to cut on the number of cigarettes you smoke won't work. You should give up completely.
3 Would you like to use the bathroom to freshen before we go out?
4 I managed to track a copy of his first album in a second-hand record shop.
5 Would you mind speaking a bit? We can't hear you at the back of the room.
6 I was only away for a week but the work has really piled in my absence.
7 The pickpocket must have sneaked behind me and taken my wallet while I was waiting in the queue.
8 They're going to spend the money Tony inherited on having their house done.
9 Calm, will you! There's no point getting angry about it.
10 I can't keep with Anna. She's got so much energy she never seems to stop to draw breath.
11 I thought the film was a rather watered version of the story in the book. It wasn't nearly as powerful.
12 She's gone to the hairdresser to have her highlights touched.
13 They had to interview everyone on the list, but they've managed to narrow it to five applicants.
14 I wish you'd liven a bit. You seem so miserable lately.
15 When Andrew was younger it was impossible to imagine him ever getting married and settling.
16 The police have managed to pin the time of the murder to between ten and ten-thirty.

English in Use: multiple-choice cloze

▶ Paper 3, Part 1

For questions 1–15, read the text below and then decide which word best fits each space. Put the letter of this word A, B, C or D into the correct box on your answer sheet. The exercise begins with an example (0).

ADVERTISING LOSES ITS SPARK

Fewer than a third of advertising executives believe their campaigns help to sell products, a(n) (0) *D* has (1) … . Instead they are (2) … by self-doubt and insecurity and dream of (3) … it all up for another career. In spite of their 'whiz-kid' (4) … , the survey of 600 advertising employees from 50 agencies found the industry weary from (5) … . Forty per cent of women said sex (6) … was rife and 73 per cent described advertising as a 'terrible career' for working mothers, because of its unpredictability and 12-hour days. Although spending on advertising by (7) … companies has increased, only 28 per cent of advertising employees were prepared to say that they (8) … believed the campaigns were (9) … . Dominic Mills, editor of the industry's trade magazine *Campaign*, which (10) … the survey, was shocked by the results. 'It is (11) … to think that so many people in advertising believe their (12) … are falling (13) … of the mark but this is (14) … what people privately think,' she said. Between 1990 and 1992 a fifth of people in the advertising industry lost their jobs. Asked what job they would most like to do instead, the (15) … said they would become barristers, writers, actors or artists.

0	D
1	
2	
3	
4	
5	
6	
7	
8	
9	
10	
11	
12	
13	
14	
15	

	A	B	C	D
0	questionnaire	research	investigation	(D) survey
1	exposed	expressed	revealed	published
2	plagued	pestered	pursued	persecuted
3	taking	putting	making	giving
4	image	view	appearance	aspect
5	overtime	overwork	overpay	overdose
6	persecution	discrimination	oppression	domination
7	greater	grander	major	leader
8	genuinely	authentically	surely	certainly
9	sufficient	capable	effective	proficient
10	made	conducted	performed	executed
11	shattering	smashing	striking	staggering
12	tries	attempts	efforts	endeavours
13	short	outside	beyond	off
14	truly	clearly	rightly	deeply
15	saved	rescued	blessed	survivors

Writing: application

▶ **Paper 2, Parts 1 and 2**

About the exam: You may be asked to write a letter of application.

Strategy

In this and all other Paper 2 writing tasks it is essential that you edit your work carefully for vocabulary, grammatical and spelling errors. Read your work through as many times as possible, checking for one type of error each time.

▶ Hot tip! ◀

Write on every second line.
This will allow you to correct errors more easily.

1 Look at this task and the answer a candidate wrote. Unfortunately, there are a number of spelling, vocabulary and grammar errors. Find and correct these errors.

TASK

You told a friend that you were interested in applying to do an MBA (Master of Business Administration) at a British university but you didn't know which one to choose. Your friend sent you a number of advertisements for MBA courses from the newspaper with a comment about what she had heard about each course. The advertisement that you found most appealing is printed on the right.

Read the advertisement and the notes your friend has made and then using the information, write a letter of application for the course (200 words) and a note to your friend telling her why you chose to apply for this course in particular (50 words).

UNIVERSITY OF HARLOW

The really modern MBA for the global market!

Apparently this is one of the most prestigious MBAs around but very hard to get into.

- flexi-study programme (distance learning, summer schools or one-year full academic year) — *One of these should suit you.*

- investment, marketing and corporate finance modules — *Sounds interesting!*

- study visits to major firms in Europe, the U.S. and the Pacific Rim

Applicants without recognised degrees or professional qualifications may be considered on the basis of extensive work experience and suitability for the course. — *Don't know what they mean here but it's worth a try.*

Applications enclosing all relevant documentation and indicating preferred study mode should be sent to:

*Sandra Henning,
Department of Business,
University of Harlow,
Harlow, Essex CM55 2UH*

Dear Ms Henning,

I am writting to apply for MBA course at University of Harlow.

It had been my intention for some time to continue my studies in field of business administration and because of my employee, Rambler Cars, is now willing to allowed me take study leave, I have decide to apply to begin your course in September.

Despite I do not hold a degree from a British university, I have a Diploma in Banking and Finance from the Institute of European Business Studies and a Certificate in Direct Marketting from the same institution. I have enclosed copies of both the diploma and certificate.

In adition, I am working for just over nine months with Rambler as trainee manager. Prior to taking up this post, I had been an Assistant Manager at English Court, a mayor clothing manufacturer.

I feel certain that your programme would be suit my needs particularly well as my main interests lay in investment, marketing and corporate finance. Your flexi-study programme and the study visits also called my attention. I would probable choose to study part-time.

I look forward to hear from you.

Yours sincerely,

Lucía Rubio Sánchez

Lucía Rubio Sánchez

2 Now write the note to your friend.

UNIT 14 It's only natural

Vocabulary: word + prepositions (2)

Study the Vocabulary section on word + prepositions (2) on p.172 of the *Advanced Gold Coursebook*.

1 Complete these sentences with the correct preposition.

1 Volcanologists say the earth might be due ... another major volcanic eruption.
2 Aircraft, capable ... carrying several tons of food supplies, were used in the emergency.
3 Daphne Sheldrick is highly critical ... the decision to lift the ban on ivory sales.
4 It sometimes seems that people in the developed world are indifferent ... the plight of those in poorer countries.
5 Many people are extremely concerned ... the introduction of genetically modified foods.
6 The guides on the Galápagos Islands are sometimes shocked ... the behaviour of visitors.

2 Complete these sentences in your own words.

1 I think I'm probably due ....
2 One thing I'm definitely not capable .... is ....
3 My friends and I are often rather critical .... people who ....
4 I think .... responsible .... a lot of the world's problems.
5 In my opinion we can't afford to be indifferent ....
6 Something I'm extremely concerned .... is ....

3 An incorrect preposition has been used in these sentences. Can you identify the mistakes and replace them with the correct prepositions?

1 We have every reason to be ashamed for our treatment of the other species on this planet.
2 The National Park is open for all visitors who undertake to obey the rules.
3 Sheldrick was baffled at the behaviour of the elephant.
4 The keeper was absent of the stall where he should have been sleeping with the elephant.
5 There's nothing wrong to punishing an elephant as long as you remember to make friends afterwards.
6 Conservationists are very anxious for the falling tiger population.

Grammar check: countable/uncountable nouns

Study the section on countable/uncountable nouns on p.176 of the *Advanced Gold Coursebook*.

There are mistakes with countable and uncountable nouns in six of the following sentences. Find the mistakes and correct them.

1 I suggest we stop for a coffee at about 10.30 if that's all right with you.
2 He published a ground-breaking research on apes and language recently.
3 Can I give you some advices? Don't buy a dog unless you're prepared to spend a lot of time with it.
4 The huge amount of information they collected on tigers had to be filed and ordered.
5 There was a very interesting news in the paper yesterday about pandas.
6 She decided to spend the rest of the money on overseas travel.
7 They're both dark but their little girl has got a lovely red hair.
8 Did you have good time at Tina's party?
9 I think I'll have to buy a new iron. This one just doesn't get the creases out any more.
10 If we're going to have children we'll need more spaces. This house is really only big enough for two people.

UNIT 14 **It's only natural**

English in Use: word formation

▶ **Paper 3, Part 4**

About the exam: You must transfer your answers to the answer sheet before the end of Paper 3.

> *Strategy*
> Fill in the words you have formed on the question paper as you go through the texts. Transfer them to the answer sheet when you finish Part 4.

> ─── **Hot tip!** ◀───
> Although word formation often involves the addition of a suffix and/or prefix, it may involve a spelling change that affects only one letter.

WHY DO ZEBRAS HAVE STRIPES?

Zebras are certainly very attractive to us and they (1) … find each other very appealing too, but it is believed their stripes evolved because they help the zebra foil its predators. Zebras have what is termed 'disruptive coloration'. The stripes break up the smooth contours of the animal's body and result in the (2) … of the zebra's true shape. When the zebra moves, the pattern may be even more (3) …, so a (4) … lion may not be sure if this is dinner after all! The ancestors of the zebra were monochrome dark-coloured animals. Through the (5) … birth of some foals with lighter coloured stripes the process of (6) … was set in motion. Since stripes were a (7) … colouring, they were an advantage. Striped animals had a better chance of (8) … and went on to have more striped foals.

1 DOUBT
2 CONCEAL
3 CONFUSE
4 THREAT
5 ACCIDENT
6 EVOLVE
7 PROTECT
8 SURVIVE

Reading: multiple choice

▶ **Paper 1, Part 3**

About the exam: In Paper 1 you will have to read approximately 3,000 words over the four parts.

Strategy
Do not spend more than 15 minutes on Part 3, which can be the shortest of the texts.

── Hot tip! ◀──
If you cannot work out the answer to a question from the text, guess or choose the answer that seems most likely to you.

1 You are going to read an article about elephants. We share a number of characteristics with elephants. Write down at least one thing we have in common. Read the text once quickly to find out if the characteristics you wrote down are mentioned.

2 Read the following newspaper article about elephants, and answer questions 1–7. On your answer sheet, indicate the letter A, B, C or D against the number of each question.

1	A B C D E F G H I J
2	A B C D E F G H I J
3	A B C D E F G H I J
4	A B C D E F G H I J
5	A B C D E F G H I J
6	A B C D E F G H I J
7	A B C D E F G H I J

AN ELEPHANT ORPHANAGE

Last October, a land cruiser truck carrying the limp body of a month-old African elephant pulled up to the gate of Daphne Sheldrick's property just outside Kenya's Nairobi National Park. It had been found wandering alone outside another park dazed and dehydrated, its floppy ears badly sunburned. 'The babies are always ill and sometimes severely traumatised,' says Sheldrick as she tends the new arrival, applying antiseptic powder to its ears and to a wound on its leg. 'Constant affection, attention, and communication are crucial to their will to live. [1]They must never be left alone.'

Remarkably, those that make it to the Sheldrick homestead never are. Until they are two, they get all the attention that a human infant would receive, including having a keeper sleep at their side every night. Sheldrick, 61, the widow of David Sheldrick, a renowned naturalist and founder of Kenya's Tsavo National Park, opened her elephant and rhino orphanage in 1977 and has become a leading authority on infant elephant behaviour. After 25 years of frustrating trial and error, she developed a system for nurturing baby elephants. Her method includes a skim milk–coconut oil formula devised for human babies – young pachyderms cannot digest the fat in cow's milk – a small amount of elephant dung to provide digestion-enhancing bacteria and round-the-clock human contact. In 1987 she became the first person to hand-raise a wild, milk-dependent baby elephant. Since then, she and her staff of eight keepers have raised 12 elephants from infancy – the highest success rate in the world.

'What Daphne gives them is hands-on care,' says Tony Fitzjohn, a Kenyan conservationist. 'It's what they need, and it's extremely hard work.' Especially when elephants arrive damaged. The newest, which Sheldrick has named Sungelai (Swahili for 'mighty warrior'), consumes about 10 litres of formula – plus 8 litres of additional fluid and salts – to help him rehydrate. He receives his bottles through a hole in a grey blanket hung between two trees, which replicates the shape and feel of a mother elephant's belly. Sheldrick's keepers rotate 6-hour shifts, playing with him, taking him on walks – and occasionally disciplining him.

'Infant elephants are very similar to human infants,' says Sheldrick. [2]They can be naughty, competitive and disobedient. When you say, "No," they want to do it.' If punishment is called for, Sheldrick gives them 'a little zing on the bottom' with a battery-powered cattle prod. 'It's an unfamiliar sensation, so it's unpleasant for them. But then,' she adds, [3]you have to be careful to make friends with them again.' Prodigious memory may explain why zookeepers are occasionally killed by elephants they have known for years. [4]"They've done something to the elephant which they've forgotten, but the elephant hasn't,' Sheldrick explains.

For every step forward, there were painful retreats. In 1974, while at Tsavo, Sheldrick achieved a breakthrough when she nursed a newborn, Aisha, to 6 months. But then she had to leave for 2 weeks to attend her daughter Jill's wedding. Aisha, who had bonded exclusively with Sheldrick – stopped eating. ⁵'She died of a broken heart,' says Sheldrick, who now rotates keepers to prevent babies from bonding with only one person.

The orphans remain at Sheldrick's Nairobi compound until the age of 2, when they are fully weaned onto a vegetable diet. Once they are able to feed themselves, they are trucked to Tsavo National Park, 150 miles away, where they are put into a stockade and gradually introduced to local herds. Eleanor, 38, who was rescued by Sheldrick's first husband and reintroduced into the wild in 1970, has become a willing adoptive mother. 'The little elephants are always welcome in a wild herd,' says Sheldrick.

But the adults can also be stern parents. 'If the matriarch gives them a smack with her trunk, ⁶they'll come flying back to their human keepers,' says Sheldrick, who makes sure the youngsters are free to come and go from the stockade. 'It takes 12 to 15 years [of their 60- to 70-year lifespan] before the baby becomes independent of his human family. Eventually they get bored stiff with people because they're having more fun with elephants.'

For their part, elephants can make it instantly clear when humans have overstepped their welcome. Last year, Sheldrick was visiting Tsavo when mistakenly she thought she had spotted Eleanor. 'I called to her, and she came over,' she recalls. 'I talked to her for about 10 minutes and touched her ear. She didn't like that at all and used her tusk and trunk to send me flying into a pile of boulders.' Despite a shattered right knee and femur from which she is still recovering, Sheldrick doesn't hold a grudge. 'On the contrary,' she says, ⁷'I'm very flattered that a completely wild elephant would come and talk to me.'

1 What is the most important element in Daphne Sheldrick's approach to rearing baby elephants?
   A Providing them with companionship 24 hours a day.
   B Feeding them with a dairy-based milk powder devised for human babies.
   C Not giving them too much attention after they turn two.
   D Getting the keepers to sleep with them.

2 Why is it important to make friends with an elephant after you have punished it?
   A They are like human children and can be naughty.
   B They might never forgive you for punishing them.
   C They will kill you if you don't.
   D They will forget the punishment too quickly.

3 Why was it a mistake for Sheldrick to nurse the baby elephant Aisha on her own?
   A She couldn't leave Aisha to attend her daughter's wedding.
   B Aisha became too attached to her.
   C The other keepers didn't know how to look after Aisha.
   D Elephants like to have a variety of people looking after them.

4 Why are the baby elephants kept in a stockade after they are taken to Tsavo National Park?
   A The wild elephants do not accept them.
   B They are still not able to feed themselves.
   C They have not yet been adopted by Eleanor.
   D The process of assimilation into a herd takes time.

5 Why do the young elephants eventually stop coming back to the stockade?
   A They prefer the company of other elephants.
   B The other elephants are too rough with them.
   C The keepers stop them because they are too old.
   D The humans get bored with them.

6 Why did Sheldrick touch the wild elephant's ear?
   A She wanted to make the elephant feel welcome.
   B She had confused her with another elephant.
   C She had already been talking to her for about ten minutes.
   D She was flattered by the elephant's attention.

7 What overall impression does the author of the article give of work with elephants?
   A It is dangerous.
   B It is depressing.
   C It is rewarding.
   D It is unpleasant.

Grammar plus: reported speech (advanced features)

Study the sections on reported speech in the Grammar Reference and on p.170 of the *Advanced Gold Coursebook*.

1 Look back at the text 'An Elephant Orphanage' on pp.108–109. In the text are a number of direct speech sentences (1–7) which have been underlined. For each gap (1–7) in the following text take the speech sentence from the text and put it into reported speech. The first one has been done for you as an example.

> Daphne Sheldrick said that constant affection, attention and communication were crucial to the baby elephants' will to live. She added that (1) *they must not be left alone* at any time. Sheldrick went on to say that elephants were like human children in that they (2) ... . Because of this it is sometimes necessary to punish an elephant, but she emphasised (3) ... . Apparently elephants occasionally kill their keepers and according to Sheldrick this was because the keepers (4) ... and the elephant had finally got its own back. Even so, elephants often grow to love their human carers – sometimes too much so. Daphne Sheldrick cared for an elephant called Aisha for the first six months of its life. When she had to go away for a couple of weeks, Aisha refused to eat. When Sheldrick got back and found Aisha dead she was convinced that the elephant (5) ... . Even when they have begun to be integrated into a herd, the orphaned elephants still seek human company. Sheldrick says that if the matriarch of the herd gives them a smack with her trunk (6) ... . But elephants raised in the wild sometimes react violently to humans. Sheldrick herself was thrown onto a pile of boulders by an elephant and broke her leg as a result. She was not the slightest bit resentful, however. In fact, she said (7) ... .

2 The sentences below are passive for one of the reasons below. In each case decide which reason applies, a) or b).

a) It reports the views of many people.
b) The speaker/writer does not want to take responsibility for a statement.

1 It is said that the elephant never forgets.
2 It is believed that the poachers may have already smuggled the dead tiger out of the country.
3 It was announced earlier today that the ban on the sale of ivory had been lifted.
4 It is widely thought that this will lead to an increase in the number of orphaned elephants.
5 It was suggested earlier today that the Environment Minister should take immediate action.
6 It is considered immoral to kill elephants for their tusks.

3 Put these reported speech sentences into the passive.

1 Lots of people think the universe is expanding.
2 Many scientists believe that the breakthrough in genetics will lead to a cure for cancer.
3 Dr Smith fears there are as few as fifteen tigers left in the region.
4 People thought that the volcano was dormant.
5 A scientist has suggested that building barriers might protect the city from eruptions.
6 A government representative announced earlier today that the use of insecticides was to be banned.

D 4 Use a dictionary to match each of the reporting verbs in the box to one of the definitions below.

whisper mutter urge stress claim retort boast concede

1 speak very quietly so that only a person very near you can hear
2 admit unwillingly that something is true or correct
3 speak in a low voice, often expressing anger or dissatisfaction
4 talk proudly about something you have got or something you have done
5 give particular importance to a matter when speaking or writing
6 say that something is true even if there is no proof
7 try very hard to persuade someone to do something
8 make a quick angry or amusing answer

Vocabulary: text-referring words

Study the Vocabulary section on text-referring words on p.171 of the *Advanced Gold Coursebook*.

1 Use the words in the box below to fill in the gaps in this text. More than one of these words may be possible in some gaps.

| topic | question | problem | issue | aspect | view |
| situation | trend | opinion |

Although Malvistan has had more than its fair share of problems, the (1) .... there seems to be really improving. I spoke, earlier this week, to the country's most distinguished journalist, Christine Patantour. The first (2) .... we discussed was agriculture, which, in her (3) .... , is likely to see dramatic increases in productivity over the next decade. Whether or not genetically modified crops should be introduced is still a (4) .... that farmers and politicians alike are asking themselves. The real (5) .... , according to Patantour, is whether these crops will benefit local farmers without damaging the environment. Environmental pollution is already a particularly serious (6) .... in urban areas and no one would want to see it spreading to the countryside. The cost of paying for seed is also a(n) (7) .... of the GM foods controversy that Dr Patantour did not feel the West had yet succeeded in adequately addressing. One particularly positive (8) .... she mentioned was the cultivation of organic fruit and vegetables.

2 Now fill in the gaps in these sentences in your own words

1 One of the most serious problems in my country is .... In my opinion, the best solution would be ....
2 .... is a topic that has always interested me. One aspect of .... that I've always found particularly fascinating is ....
3 .... is a really controversial issue where I live.
4 A growing trend among people of my age is ....
5 One situation that has certainly improved lately is ....

Listening: sentence completion

▶ **Paper 4, Part 2**

About the exam: The recording in this part of Paper 4 is shorter than the other recordings. Sometimes you hear the information you need to complete an item (e.g. a date or a place name) more than once.

Strategy

Fill in the gap as soon as you hear the information the first time.

— **Hot tip!** ◀

Under no circumstances should you listen to Part 2 and then attempt to answer the questions from memory. You <u>must</u> answer as you listen.

You will hear a tour representative talking to a group of visitors to the Galápagos Islands. For questions 1–10, fill in the missing information.

Listen very carefully as you will hear the recording ONCE only.

Galápagos National Park Rules

All visitors receive a printed copy of (1) ....

Removing any plant, animal or natural object from the islands (2) ....

Check your clothing for (3) .... when arriving and leaving islands.

Do not take food to the (4) ....

Do not touch the animals even though they seem (5) ....

You may threaten the animals' social system and breeding habits if you try to (6) .... them so don't.

Don't leave (7) .... on the islands: bring a bag in which to dispose of it.

Do not buy (8) .... made of plants or animals from the islands.

Follow (9) .... at all times.

111

Writing: report

▶ **Paper 2, Parts 1 and 2**

About the exam: You may be asked to write a report either in Part 1 or as an option in Part 2. Sometimes you are given information on which to base your report, sometimes you are expected to invent the content or draw on your background knowledge.

> **Strategy**
>
> Plan your report to ensure coverage of all aspects of the question. If you leave something out you will lose marks.

> ◀ **Hot tip!**
>
> In Part 2 a question asking you to write a report may require some business experience. If you don't have this choose another question to answer.

1 Look at the task below, the answer a student wrote and the comments an examiner made on the student's answer. Find examples in the student's answer of each of the areas the examiner has commented on.

> **TASK**
>
> An international conservation organisation is compiling information on environmental problems around the globe. You have been asked to contribute a **report** on three major environmental issues affecting your country or region and to make recommendations about what action you believe should be taken. Write your **report** (200 words).

BAND 2	
Content *Not all points covered. Some irrelevancy.*	**Register** *Mostly appropriate but sometimes a bit dramatic.*
Organisation and cohesion *Good organisation and cohesion.*	**Target reader** *Would be informed but see comment on 'content'.*
Vocabulary *Adequate but sometimes repetitive.*	**Accuracy** *Some non-impeding errors.*

REPORT: ENVIRONMENTAL ISSUES IN TENERIFE

INTRODUCTION
The purpose of this report is to provide information on three serious problems here in Tenerife that affect our environment and all of us who live here. They are:
- noise pollution
- rubbish
- the oil refinery

NOISE POLLUTION
Every day we face with more and more noise in our daily life. This causes stress and can even result in permanent damage to people's hearing. The main sources of noise pollution here in Tenerife are the following:
1 Traffic noise (motorcycles, cars and trucks)
2 Building and road work
This kind of noise is terrible for people who live in the cities where it goes on almost 24 hours a day.

RUBBISH
There is also a very serious problem with rubbish here. Apart from glass, there is almost no recycling and all the other things that people throw are taken down to a big area in the south of the island. In the summer the smell from this place is terrible. What is more it attracts millions of flies.

THE OIL REFINERY
Despite the fact that this provides employment for many people, it also causes a frightful contamination. People who live in Santa Cruz often have trouble breathing because of the horrible smells coming from this place. When it is hot and the wind blows in a certain direction I can even smell it in my bedroom!

CONCLUSION
Tenerife is a beautiful island and we must sure that it is a reasonable place for us all to live. Furthermore, if something is not done quickly about these problems the tourists will stop coming. Then where will we be?

2 Look at the banding system used by UCLES examiners on p.211 of the *Advanced Gold Coursebook*. Now use the examiner's comments to help you rewrite the answer so that it would satisfy the requirements for a higher band.

112

UNIT 15 It's all in the past

Listening: multiple choice

▶ **Paper 4, Part 4**

About the exam: In Part 4 of Paper 4 you will listen to five short extracts of about 30 seconds each. You will hear the five extracts twice. The speakers will all be talking about a similar topic. You will either have a multiple-matching task or a multiple-choice task. In multiple-choice questions there are two questions for each extract and these occur in the same order as the extracts.

> **Strategy**
> 1 Read the stem and the options for each question before you listen. (Remember there will be two questions for each extract.)
> 2 Listen out for key words which relate to the options. Listen to the complete context in which you hear the key words; sometimes they can mislead you.

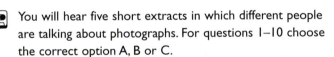

Hot tip!

As with all multiple-choice tasks, if you don't know an answer, GUESS!

You will hear five short extracts in which different people are talking about photographs. For questions 1–10 choose the correct option A, B or C.

1 Who wants him to put the photograph in the cupboard?
   A The subject of the photograph.
   B The speaker's mother.
   C The speaker's grandmother.

2 How does the photographer feel about the photograph?
   A He is ashamed of it.
   B He finds it embarrassing.
   C He is very fond of it.

3 Who are the subjects of the photo?
   A A family.
   B A married couple.
   C A class and their teacher.

4 What does the speaker know about the photograph?
   A Who four of the people are.
   B The names of all the people.
   C Who took the photograph.

5 Who appears in the photograph?
   A The speaker and her parents.
   B The speaker and her mother.
   C The speaker and her father.

6 Why is the photograph memorable for the speaker?
   A It was taken by someone she loved very much.
   B She had just received a much appreciated gift.
   C She had just come back from America.

7 Where was the photograph taken?
   A In a photographer's studio.
   B Outside a villa.
   C In the countryside.

8 What has happened to the clothes and jewellery in the photograph?
   A They have disappeared.
   B They have stayed in the speaker's family.
   C They have been given away.

9 What is shown in the photograph?
   A A woman standing outside a house.
   B A couple in the living room of their house.
   C A couple with their car.

10 How does the speaker feel about the subject of the photograph?
   A proud
   B guilty
   C regretful

113

g: gapped text

▶ **Paper 1, Part 2**

About the exam: You will read a text from which six or seven paragraphs have been removed and placed in jumbled order after the text. You must decide from where in the text the paragraphs have been removed. Only one answer is correct in each case and there is one extra paragraph that does not fit in any of the gaps.

Strategy

1 Read the main part of the text through to get a general idea of the structure and the content. Pay attention to the information and ideas before and after each gap. Highlight any linking or referencing words e.g. *However, Consequently, This idea*, which will help you put the paragraphs in the right order.
2 Read the missing paragraphs to see if any of them obviously fit into the spaces in the main text.
3 Go through the main part of the text again. Stop at each gap and check each missing paragraph. Look for grammar and vocabulary links. If you are not sure about a particular gap, leave it and go on to the next one.
4 Go back and make sure that you have decided on one paragraph for each gap.
5 Check your ideas by reading the complete text in sequence. Make sure your answers make sense.
6 Transfer your answers to the answer sheet.

── **Hot tip!** ◀──

As you fill each gap, cross out the paragraph in question on your question paper.

1 For questions 1–6, choose which of the paragraphs A–G fit into the numbered gaps in the following text. There is one extra paragraph that does not fit in any of the gaps.

A Threat to the New World Order

Academics say the first Americans crossed the ice from Asia about 12,000 years ago, but cave paintings in Brazil tell a different story.

Gaining entry to the oldest archaeological sites on the American continents would challenge even the most intrepid explorer. Intense dry heat, treacherous rocky ground, flash floods, boulders falling from cliffs, aggressive snakes, swarms of mosquitoes and plagues of deadly bees must all be overcome if you wish to glimpse the ancient trophies of Pedra Furada, located near the town of São Raimundo Nonato, deep in a scrubby, mountainous area of north-eastern Brazil.

| 1 |

The rock paintings, depicting prehistoric ways of life, including dancing, hunting, war and mating rituals, turned the world of American prehistory on its head. For they suggested that the first people in the New World arrived not via a bridge from Russia but by the sea from Africa or possibly even Australia.

| 2 |

However, in 1970 she was more successful. After three gruelling months, trekking 700km through an arid landscape of rugged canyons, low thorn trees and merciless scrub she managed to unearth the first of many prehistoric sites and to locate the paintings. She found them in huge sandstone rock shelters and deep ravines. She didn't expect them to be very old and they weren't.

| 3 |

In the field of archaeology few things fire people up more than the subject of dating. There are countless examples of ancient

A Guidon has attracted her fair share of this. It is not uncommon for archaeologists to pretend never to have heard of her finds, but it is more likely that they will dismiss them outright. The main reason for this stiff resistance is that her discoveries seriously undermine the Clovis theory which states that the first people in America arrived from Asia across a 1,200-mile bridge which formed across the Bering Straits when sea levels dropped during the last ice age.

B Recently, in an attempt to convince the hard-liners, she invited a number of them to see the sites and dating results for themselves. Although they seemed impressed by what they saw, when they got home three of them wrote a very critical paper raising [4]questions that could have been answered at the site. The article got massive publicity but when Guidon wrote a furious reply, it got none.

C But how did they get there? Guidon suggests they must have come in from the sea. But from where? Africa is the obvious assumption. One theory, based around a skull called Luzia,

114

relics being heralded as tens of thousands of years older than they finally turned out to be. Their excavators write lengthy papers in reputable journals on how their finds have changed the history of the world, only for it to be later discovered that they got their dates wrong. The subject is steeped in controversy.

4

The case for this rests on some 12,000-year-old fluted spears, [1] which were found in the 1930s scattered in various places around North America including Clovis, New Mexico. [2] The theory was cemented when similar tools were found in Siberia.

5

As in many areas of science, the longer a theory has stood the test of time, the harder it is to overturn. If archaeological experts want to resist new discoveries, the easiest way to do it is to kick up a fuss over how the finds have been dated. Some say that in relation to Guidon's work these experts have been overly critical. In the highly contentious world of dating archaeological artefacts, proof lies in arriving at the same date by using several techniques. This is exactly what Guidon has done and she has also had a number of other laboratories confirm her results. Yet still the sceptics hold their ground.

6

The archaeological establishment seems determined to protect their cherished theory of Clovis from any serious challenge. [3] When you consider the extraordinary level of hostility to which Guidon has been subjected and the near-total lack of regard for her 30 years of hard research, excavation, mapping, dating, conserving and education, it seems safer to brave the poisonous spider webs, killer bees, bouncing boulders and torrential flash floods for yourself than to believe what you read about Pedra Furada.

found in South America, suggests they could have come from Australia. However this has met with disbelieving frowns from the archaeological profession.

D Dr Guidon had first been inspired to explore the São Raimundo Nonato region in 1963 after seeing pictures of some rock paintings, known locally as 'stone embroidery'. But her efforts in that year were halted by floods which tore down bridges, making the area inaccessible.

E But when she dug deeper, she started to find bits of sandstone wall which were extremely old – more than 12,000 years old. When she dug further still, [5] she found red pigments, which had been used in paints. Microscopic analysis revealed that these pigments were over 30,000 years old. Over 30 years, she has dug up around 400 sites, containing an estimated 25,000 paintings. If the dates are accurate, these are some of the earliest examples of rock art in the world.

F Today, archaeology is filled with experts who have built their work and ideas around the Clovis theory, which says [6] that America was first populated by big game hunters 11,000–12,000 years ago. Throughout the last century the belief has been that nobody existed in the New World before then.

G For it was in this extremely remote part of the country that Dr Niéde Guidon, a French-Brazilian archaeologist, unearthed her extraordinary finds in 1970. [7] These included rock paintings which are thought to be more than 12,000 years old and some curious pebble structures and early stone tools which could be up to 50,000 years old.

115

2 Now transfer your answers from the boxes on pp.114–115 to the answer sheet that follows.

1	A B C D E F G H I J
2	A B C D E F G H I J
3	A B C D E F G H I J
4	A B C D E F G H I J
5	A B C D E F G H I J
6	A B C D E F G H I J

Vocabulary: idiomatic language connected with talking/communication

Study the Vocabulary section on idiomatic language connected with talking/communication on p.183 of the *Advanced Gold Coursebook*.

Fill in the gaps in these sentences.

1 I knew I had to ...*get*... to the point quickly or the audience would lose interest.
2 You shouldn't let her ...*talk*... down to you like that. Who does she think she is?
3 Don't expect me to sit around ...*making*... small talk with your friends while you're out in the kitchen cooking the dinner.
4 She ...*gave*... them a good talking to when she heard how badly behaved they'd been with the supply teacher.
5 I tried to tell her I wouldn't be there but she was talking so much I just couldn't ...*get*... a word in edgeways.
6 We were disappointed with the accommodation to ...*say*... the least.
7 I think I might have ...*got*... the wrong end of the stick. Didn't you say you were arriving on the morning of the 17th?
8 I don't want to ...*talk*... shop, but now that we've got a few minutes can I just show you this article I've been working on?
9 Everyone says she's brilliant but I can't ...*make*... head or tail of half the things she writes.
10 We seem to be ...*talking*... at cross purposes. The book I'm referring to is the one she edited not the one she wrote herself.

Grammar plus: passives (advanced features)

Study the section on passives (advanced features) on p.180 of the *Advanced Gold Coursebook* and Grammar reference p.195.

1 Match the uses of the passive a)–d) to the examples of the passive 1–7 in 'A Threat to the New World Order' on pp.114–115.

Uses of the passive

a) We use the passive when the active form would require the use of an indefinite of vague pronoun e.g. *someone, they, people*.
b) We often use the passive with verbs such as *think, believe, know, say* to give a general opinion.
c) Using the passive means we can make a statement sound more impersonal and less connected to the speaker.
d) Using the passive means we can avoid an awkward change of subject in the middle of the sentence.

2 Decide whether it is possible to make the underlined part of the following sentences passive. If so, make the transformation.

1 You <u>seem to have added the bill up incorrectly</u>. It doesn't come to £75.30.
2 Scientists <u>have known</u> for some time that smoking causes lung disease.
3 Someone <u>left the front door unlocked</u> last night.
4 Everyone <u>often says</u> that things were better in the 'good old days'.
5 People frequently <u>ask me</u> if parapsychology is recognised by universities.
6 The university <u>is going to send more than forty students abroad to study</u>.
7 <u>They've been telling me</u> you are planning to get married.
8 <u>They had warned us</u> that it was difficult to find somewhere cheap to stay in Rome.
9 <u>You must switch off</u> the power before you connect the screen to your computer.
10 Someone will come in once or twice a day <u>to feed our cats and water the plants</u> while we're away.

116

UNIT 15 I'ts all in the past

English in Use: error correction (extra word)

▶ **Paper 3, Part 3**

About the exam: In Paper 3, Part 3 you have to check a text of about 15 lines for errors. There are always example lines numbered 0 and 00 (one that is correct, one with an extra word). There is usually an unnumbered line or part of a line at the end of the text that you don't need to correct.

Strategy

1. Read the instructions carefully to find out which kind of task you have to do.
2. Read the title and text through to get a general idea of the meaning. If you notice any errors circle them.
3. Read the text again sentence by sentence.
4. If a sentence sounds ungrammatical check each line for extra words such as:
   - articles
   - auxiliaries
   - more, most
   - conjunctions
   - prepositions
   - pronouns
   - modifiers e.g. *too, so, quite, rather, such*
   - relative pronouns

─ Hot tip! ◀

There are never more than five correct numbered lines. Don't forget to tick these and to transfer the ticks and extra words to the answer sheet.

In most lines of the following text, there is one extra unnecessary word. It is either grammatically incorrect or does not fit in with the sense of the text. For each numbered line (1–16) find this word and then write it in the box on your answer sheet. Some lines are correct. Indicate these lines with a (✓) in the box. The exercise begins with two examples (0).

0	*been*
00	✓
1	
2	
3	
4	
5	
6	
7	
8	
9	
10	
11	
12	
13	
14	
15	
16	

THE SHAKESPEARE CONTROVERSY

0 The alleged mystery of William Shakespeare has been
00 fascinated the world for more than a century. Did a lowly
1 commoner from Stratford-on-Avon with only a few years
2 of public schooling really could write some of the greatest
3 works in the English language? Was he just a front man for
4 an aristocrat who wanted the anonymity? Today's authorities
5 say that without a doubt, Shakespeare who was the true author.
6 It is important to remember at the same time as that he did not
7 just create plays on his own. He had fulfilled commissions, he
8 contributed to plays which had scenes written by such different
9 dramatists and he revised other writers' work. Nor did Shakespeare
10 own of his manuscripts: they were the property of whichever acting
11 company he was writing it for. He probably got his information
12 on court intrigue from books and gossip but it is quite harder to
13 imagine that an aristocrat reproducing the slang of the common
14 tavern which is as much characteristic of Shakespeare's plays as
15 courtly language. Most readers find out more questions than
16 answers in Shakespeare's plays, but whether they were written
   by a certain hard-working man from Stratford is no mystery at all.

Writing

▶ **Paper 2, Part 2**

About the exam: Part 1 is compulsory, but in Part 2 you choose one of four options. The following task types can occur in either part of Paper 2: an account, an application, an article, a contribution to a leaflet or brochure, a notice, an announcement, a personal note or message, a formal or informal letter, a report, a review, instructions, directions, a competition entry, an information sheet, a memo.

Strategy
1 Read the instructions very carefully, underlining key words.
2 In Part 2 choose a question which you are confident you understand and can complete well.
3 Plan your answer carefully so that you cover all the things you are asked to do.
4 Think about the audience you are writing for and the organisation of your ideas before you start.
5 Check your answer carefully for number of words, spelling and grammatical errors.

Choose a task, plan and write your answer.

TASK
1 A business magazine has commissioned you to write an **article** on the various ways in which the information technology revolution has affected your particular industry and what possible future developments might occur. Write your **article** (250 words).
2 You have agreed to write part of a brochure for international students coming to study in your country or region. You have been asked to cover accommodation, food and extra-curricular activities. Write your part of the **brochure** (250 words).
3 The annual budget for extra-curricular activities at your college has been cut by 20%. The college principal has asked you to look into how important the various extra-curricular activities are to students. She has asked you to prepare a report making recommendations about any activities you think could be eliminated to save money. Write your **report** (250 words).
4 The editor of an English language newspaper aimed at young people visiting your country has asked you to write a review of two events (concerts, theatre or exhibitions) you have seen recently that such visitors might also enjoy. You should describe two <u>different</u> events, discussing their strengths and weaknesses and making a recommendation. Write your **review** (250 words).

Grammar check: *have/get something done*

Study the section on *have/get something done* on p.183 of the *Advanced Gold Coursebook*.

1 Complete these sentences using the appropriate form of the structure *have/get something done*.

1 I haven't finished writing the report yet and if I .... by Monday the boss will kill me.
2 When I was a student I used to cut my own hair but now I .... at a salon near here.
3 .... that bed .... and your room tidied up or you won't be allowed to watch television tonight!
4 Please make sure you .... your suitcase .... and ready to take downstairs by 10 a.m..
5 I wish they .... the aerial on the roof .... No one has been able to get the first channel for months.
6 Every time Micky goes away on holiday he manages to lose his passport or ....
7 You wouldn't know we .... the windows .... two months ago. You can hardly see through them now.
8 The restaurant is now closed. If you don't leave of your own accord, I .... you .... out.

2 Match the sentences in Exercise 1 to these rules.

a) *Have/get something done* usually describes a service performed for us by someone else.
b) *Have/get something done* can also refer to 'experience', particularly to describe something unfortunate that has happened to somebody.
c) *Get something done* can also be used to mean 'finish doing something'.
d) *Get something done* is often used in orders and imperatives.
e) *Have something done* is used in more formal contexts than *get something done*.

UNIT 15 It's all in the past

Vocabulary: revision

Study the Vocabulary sections of each of the units 1–15 in the *Advanced Gold Coursebook* and *Exam Maximiser*. Try to complete this crossword from memory.

Across
1 having or showing the ability to make decisions
6 The hospital has a .... of 20 doctors and 60 nurses.
7 a person who is in charge of a meeting
9 very valuable
11 faithful to one's friends, principles, country etc.
13 She always dressed extremely .... in tasteful clothes she designed herself.
16 She .... regretted ever having married him.
17 Despite their long-................ friendship, they fell out over a very small amount of money she had lent him.
21 I felt like a .... out of water at Mary and Jeff's party.
22 Tom is one of those ....-minded professor types.
24 Don't worry about me. I'm as strong as an ....
27 morally good or correct
28 He has some very ....-fetched ideas but some of them actually work.
29 say you will do something bad or hurtful
30 in a silly manner unsuitable for someone who is not a child

Down
2 Since the beginning of the 20th century there has been a steady .... in the number of cars on our roads.
3 The .... from my hotel window completely took my breath away.
4 a person who illegally gains access to and sometimes tampers with a computer system
5 Immigration is an increasingly controversial ....
8 .... down, will you! There's no point getting angry about it.
10 Having .... work increases the factory's production.
12 a leather seat made to fit over the back of an animal, especially a horse
14 a piece of glass or other transparent material which makes a beam of light passing through it bend, spread out, become narrower, change direction etc.
15 a rubber garment worn by underwater swimmers, surfers etc.
18 We've .... got a lot in common. The problem is no one seems to notice.
19 transfer a file from one computer to another
20 You can take it for .... that Tim will be on time. He's the most punctual person I know.
23 .... you're not serious about marrying Jane. You're hopelessly incompatible.
25 A .... of lightening illuminated the whole room.
26 the parts of a company that people can buy and own

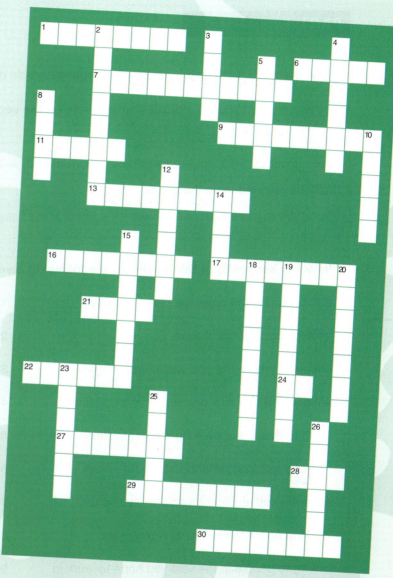

119

Practice exam

PAPER 1 – READING

PART 1

Answer questions **1–15** by referring to the magazine article on page **121** about changing jobs.

In the actual exam you will indicate your answers **on the separate answer sheet**.

For questions **1–15**, answer by choosing from the list (**A–E**) on the right below. Some of the choices may be required more than once.

Note: When more than one answer is required, these may be given **in any order**.

In which section(s) of the article are the following mentioned?

rising through the organisational hierarchy	1 ....
uninspiring aspects of a job	2 ....
changing jobs within the same organisation	3 ....
an ideal job that was ultimately disappointing	4 ....
liking the work but disliking the organisation	5 ....
working with people who share your values	6 ....
accepting other people's advice uncritically	7 ....
learning about the nature of working life	8 ....
talking to people in the field you hope to work in	9 ....
being realistic about your potential contribution	10 ....
lack of success due to the wrong attitude	11 ....
finding out about careers before you finish college	12 ....
staying in a job even if you find it dull	13 ....
getting to know people in the field	14 .... 15 ....

A drudgery

B expectations

C unhappiness

D initial appeal

E new career

HELP! I THINK I CHOSE THE WRONG CAREER.

There is life after a first job (even after a first or second career), so you really don't have to feel stuck. Before making a major move, however, there are vital questions you should ask yourself. Here are the top five.

A Is it the drudgery that's driving you mad? Opening mail, answering phones, filing ... such tasks are typical of all entry-level positions. But a lot of young people have trouble accepting that fact. 'Too many new graduates begin first jobs with the wrong attitude,' says Adele Scheele, author of 'Career Strategies for the Working Woman'. 'They quickly become frustrated because the work isn't challenging, and write off an entire industry. But junior jobs in any field have their share of unimaginative tasks. The only way to eliminate them is to be promoted.'

Barbara McDonald, vice president of a career-management firm, recommends digging in for at least two years, if at all possible. 'If you can tolerate your present situation, you'll acquire skills that will be valuable throughout your working life, plus make contacts, see how the business world really operates,' says McDonald. 'Also, remember that many opportunities exist within a company. You may not have to make a drastic career switch to get where you eventually want to go, just fine-tune your choice a bit.'

B Are your expectations realistic? Another reason many young people change jobs frequently is that they expect too much too soon. 'Even in this tight job market, bright new graduates often feel they should enter companies at much higher levels than they're prepared for,' comments Belinda Plutz, a partner at a career-consulting firm. 'Such a sense of entitlement often dooms them to failure, and their only solution is to change fields completely. I ask clients who are frustrated in their careers, "Are your expectations reasonable, given your current skills and the needs of the industry you're in?" Often they're not.'

C Is your unhappiness caused by what you do or where you do it? Studies show that frequently, people who are miserable at work don't necessarily hate the job itself but the office atmosphere. 'Try to separate day-to-day tasks that define your position from the environment in which they're performed,' advises Plutz. 'You might be quite happy doing the same type of work with different people in a different place.'

That's exactly what twenty-six-year-old Barbara Benson discovered when she changed her work environment. After finishing university, she spent several years as a public-relations assistant in an agency that dealt with celebrity clients. But increasingly, the job's glamour aspect bothered her. She eventually switched to the communications department of a large hospital that was involved in cancer research. 'Even though I'm still in PR, going to work means a lot more to me now,' says Benson. 'I'm surrounded by people like myself, plus there's a satisfaction level I never felt at my old job.'

D Think back to what initially appealed to you about your chosen field. Are those reasons important to you now? 'Reconsider what led you to go into your career in the first place,' advises Karen Danziger, executive vice president of a recruiting firm. 'Then determine whether the particular position or industry is still suitable for you.'

Take Sarah Jones, a fine arts graduate who became a freelance illustrator and, at first, thought she'd chosen the perfect career. 'Ever since I was a kid, people had told me how good I was at drawing and painting – that I'd be wasting my talents if I didn't do something involving those areas,' she remembers. 'Also, freelancing seemed perfect because I'd have time for serious artwork. But I soon discovered that the freelance illustrator's life, with its isolation, unsteady income, frequent rejections, was not for me.' Sarah then did some graphic-design courses, talked with art directors and designers who bought her work about job possibilities, and ended up joining a small graphics company as an assistant, eventually working her way up to art director. 'While it all worked out, I could have saved myself a lot of floundering if I'd talked to illustrators about the reality of their working lives while I was still a student,' she says.

E If you've set your sights on a new career, have you thoroughly investigated the field? 'When making a switch, do the necessary research to find out exactly what a new job would entail,' says recruiting firm VP Karen Danziger.

To explore a particular profession, go directly to people who do what you think you'd like to do. 'Set up as many informational interviews as possible,' advises Phyllis Tama, president of an executive-recruiting firm. 'Such sessions give you an insider's look at a field, help you establish a fledgling network within it, and may also make you aware of jobs you never knew existed.'

PART 2

For questions **16–21**, choose which of the paragraphs **A–G** on page **123** fit into the numbered gaps in the following newspaper article. There is one extra paragraph which does not fit in any of the gaps.

In the actual exam you will indicate your answers **on the separate answer sheet**.

Where insects fear to tread

About five-sixths of known animal life is made up of insects. They flourish almost everywhere, from the Antarctic to the Arctic, in caves, lakes, deserts, and rain forests, in hot springs, and even in pools of petroleum. But oddly enough, not in the ocean. Why this should be has always been something of a mystery.

16

It's not as if insects are completely averse to life in water. On the contrary, some 3 to 5 per cent of all insect species actually live in lakes and rivers and some have even adapted to the salinity of salt marshes. Yet almost none live beneath the surface of the open sea.

17

Previous attempts to explain the dearth of marine insects have all been unsatisfactory, according to Van der Hage. Some theories have suggested that physical barriers such as waves and salt have prevented an insect invasion; others proffer the view that predatory fish were a deterrent. Van der Hage points out that such obstacles have not hindered other arthropods, such as arachnids, in the slightest. Around 400 different sea spiders and many mites live quite happily in the sea.

18

The reason flowering plants, which evolved on land, have been unable to colonize the sea, says Van der Hage, has to do with the movement of particles in a fluid. If a pollen grain is immersed in a fluid of the same density, such as water, then pollen released from an underwater flower will be swept away by the water flow.

19

According to the conventional view, to which Van der Hage subscribes, insects as a group languished for some 250 million years, eking out an existence foraging in detritus. But when flowering plants appeared some 115 million years ago, the fortunes of insects changed dramatically.

20

Unfortunately, his argument fails to convince paleobiologist, Conrad Labandeira. Some years ago, Labandeira advanced the idea that insects diversified long before the advent of flowering plants, evolving highly-specialized mouth parts to feed, not on flowers, but other more primitive plants.

21

By comparison, seaweed often consists of just a few spongy leaf-like tissues. What gives terrestrial ecosystems such a unique habitat for insects is the tremendous architectural diversity of plants. In the ocean, that diversity is simply not there.

122

A Even if an animal or fish were to carry a few pollen grains to a flower's stigma, flowing water would wash them off. Pollination thus becomes extremely difficult and this is why flowers are rare underwater.

B Of course there are sea creatures with insect names. There is the 'sea wasp'; no more a wasp than the sea horse is a horse. Instead, it is a jelly fish named for its terrible sting rather than for any resemblance it might bear to an insect.

C He explains the oceans' lack of insects very simply: 'There are no trees in the sea. An average tree contains a multitude of habitats for insects: roots, bark, strengthening tissues, seeds, leaves,' he says.

D They might thrive but flowering plants, or angiosperms, don't. The vast majority of plant life in the ocean consists of simple plants that lack true leaves, stems, or roots. There are only about 30 marine angiosperms, and all live in coastal regions.

E Jeroen van der Hage, a physicist at Utrecht University, thinks he may have solved it. There are few marine insects, he says, because there are almost no flowering plants in the sea. And because the two have evolved together, the absence of flowers made life in the sea impossible for insects.

F A rare exception is Pontomyia, a midge that lives as a larva submerged in Pacific tide pools, but even this unusual insect must emerge to mate and lay eggs before dying. Some coastal insects live on sand and seaweed, but none of these species are fully marine.

G They exploded across the planet, developing a variety of specialized mouth parts for feeding on pollen and nectar, until most became dependent on some flower for survival. And those insects that didn't feed on flowers probably fed on insects that did. Since flowering plants failed to colonize the ocean, insects, says Van der Hage, remained landlubbers.

PART 3

Read the following newspaper article and then answer questions **22–28** on page **125**. Indicate your answers **A, B, C** or **D** to each question **22–28**. Give only one answer to each question.

In the actual exam you will indicate your answers **on the separate answer sheet**.

The man who battled infinity

For three centuries the greatest minds on the planet were baffled by a seemingly simple equation set by an amateur 17th century mathematician, Pierre de Fermat. The battle to prove Fermat's theory about this equation was a long and hard one and it was not until 1997 that Professor Andrew Wiles received the prestigious Wolfskehl Prize, in recognition of his epic struggle with this 'simple equation' which had become one of the most notorious problems in mathematics: Fermat's Last Theorem.

Wiles first read about Fermat's Last Theorem when, as a schoolboy, he visited his local library: 'One day I borrowed a book about this ancient and unsolved problem. It looked so simple, and yet the greatest mathematicians in history couldn't solve it. Here was a problem I, a 10-year-old, could understand; and I knew from that moment I would never let it go.'

The theorem's creator was a civil servant and mathematician. Having studied an equation, he realised that it was impossible to find a solution to it. Indeed, he claimed that he could prove it was impossible to solve this particular equation, but the mischievous Frenchman never committed his proof to paper.

For thirty years, teachers, lecturers and then colleagues told Wiles he was wasting his time but he never gave up. When he eventually spotted a potential strategy, the maverick mathematician did not publicise his idea. Instead he worked in complete isolation. Only his wife knew of the new direction his work had taken.

He believed his approach was right, but feared that rival mathematicians might beat him to the proof if they discovered his plan. Making his strategy succeed would take seven years of dedicated effort, conducted in complete secrecy. During this period, Wiles continued to publish papers of conventional calculations every year to put his peers off the scent.

To show that no numbers fitted the equation, Wiles had to confront infinity – the mathematician's nightmare. He likens his experience to a journey through a dark, unexplored mansion: 'You enter the first room and it's completely dark. You stumble around, bumping into the furniture. After six months or so you find the light switch and suddenly everything is illuminated. Then you move into the next room and spend another six months in the dark. Although each of these breakthroughs can be momentary, they are the culmination of many months of stumbling around in the dark.'

In June 1993, Wiles revealed to the world that he had proved Fermat's Last Theorem. The achievement was the mathematical equivalent of splitting the atom. However, within a few months referees spotted an error in the proof. Wiles attempted to fix it before news of the error had leaked out, but he failed. By the end of 1993, the mathematical community was full of gossip and rumour, with many academics criticising Wiles because he refused to release the flawed calculations, thus preventing others from fixing the error.

Wiles spent an agonising year before making the final breakthrough that resurrected his proof. 'It was so indescribably beautiful. I stared at the calculation in disbelief for 20 minutes. It was the most important moment of my working life.'

The sheer complexity of the proof shows it can't possibly be the proof Fermat had in mind, and some mathematicians are continuing the search for the original 17th century proof. For Wiles it's finally all over. 'I was obsessed with this problem for eight years. This particular odyssey is over. My mind is at rest.'

22 How did Wiles feel about Fermat's Last Theorem?

    A He was obsessed with it.

    B He couldn't understand it.

    C He was worried about it.

    D He didn't think he could solve it.

23 Why is Fermat described as 'the mischievous Frenchman'?

    A He said it was impossible to find a solution to the equation.

    B He only did mathematics in his spare time as a hobby.

    C The proof he claimed to have discovered was not written down.

    D He would not say whether he had found a proof or not.

24 Why were Wiles' teachers and colleagues discouraging about his project?

    A They thought he had adopted the wrong approach.

    B They did not know he had found a strategy.

    C They did not know his wife knew about it.

    D They thought the problem was unsolvable.

25 How did Wiles avoid attracting suspicion?

    A He was very secretive about his work.

    B He carried on doing his normal work.

    C He was extremely dedicated to his work.

    D He published papers about the proof.

26 What did the process of arriving at a proof involve?

    A Long periods of bewilderment followed by flashes of understanding.

    B Careful, painstaking work which gradually began to reveal a solution.

    C A series of sudden realisations leading to a final answer.

    D A long journey of exploration at the end of which the solution was revealed.

27 Why did other mathematicians criticise Wiles in 1993?

    A There were errors in the original proof.

    B He could not fix the errors in the original proof.

    C He would not let others work on his original proof.

    D He allowed rumours about the original proof to circulate.

28 The equation Fermat and Wiles studied

    A was solvable but Wiles couldn't work out the solution.

    B was solvable and Wiles eventually worked out the solution.

    C was unsolvable but Wiles couldn't prove this.

    D was unsolvable and Wiles eventually proved this.

PART 4

Answer questions **29–41** by referring to the magazine article on page **127** about collecting.

In the actual exam you will indicate your answers **on the separate answer sheet**.

For questions **29–41** choose your answers from the list of collectable items (**A–E**).

Some of the choices may be required more than once.

Note: When more than one answer is required, these may be given **in any order**.

Which items

depend on collectors' tastes for their value?	29	
may vary in value according to where they were produced?	30	
can be valuable although large numbers of them are produced?	31	**A** Toys
will be worth less if they have been cleaned?	32	**B** Newspapers
can be more valuable if they are defective?	33	
have become more popular among collectors recently?	34	**C** Coins
are more valuable if they are out of the ordinary?	35	**D** Stamps
can lose value over time?	36	**E** Shaving items
can be twice as valuable if their past owners were powerful individuals?	37	
are best acquired from those with large, well-organised collections?	38	
are more valuable if they have never been used?	39 .... 40	
will become more popular with collectors in the near future?	41	

126

WHAT TO COLLECT AND WHY YOU SHOULD COLLECT IT

Thinking of starting a collection? Hoping to make a fortune? Sandra Whitty tells you what to collect and how likely you are to make any money out of it.

A TOYS

Hundreds of thousands of people around the world collect toys. When it comes to older toys, dolls are the most consistently expensive items and regularly fetch from £1,000 to £20,000, followed by trains and early tinplate cars and boats.

Unfortunately, even antique toy specialists can't predict which of this year's toys will be fetching thousands in a few years' time. One tip is that most of the toys from the 60s and 70s which have risen in value are linked to characters from cartoons, films or TV series. The cardinal rule is to keep the toy in its box and never let your child play with it, which rather defeats the object of a toy.

Most modern toys are produced in such numbers they are unlikely ever to be worth much. Daniel Agnew from Christie's, a famous British auction house, says: 'If a toy is in short supply and you have to struggle to find one, it probably means it will never be valuable as a collectable item because so many have already been sold and more will be manufactured to meet demand.'

Paradoxically, however, rarity does not ensure value. Auction houses are often offered extremely rare objects, but if it doesn't spark the imagination of collectors the rare object may be worth only a few pounds. Some mass produced toys, on the other hand, are still in huge demand because they are remembered with such affection.

All toy experts insist that the only reason for starting a collection of modern toys is because you like them. There is no certainty that they will ever sell for large sums.

B NEWSPAPERS

What makes a newspaper valuable? Generally the price of a newspaper reflects its age, condition, the events it covers and its geographic proximity to historical events.

Because newspapers seem so fragile people are often amazed to discover that they can buy one which is over 200 years old. Actually, newspapers printed before 1880 are often in better condition than those printed after that date because the quality of the paper and the ink used was better in the past.

Many old papers are reasonably priced. So-called 'atmosphere' papers, which are old enough to be collectable but do not have specific news of the type that interests most collectors, can be very inexpensive. So don't expect those old papers piling up in the attic to turn to gold. 'You really don't find many good items or extensive collections lying around in attics,' says Tim Hughes, a major dealer. 'Most come from book dealers, libraries, or institutions that decide they no longer want to have certain holdings.'

Collecting papers can be an investment for those willing to do the research and legwork necessary to buy and sell wisely – it's all a matter of persistence. But as collectors will tell you, the best reason for collecting is the thrill of making a real connection with the past through the pages of a newspaper.

C COINS

Although rarities can cost thousands of pounds, for every expensive coin, there are many that can be purchased for more modest sums. Contrary to popular opinion, a coin's value is not influenced by age. A reasonable example of a Roman or medieval coin can be purchased for only a few pounds.

The most important factor in determining a coin's value is its condition, which can range from mint state to poor. An uncirculated 1887 silver crown, bearing the portrait of Britain's Queen Victoria, would sell for £60. However, one with considerable signs of wear on its raised surfaces would be worth only £10. Incidentally, never clean a coin as this slashes its value.

The future of coin collecting looks promising. The adoption of a single European currency will generate considerable new collector demand and prices will undoubtedly rise. However, there is one lesson to be learnt from the past: coins are not an investment. Collectors merely interested in making money may be very disappointed and are certainly missing the main point, which is that coins are a fascinating subject in their own right.

D STAMPS

In 1945 a block of stamps was found wrapped in an old writing set in a desk at Dalkeith Palace, near Edinburgh in Scotland. Known as the Buccleuch Find, the stamps are now on sale for £2.75 million – more than a million times their face value. However, investors hoping for similar gains from mint modern stamps will be disappointed. Stamps are issued in such huge quantities today that hoarding for investment purposes usually leads to losses not profits. A good example was the stamp issued in Britain in 1966 to celebrate the World Cup Football Championships. The stamp was expected to become a valuable collector's item. It changed hands for 20 times its face value and was even traded on the London Stock Exchange. However, the Post Office issued tens of millions of the stamp, which was more than enough to satisfy demand from speculators and collectors, and so its value did not rise as anticipated, and today the stamps change hands for 5 pence (considerably less than the price of the new stamp in 1966).

Modern issues of stamps seldom rise in value faster than the rate of inflation, so unless stamps have an unusual postmark or illustration, they are unlikely to become valuable. But there can be some exceptions, particularly where there has been a printing error or a stamp is withdrawn because of a design problem.

Leading dealers and auctioneers warn against collecting solely for investment; however, you can make what may prove to be good investments if you use your knowledge. You have more chance of finding something in an old collection or a box of stamps from a jumble sale or car boot sale than from buying new issues.

E SHAVING ITEMS

The number of razor collectors has risen very fast in the last five years and prices for shaving items have doubled and sometimes even tripled. Top quality, cut-throat razors made from mother-of-pearl can change hands for £300 and recently, electric shavers have also become very popular. An early fifties electric shaver in its box with a good quality cable will command between £15 and £20.

Because shaving items are made from a wide range of materials, shaving collectors often have to compete with collectors from other fields. Ceramic collectors are also attracted to shaving items, particularly shaving bowls from the 18th and 19th century decorated with country scenes, flowers and shaving paraphernalia. There are many copies on the market, but a genuine, plain 19th century shaving bowl will fetch at least £55. Imported varieties dating from the 18th century will fetch £3000 or more.

Obtaining a shaving item that originally belonged to a member of the royal family or to a famous historical figure, is in collecting terms, the equivalent of winning the National Lottery. A pearl razor that once belonged to Britain's King William IV, for example, will be double the price of one which belonged to any of his subjects.

PAPER 2 – WRITING

PART 1

1   You are a member of the Port Halbut environmental protection group. The group has recently received a letter from the Mayor stating that the local authorities intend to develop a beach near your town. Your group is opposed to the development and has recently completed a survey indicating that many local people share your concerns. You have produced the poster shown below to advertise the results of your survey to the public and to invite them to a meeting to discuss the issues.

You have offered to write an article for a local newspaper to publicise your views and win more support. You have also been asked to write a brief reply to the letter from the Mayor informing her of the results of your survey and making her aware of the group's opposition to the development.

Read the survey below and the Mayor's letter on page **129**, to which you have added your comments. Then, **using the information carefully**, write the article and letter as instructed on page **129**.

SAVE LEAMOUTH BAY!

Make your views heard. Come to the public meeting on 5th July.

Did you know that your local government plans to develop Leamouth Bay as a tourist resort?

They intend to:

- build a major hotel complex behind the beach.
- provide hotel guests with priority access to the beach.
- charge non-hotel guests a fee of £3.50 for access to the beach.
- build bars and restaurants on the beach itself.

HOW DO YOU FEEL ABOUT THIS?

Our survey shows that most citizens of Port Halbut use the beach regularly and object to the development.

Citizens visit the beach:

- at least once a week throughout the year. (7%)
- at least once a week in summer. (33%)
- at least once a month throughout the year. (60%)

Citizens opposed to:

- the development of Leamouth Bay in any form. (25%)
- the priority access to hotel guests. (90%)
- the charging of an entry fee. (85%)
- building on the beach itself. (30%)

6 p.m. at the Floral Clock in Williams Park.

Dear fellow-citizen,

I am writing to inform you of an exciting project the Port Halbut Council plans to put into action. I very much hope you will give this project your full support.

For some time now we have felt that the Leamouth Bay beach is an under-developed feature of our local environment. The beach is also underused, a fact that is attributable to the poor facilities it offers.

Not true. See our survey!

We estimate that as few as 5% of the citizens of Port Halbut regularly use the beach and those that do seldom visit bars or restaurants in the streets nearby. Since local business people are anxious to see this situation change, we have decided to build a major hotel complex in the area immediately behind the beach. Guests at the hotel will be given priority access to the beach and non-guests required to pay a £3.50 fee. The income generated will be used for the development and maintenance of more facilities on the beach. At present we envisage toilets, showers and changing rooms as well as a beach sports centre.

Why not improve them?

What does this mean? To the whole beach or a special area?

We are convinced that this development will be of benefit to local businesses and indeed, to all the citizens of Port Halbut. Every effort will be made, at the same time, to protect the environment.

For example?

Should you wish to raise any objections to the project, I would be grateful if you would notify me in writing.

Yours sincerely,

Stephanie Barnett

Now write:
a) an **article** for the newspaper (approximately 150 words);
b) an appropriate **letter** to the Mayor (approximately 100 words).

You should use your own words as far as possible.

PART 2

Choose **one** of the following writing tasks. Your answer should follow exactly the instructions given. Write approximately 250 words.

2 An English language magazine has just run a competition for the best story about the importance of friendship. You were asked to judge the competition, which attracted more than 500 entries. The editor of the magazine now wants you to write an article naming the prize winner and the runner-up*. Write about the story of each of the two people selected and give your reasons for choosing them as prize winners.

Write the **article**.

* *runner-up: the person who comes second in a competition*

3 You have been asked to write an information leaflet for prospective students at a college. You should give a brief history of the college, describe its main activities and plans for the future and mention any other points you think are important.

Write the **leaflet**.

4 You see this competition in an English language magazine.

> 'Computers are the way forward in language learning. Who needs teachers and books when we've got computers?'
>
> Do you agree with this opinion? Give us your reasons why or why not. The best answer will win a ticket to Seattle.

Write your **competition entry**, giving your views.

5 Your company or organisation is considering the possibility of sending staff on weekend residential training programmes but has not yet decided which programmes would be most popular and beneficial. You have been asked to write a report recommending a training programme you feel would be suitable.

Write the **report**, describing the programme you have chosen and explaining why you feel it would be suitable.

PAPER 3 – ENGLISH IN USE

PART 1

For questions **1–15**, read the text below and then decide which word on page **132** best fits each space. The exercise begins with an example (**0**).

In the actual exam you will indicate your answers **on the separate answer sheet**.

PICTURES AT AN EXHIBITION

There is a tendency to think of each of the arts as a separate (**0**) … of activity. Many artists, however, would testify to the fact that there has always been a (**1**) … relationship between the various spheres of human activity. For example, in the late nineteenth century the connections between music and painting were particularly close. Artists were commissioned to design (**2**) … and sets for operas and ballets, but sometimes it was the musicians who were (**3**) … by the work of contemporary painters. Of the musical compositions that were (**4**) … as responses to the visual arts, perhaps the most famous is Mussorgsky's *Pictures at an Exhibition*. Mussorgsky composed the piece in 1874 after the death, at the age of 39, of the artist Victor Hartmann. Though their friendship had not been a particularly (**5**) … one, Mussorgsky was shattered by Hartmann's untimely death. The following year the critic, Vladimir Stasov, decided to (**6**) … an exhibition of Hartmann's work. He (**7**) … that Mussorgsky try to soothe his grief by writing something to (**8**) … Hartmann's life and work. The exhibition served as Mussorgsky's inspiration. The ten pieces that make up *Pictures at an Exhibition* are intended as (**9**) … rather than representations of the paintings in the exhibition. Between each is a promenade, as the composer walks from one painting to another. The music is sometimes (**10**) … and playful, sometimes almost (**11**) … and frightening, but always spellbinding. Through a range of startling (**12**) …, Mussorgsky manages to (**13**) … the spirit of the artist and his work. Although it was originally (**14**) … as a series of pieces for solo piano, the composer Ravel, who had already managed to carry (**15**) … successful adaptations of many works for solo instruments, wrote an orchestral version of *Pictures at an Exhibition* in 1922.

0	A	entity	B	article	C	item	D	area
1	A	thick	B	private	C	warm	D	personal
2	A	outfits	B	costumes	C	disguises	D	ensembles
3	A	spurred	B	animated	C	enlivened	D	inspired
4	A	originated	B	initiated	C	begun	D	conceived
5	A	long-sighted	B	long-lived	C	long-standing	D	long-suffering
6	A	inaugurate	B	hold	C	offer	D	put
7	A	advised	B	suggested	C	assured	D	encouraged
8	A	memorise	B	remember	C	commemorate	D	recollect
9	A	signs	B	logos	C	symbols	D	passwords
10	A	witty	B	cunning	C	intelligent	D	clever
11	A	horrifying	B	alarming	C	appalling	D	dreadful
12	A	contrasts	B	differences	C	comparisons	D	distinctions
13	A	bring	B	carry	C	convey	D	bear
14	A	supposed	B	thought	C	meant	D	intended
15	A	on	B	through	C	away	D	off

PART 2

For questions **16–30**, complete the following article by writing each missing word in the correct space. **Use only one word for each space**. The exercise begins with an example (**0**).

Example: | 0 | of |

In the actual example, you will write your answers **on the separate answer sheet**.

TALENTS OF GIFTED CHILDREN NOT RECOGNISED

A recent report has shown that conventional intelligence tests may not be the best way (**0**) ... identifying gifted children. It seems that the tests fail to pick up specific aptitudes and (**16**) ... important factors, such as motivation. Another problem is that (**17**) ... it is difficult to test intelligence without relying (**18**) ... vocabulary knowledge, the results of the tests are inevitably influenced by (**19**) ... a child has already learned at school. The report, a review of international research on (**20**) ... gifted child, suggests that while many child prodigies fail to maintain (**21**) ... success into adult life, both parents and teachers tend to pick the wrong children. Primary teachers in England tended to label children (**22**) ... very able on the basis of their ways of working (**23**) ... than their cognitive ability. A study (**24**) ... 1984 showed that 40 per cent of potential high-achievers (**25**) ... been under-estimated by their teachers. Furthermore, parents and teachers were far (**26**) ... likely to see boys as gifted. Studies in America, China and England all showed a stable ratio of two boys for (**27**) ... girl identified as highly able. The report's author, Professor Freeman, urges schools to provide extra activities (**28**) ... able pupils. Instead of just teaching gifted children in the same (**29**) ... as other children, but more quickly, these extra activities would be aimed (**30**) ... stimulating the child's special aptitudes and interests.

PART 3

In **most** lines of the following text, there is **one** unnecessary word. It is either grammatically incorrect or does not fit in with the sense of the text. For each numbered line **31–46** find the word and then write it in the space provided. Some lines are correct. Indicate these with a ✓ in the space. The exercise begins with two examples (**0**).

Examples:

0	the
0	✓

In the actual exam you will indicate your answers **on the separate answer sheet**.

THE HEALING POWER OF HERBS

0   Although herbs are generally thought of as the mild, inexpensive
0   ✓ remedies against minor ailments such as sore throats and coughs,
31 some doctors are now believe they can also be powerful
32 treatments for more serious illnesses. Herbs may take bit longer
33 to work, and the effects may be little less dramatic at the outset,
34 but they can be just as potent as conventional drugs. For patients
35 who have had the bad side effects with drugs, herbs become
36 very attractive. Experts say, however, that not all herbal medicines
37 are risk-free. They may not have be subject to the same safety
38 standards as conventional drugs are. When they taken in high doses,
39 some herbs can even have dangerous consequences. There are no
40 statistics about the number of doctors who prescribe of herbal
41 remedies, but they are in the minority. That means some consumers
42 are often on their own and unfortunately, misinformation abounds.
43 Manufacturers are allowed to make out health claims for their HERBAL products
44 whether these have been proven or not. Many have not been
45 subject to scientific scrutiny, though there is a reliable data about the
46 safety and efficacy of herbal medicine, more largely as a result of
    research carried out by European scientists.

PART 4

For questions 47–61, read the two texts below. Use the words in the boxes to the right of the two texts to form **one** word that fits in the same numbered space in the text. Write the word in the space. The exercise begins with an example (**0**).

In the actual exam you will write your answers **on the separate answer sheet**.

PHARMACEUTICAL LEAFLET

TAKING *FLU-AWAY*

For the (0) *relief* of the symptoms of colds and flu, take three times daily at mealtimes or as directed by your physician. In severe cases the dosage may be increased to every three hours. Some patients experience (47) … of appetite and (48) … but if any of the following side effects occur the (49) … should be immediately discontinued and professional medical (50) … sought: dizziness, dry mouth, tingling or cramps in lower limbs. *Flu-away* is (51) … for children under sixteen and should not be used by pregnant women. Elderly patients or those with a history of (52) … reactions or (53) … to aspirin should consult their physician before taking *Flu-away*. It should not be taken (54) … for a period greater than one week. If symptoms persist, see your doctor.

0	RELIEVE
47	LOSE
48	REST
49	TREAT
50	ADVISE
51	SUIT
52	ALLERGY
53	SENSE
54	CONTINUE

MAGAZINE EXTRACT

MUSIN: THE CONDUCTORS' MAESTRO

Musin did not come from a musical family but in 1919, at the age of 16, he entered the St Petersburg Conservatory. He went in as a (55) … but injured his hands practising in the cruel cold of the (56) … Conservatory. As a result, he became the first student in the Conservatory's first conducting class, led by the (57) … Nikolay Malko. A year later, Yevgeny Mravinsky, with whom Musin was to develop an intense (58) … , also completed the course. At the time, they were seen as (59) … equals, and both became assistant conductors of the Leningrad Philharmonic. In 1937, Musin accepted an invitation to become music director of the Minsk Philharmonic. Just one year later, a (60) … for the position of principal conductor of the Leningrad Philharmonic came up. Mravinsky got the job. Was it bad luck, bad (61) … or something else?

55	PIANO
56	HEAT
57	LEGEND
58	RIVAL
59	ART
60	VACANT
61	TIME

For questions **62–74**, read the following letter from a camp director. Use the information in the letter to complete the numbered gaps in another letter, which follows. **Use no more than two words for each gap**. The words you need do not occur in the first letter. The exercise begins with an example (**0**).

In the actual exam you will write your answers **on the separate answer sheet**.

LETTER 1

Dear Ms Riley,

We are pleased to inform you that your booking has been accepted

General Information

Arrival
Reception is open from 12pm–3.30pm daily and we would appreciate you arriving between these times. If you are planning to arrive later, please notify us.

If you are coming by car we urge you to share transport with another camper if at all possible. Parking for private vehicles is limited.

The camp can be easily reached by train. The nearest railway station is at Totnes and return tickets can be purchased from London, Paddington for £70. Off-peak tickets are also available and are less expensive. We run a complimentary bus service between Totnes and the TGL campsite.

Fire prevention
Fire is a major hazard during the summer months. To minimise the risk of fires, smoking is prohibited on the campsite except in <u>one</u> designated area.

What to bring
We recommend that you bring clothing that can be layered for different weather conditions.

Departure
We ask you to depart promptly at the end of the camp so that we can start preparations for the next group of campers.

Yours truly,

Rex Mossop

Camp Director

LETTER 2

Dear Sue,

I've just had a letter from TGL Sports Camp (**0**) *saying/to say* that our booking has been accepted.

They would (**62**) … us to arrive between 12pm and 3.30pm and if we're going to be late we're supposed to (**63**) … know. They suggest that people driving to the camp should (**64**) … to carshare because there isn't (**65**) … parking space. I think it's probably better to (**66**) … the train anyway. Return tickets from London are expensive but if we travel after the (**67**) … hour there are special deals available which work out a (**68**) … and at Totnes there's a (**69**) … bus to the campsite.

Because of the (**70**) … fire in summer there is a (**71**) … on smoking except in one place – so you'll have to give up the weed for the summer! They say the weather can be a bit unpredictable and it's a (**72**) … to bring clothes you can layer. You know, sweaters and things like that. At the end of the camp they want us to (**73**) … as quickly as possible because they have to get the camp (**74**) … for the next lot of campers.

See you on 5th July.

Love,

Bernadette

PART 6

For questions **75–80**, read the following text and then choose from the list **A–J** the best phrase given below it to fill each of the spaces. Write one letter (**A–J**) in the correct space. Each correct phrase may only be used once. **Some of the suggested answers do not fit at all**. The exercise begins with an example (**0**).

In the actual example you will indicate your answers **on the separate answer sheet**.

MONA LISA SCENERY MAY BE AS REAL AS HER SMILE

Behind the Mona Lisa, Leonardo da Vinci painted a fantastic topography of jagged mountains, with a misty lake and a winding river. The only man-made object in sight is a rustic bridge (**0**) .J.. . Over the years, there have been plenty of claims for the location, as cities and regions vied to call Leonardo their own. Some art historians said it was simply an invented landscape but now two amateur art sleuths claim (**75**) ... . They have combined simple observation, historical research and computer technology to pinpoint the location in eastern Tuscany, near Arezzo, 40 miles southeast of Florence. Carlo Starnazzi, a University of Florence paleontologist, says of the landscape in the famous painting (**76**) ... , that what seems to be a winding road leading to the lake is a canal (**77**) ... and that to the right is the Burgiano Bridge, a medieval stone structure (**78**) ... . He also believes that the mysterious peaks in the painting are not mountains at all, but a group of eroded hills unique to Tuscany. Starnazzi began his research after a friend surmised (**79**) ... . But how might Leonardo have got such an interesting view? Starnazzi discovered (**80**) ... , and he decided that Leonardo would probably have surveyed the terrain from it. Starnazzi then rigged up computer models to approximate how the area might have looked from the castle vantage point. 'It looks,' he said, 'pretty much like the scene in Mona Lisa.' Some experts are sceptical. John Sherman, a Renaissance art professor at Harvard University, points out that the kind of landscape painted by Leonardo had precedents in works by previous artists.

- **A** which links the lake to the Arno River
- **B** that an old castle once stood about 1½ miles from the bridge
- **C** that spans the Arno and is still open to traffic
- **D** that he had been there himself
- **E** that the landscape is as real as the Mona Lisa herself
- **F** that the lake to the left of the painting is Lake Chiana
- **G** that was not built until the late nineteenth century
- **H** that someone else may have painted the landscape
- **I** that the Burgiano Bridge might be the one painted in the 'Mona Lisa'
- **J** which is visible over Mona Lisa's shoulder.

PAPER 4 – LISTENING

PART 1

You will hear part of a radio programme about sleep and dreaming. For questions **1–8** fill in the missing information.

You will hear the recording twice.

Silvia Johnson believes people can [_____1_____] at a particular time by deciding on this in advance.

In the past researchers believed sleeping was not a [_____2_____] activity.

Environmental factors including the number of [_____3_____] were thought to affect people's sleeping patterns.

Researchers [_____4_____] of a particular stimulating hormone in each of the sleepers throughout the night.

The results of Dr Johnson's research indicate that [_____5_____] can influence bodily mechanisms.

Sleep research is difficult because people can't tell researchers what is happening [_____6_____] while they are asleep.

Lucid dreams are different from ordinary dreams because we [_____7_____]

With practice lucid dreamers can experience amazing physical sensations such as leaving their bodies and [_____8_____]

PRACTICE EXAM

PART 2

You will hear the chairperson of a sports club speaking at the club's annual general meeting. As you listen, complete the notes for questions **9–17**.

Listen very carefully as you will hear the recording ONCE only.

<u>Annual General Meeting 7/1/02</u>

Apologies

Treasurer Greg Wilson:

Reason for absence: playing in [_____9_____]

Doug and Nancy Peppard

Reason for absence: Abroad

Balance at 1/1/01 = [____10____]

Sources of revenue: [____11____] and interest on investments

Repairs to clubhouse

- burglar alarm: £200 +

  Justification:

  state-of-the-art alarm goes off at local [____12____]

  [____13____] the alarm included in fee

- replacement keys: £55

  Justification:

  [____14____] had to be replaced as well

- shower curtains: [____15____]

  Explanation:

  member obtained discount

Other expenses:

£100 on [____16____] for tennis courts

£69.75 on [____17____] as wedding gift for Julie Peppard

139

PART 3

 You will hear part of an interview with two people who organise music festivals. For questions **18–26**, complete the sentences.

You will hear the recording twice.

Andrew agrees that he was [_____ **18**_____] with the music industry.

Andrew says that the members of Metamorphosis stopped one another developing [_____ **19**_____]

After Andrew left Metamorphosis he realised his interest in world music was very [_____ **20**_____] to him.

Juliet helped Andrew launch his second career by introducing him to some [_____ **21**_____]

Andrew says that nowadays he and Juliet concentrate their energies on [_____ **22**_____] music festivals.

The presenter says that Juliet and Andrew's most recent festival was [_____ **23**_____]

According to Andrew it is easy to ensure that a festival has [_____ **24**_____]

To make sure everything will run smoothly, Andrew and Juliet have a [_____ **25**_____] two days before the festival.

Andrew and Juliet [_____ **26**_____] all the people they employ to work at the festival.

PART 4

 You will hear five short extracts in which different people are talking about jobs they have had. For questions **27–36** choose the correct option **A**, **B** or **C**.

You will hear the recording twice.

27 Why did the speaker go and work for her parents?

- A   They assumed she would.
- B   Her sisters worked there.
- C   They needed more staff.

28 How did the speaker feel about the work?

- A   She found it challenging.
- B   She liked the variety.
- C   She disliked the working hours.

29 What does the speaker say about his spare time?

- A   There wasn't much of it.
- B   There was nothing to do.
- C   There was plenty to do.

30 How did the kitchen staff regard the student waiters?

- A   with respect
- B   with contempt
- C   with resentment

31 What attracted the speaker to the job?

- A   The training course she would do.
- B   The salary she would be paid.
- C   The amount of money she would make.

32 When she started the job the speaker was surprised by

- A   how successful she was.
- B   how unfriendly people were.
- C   how few mistakes she made.

33 What advantage does the speaker say the job offered?

- A   It was run by the local council.
- B   It allowed him to continue to study nursing.
- C   It was relevant to the work he hoped to do later.

34 Who decided what work needed to be done on each visit?

- A   the volunteers
- B   the elderly people
- C   the council

35 How did the speaker feel about the job?

- A   She enjoyed it despite the supervisor.
- B   She didn't enjoy it because there wasn't enough work to do.
- C   She didn't enjoy it because of the supervisor.

36 Why did the shop assistants fold T-shirts?

- A   To avoid serving the customers.
- B   To give the impression they were busy.
- C   To keep them neat and tidy.

PAPER 5 – SPEAKING

PART 1

The interlocutor will ask you and the other candidate(s) about yourselves.

Listen to the recording and answer the questions. Pause the cassette after each bleep.

PART 2

The interlocutor will ask you and the other candidate to talk about some photographs.

Listen to the recording. When you hear two bleeps, pause the cassette for one minute and answer the question. When you hear one bleep, pause the recording for 20 seconds and answer the question.

Candidate A

Candidate B

PART 3

 The interlocutor will ask you and the other candidate to discuss something together.

Look at the pictures and follow the interlocutor's instructions. When you hear the bleep, pause the recording for 3 minutes and do the task. After three minutes, listen to the recording again and answer the interlocutor's final question.

PART 4

 The interlocutor will ask you and the other candidates questions related to the theme of Part 3.

Listen to the recording and answer the interlocutor's questions. Pause the cassette at the end of each question, when you hear the bleep, and discuss it with the other candidate.

Answer key

UNIT 1

Reading pp.8–9

2 1 B 2 C 3 B 4 A 5 A 6 C 7 B

Vocabulary p.10

1 a 2 g 3 c 4 e 5 d 6 f 7 b

Grammar plus p.10

1 a 5 b 4 c 3 d 1 e 2

2 1 ✓
2 Could you describe your ideal holiday **to us**?
3 ✓
4 A strange thing happened **to me** the other day.
5 ✓
6 He didn't explain the problem **to us** very clearly.
7 ✓
8 ✓
9 ✓
10 ✓
11 ✓
12 Could you suggest a good restaurant near here **to us**?
13 He shouted something **to/at me** as the train was leaving the station.
14 They were kind enough to provide a meal **for us** when we arrived.
15 They recommended his latest play **to us**.
16 ✓

3 1 My mother always hated *sewing*. ✓
2 I'm so clumsy! I keep *dropping* **things**.
3 I wish I could *sing*. ✓
4 They plan to *sail* from here to Brazil. ✓
5 Shall I *close* **the window/the door**? It's quite cold in here.
6 It's my turn to *pay*. ✓
7 He has never learnt to *drive*. ✓
8 I spent the whole morning *drawing*. ✓

Listening p.11

1 'Mona Lisa'

2 1 at the top 2 more famous 3 five million / 5,000,000 / 5 million people 4 painted it 5 good fun
6 appreciate the painting 7 crowds of people 8 ten seconds 9 impossible to see 10 unresolved mysteries
11 meaningful image.

Tapescript

**I = Interviewer AS = Ann Summer
JH = Joseph Harris**

I: Welcome to Art for Art's Sake, the programme that keeps you abreast of what's going on in the arts around the globe. Tonight I have with me in the studio art experts Ann Summer and Joseph Harris. The question we'll be discussing is what are the world's most looked at works of art … and do they deserve the attention they get. Ann, let me start off by putting the first question to you.

AS: Well, I'm sure Joseph will agree that top of the list we'd have to put the 'Mona Lisa', but after that I'd put as equal second Van Gogh's 'Sunflowers' and the Taj Mahal, and then equal third Hokusai's 'The Wave' and Munch's 'The Scream'.

I: And Joseph?

JH: I don't know about second and third place, but I agree with Ann that the 'Mona Lisa' is number 1.

AS: Actually, the Norwegians have claimed recently that 'The Scream' is now more famous. [JH: Really?] But when it comes to seeing the original, the 'Mona Lisa' wins hands down. The figures make that absolutely clear. Nearly five million people visited the Louvre last year and presumably a very high proportion of them saw the 'Mona Lisa'. Only 300,000 went to the National Gallery in Oslo.

I: So, on what grounds do the Norwegians claim 'The Scream' is more famous?

AS: On the basis that the image has been reproduced in a wider variety of forms. And they might have something there. I think there are probably very few people in the developed world who haven't seen it.

JH But would they know who painted it?

AS: Probably not. No. And they'd also be unlikely to know where the original painting is. But you have to admit there are a lot of reproductions around.

145

JH: Yes, but I'm sure there are even more of the 'Mona Lisa'. There've been T-shirts, posters, ball pens, coffee mugs, coasters, tights, watches, match boxes, thimbles … even a giggling pillow … you name it.

AS: I read the other day that the Artists' Rights Society has been trying to get reproductions like this suppressed on behalf of Munch's heirs. I think that's so pompous! Parodies and reproductions are good fun if you ask me. They make me laugh, anyway.

I: What's your view, Joseph?

JH: Well, there have, of course, been parodies of the 'Mona Lisa' painted by famous artists. Marcel Duchamp's is probably the best known. But it seems to me that it's all gone rather too far. Nowadays, whenever you want to make fun of somebody, you paint them as the 'Mona Lisa', and the image has been used in literally hundreds of advertisements. I think that's made it even harder for us to really appreciate the painting.

AS: Yes. Absolutely. Over-exposure makes us kind of artistically deaf and blind. But the other thing about the 'Mona Lisa' is that even if you go to the Louvre, it's almost impossible to get a proper look at the painting behind all that bullet-proof glass. Not to mention the crowds of people all pushing and shoving to take photos.

JH: Yes, it's terrible. When the painting was shown in the Tokyo National Museum there was actually a guard to direct the traffic, so to speak. Most of the million and a half people who saw her really only caught a glimpse because they were moved on every ten seconds.

I: When I saw it, I was struck by how yellowish it looked, and then someone explained that that was the varnish. Are there any plans to clean the 'Mona Lisa'?

AS: No, the people at the Louvre simply wouldn't dare. They say we've all got so used to her looking like that, but she's almost invisible. There's an exquisite landscape of mountains and rivers behind her which has been impossible to see properly now for decades.

I: Why are we all so obsessed with her then?

JH: I think partly because so many unresolved mysteries surround the painting. Who commissioned it? Who was she? Was the landscape painted from life? And is the 'Mona Lisa' in the Louvre the original? The painting was stolen, you know.

AS: I think her super-star status is really a 19th century idea. Then Leonardo da Vinci was regarded as one of, if not the, most glorious Renaissance artist and the 'Mona Lisa' was seen as his most mysterious and romantic work – therefore, the thinking went, the 'Mona Lisa' was the greatest painting in the world.

I: So do you prefer 'The Scream'?

AS: Oh, yes, I do. I think it's a much more meaningful image today: a tormented image for a tormented century. And 'The Scream' also had the good fortune to be stolen.

I: Oh really. When was that?

AS: In 1994. It was found six months later, but in the meantime it had enjoyed plenty of free publicity.

JH: But surely you don't actually believe …

Speaking p.12

1 A Have you always lived there? What's it like living there? Would you like to live anywhere else? Are there any interesting places to visit in your area? Where were you born?
B Have you got any brothers or sisters? Do you live in a house or an apartment?
C What do you like doing in your spare time? What kind of music do you like?
D Do you enjoy your work? Do you need any special qualifications to do that?
E What other languages would you like to learn?
F What do you think you will be doing five years from now? Are you doing anything special this summer?

2 1 Where are you from? 2 Have you got any brothers or sisters? 3 What do you like doing in your spare time? 4 Are you working or studying at the moment? 5 Why are you learning English? 6 Are you doing anything special this summer? 7 Have you got any special plans for the future?

English in Use p.13

1 ✓ 2 most 3 The 4 for 5 are 6 you 7 too 8 have 9 they 10 ✓ 11 a 12 but 13 had 14 of 15 it 16 ✓

Writing pp.14–15

2

Dear Sarah and Pete,

This is just a quick note to thank you for letting us **to use** (use) your circus tickets. We know how much you were both looking forward to it and wish **you could use** (you could have used) the tickets yourselves. I hear that Irish folk group you like will be in town **the** (–) next month. Marcus knows someone **who's** (whose) sister used to **playing** (play) with them so he might to be able to get free tickets. Would you like to go?

All the best,

Nadja

146

Dear Sir/Madam,

My partner and I attended a performance of the Chipperhall Circus on Tuesday 23rd November. I am very sorry to inform you that we were both angered and disappointed by our experience.

Firstly, your circus **is not representing** (does not represent) good value for money. We were given our tickets but **if we would have bought** (if we had bought) them we would have asked for our money back. We could barely see some of the acts as there was a large pillar in front of our seats. What is more, although you state on your leaflet that performances last two hours, the one we saw was a lot **more shorter** (shorter). We had been waiting **since twenty minutes** (for twenty minutes) before the performance began and we were on our way home before 9 p.m.

A second criticism we have concerns standards of safety. We were all horrified to see that one of the lions managed **getting** (to get) outside the ring. People sitting in the front rows **must have being** (must have been) **absolutely frightened** (absolutely terrified).

Finally, I wish to draw your attention to the poor **facility** (facilities) your circus provides. there was **a so long** (such a long) queue for drinks at the interval that we eventually gave up. **I wonder do you imagine** (I wonder how you imagine) two inexperienced bar staff are sufficient to deal with several hundred customers. We were also infuriated to discover that we had to walk through very muddy ground outside the marquee to reach the car park. I doubt that I will ever be able to wear the shoes I was wearing that night again.

Your circus **may performed** (may have performed) internationally but if last Tuesday was at all typical, I am certain those who have attended these shows have been as disappointed as we were.

Yours sincerely,

Nadja Höbling

3 1 before Friday, because they wanted to go to another concert 2 views of stage, seats 3 three 4 your favourite piece was played, universally appealing programme, two encores

4 The note should include both apology and thanks; the letter will be read by the general public; the desired effect would be to get the readers to attend performances at the concert hall.

UNIT 2

Reading pp.16–18

3 1 A 2 C 3 B 4 C 5 A 6 B 7 E 8 B 9 C 10 A 11 D 12 B 13 D 14 A 15 C 16 D

4 1 b 2 a 3 b 4 a 5 a 6 b 7 a 8 b

5 1 booming 2 caught on 3 spawned 4 mock 5 lingers 6 prompted

Speaking p.18

1 Gerda does not say how the people are feeling, she simply describes what she sees. She speaks for less than a minute.

2 Key vocabulary: formal evening clothes, dinner jackets, bow ties, beards, velvet, satin, celebrate.

Useful expressions: I'd imagine that they feel …, Perhaps they've been …

Tapescript
First candidate

I = Interlocutor   G = Gerda

I: In this part of the test I'm going to give each of you the chance to talk for about a minute and to comment briefly after your partner has spoken.
First you will each have the same set of pictures to look at. They show people dressed up in various ways. Gerda, it's your turn first. I'd like you to describe these two pictures, saying why you think these people are dressed up and how they might be feeling. Don't forget, you have about one minute for this. All right? So, Gerda, would you start now, please?

G: In the first picture I can see a group of people in formal evening clothes. The women are wearing long dresses and the men are dressed in dinner jackets and bow ties. I think the women's dresses are probably made of fabrics like velvet or satin. The women have probably been to the hairdressers to have their hair done that day. The second picture shows some men dressed up as Santa Claus. They are all wearing false beards and moustaches. These are made of white cotton wool or perhaps some kind of synthetic material. They are wearing red suits with big thick belts and high boots. The belts and boots look as if they are made of black leather or vinyl. Some of the men seem to have padding under the suit jacket to make them look fatter than they really are … umm … (SILENCE)

I: Thank you.
Now, Marta can you tell us which of the outfits you would prefer to dress up in?

147

Second candidate

I = Interlocutor   A = Alberto

I: In this part of the test I'm going to give each of you the chance to talk for about a minute and to comment briefly after your partner has spoken.
First you will each have the same set of pictures to look at. They show people dressed up in various ways. Alberto, it's your turn first. I'd like you to describe these two pictures, saying why you think these people are dressed up and how they might be feeling.

A: Well, in the first picture there's a group of people who are very formally dressed. The men are wearing smoking … no … dinner jackets and black bow ties and the women are in ball gowns. They might actually be going to a ball. They all look quite young, so it could be a university ball or even a formal 21st birthday party. In Spain people also get dressed up like this to celebrate New Year's Eve, so that could be what's happening here. I imagine they feel excited and happy to be together celebrating, and that they are rather pleased with the way they look … they all look very elegant to me, and I think most people enjoy getting really dressed up once in a while. The second picture is similar in that it also shows a group of young people and – if I'm right about the first picture showing a New Year's Eve celebration – then we could say that the two pictures were taken at the same time of the year … I mean the Christmas holidays. This picture is more unusual than the other one because we don't generally see groups of people dressed as Papa Noel … I mean Father Christmas … with the typical red suit, boots and belt, false beards and fur-trimmed caps. One explanation I can think of for why they might be all dressed like this is that they work for a chain of shops or perhaps a department store – and they have just finished work for the day and are having a drink together. If that's the case, then I suppose they feel a little tired and glad that the working day has come to an end. At the same time, like people in the first picture, they look as if they enjoy being together and that they are getting into the spirit of the festive season.

I: Thank you.
Now, Simone, which group of people look happier to you?

Vocabulary p.19

1 A 2 B 3 C 4 D 5 C 6 A 7 B 8 D 9 D 10 C
11 D 12 B 13 D 14 B 15 B

Grammar check p.20

1 1 he might/could have been   2 Could you ride
3 may/can visit   4 I didn't need to buy
5 You should take up   6 It must be   7 You must not/should not carry   8 You may not/cannot/must not leave   9 I had to stay   10 I may/might be

2 2 Sally said we could stay in her flat while she's/she was away.
3 Pete asked if I would be home by ten thirty.
4 The woman asked if she might/could smoke.
5 Mark said he had to look after his nephews this weekend.
6 The man said he could not/couldn't lift the heavy boxes in his condition.
7 Alice said she had to go.
8 My friends said I needn't write to accept the invitation.

3 2 e 3 h 4 f 5 d 6 g 7 a 8 c

Listening pp.20–21

1 A 2 C 3 A 4 B 5 C 6 C 7 A 8 C 9 B 10 C

Tapescript

**A = Australian woman   ME = Middle Eastern man   S = Spanish man   E = English woman
V = Venezuelan woman**

A: I think the first thing business visitors need to know is that Australians always say what's on their minds and they probably expect you to do the same. Another important characteristic is that it's a very egalitarian society and people don't like it if you try to pull rank … you know, to try to impress them or imply that you're somehow superior. For example, for men, if you get into a taxi on your own, the taxi driver will expect you to sit in the front seat with him, as if you were getting into a car with a friend. When we meet we shake hands and use first names. Men, well they quite often call each other 'mate'. Something you definitely should NOT do in Australia is drop litter in the street. It's actually against the law! Oh and also we're very punctual, so be on time!

ME: In the Middle East there are important differences in the timetable of the working day and working week, and business visitors need to be aware of these. During the month of Ramadan – the ninth month in the Islamic calendar – the working day finishes at 12 o'clock, so don't expect to do business after that. The working week runs from Saturday to Wednesday or Thursday … Friday is a day for religious observance. We're very hospitable people, and if you're invited home for a meal, you can expect the food to be delicious, but it will probably be served a little later than in some other parts of the world. A good gift to give is a fountain pen … they're wonderful for writing in Arabic script. It's also a good idea to take a supply

148

of business cards, and even to have them printed on one side in English and on the other in Arabic.

S: Our timetable here in Spain is a little different from the UK, and business visitors need to bear this in mind. We stop work in the middle of the day, so it's wise not to schedule any meetings after 1.30 or before 5 in the afternoon since most people like to go home to eat lunch … the main meal of the day … with their families. If you are taken out to lunch, you should expect the meal to go on well into the afternoon. That's why you'll also find the evening meal is eaten much later … often not until 10 or 11 … so don't expect to find many restaurants opening their doors until 9. If you're invited to someone's home for a meal, you can take gifts like chocolates, cakes and pastries or flowers … but not chrysanthemums, please, we associate them with death. We're very affectionate people. If we've met someone before, we usually give each other a little hug, and women kiss each other on the cheek.

E: I think most visitors find Thai people very polite. There are several things that you should know so as to make the same impression on your Thai business associates. For example, it is considered very rude to lose your temper in public. So, keep your cool … even if you're stuck in a traffic jam in Bangkok. Another thing you should never do is to touch another person's head … even a child's … so don't be tempted to pat your host's little girl or boy on the head. They think of the head as the highest part of the body … and the feet, on the other hand, they regard as the lowest, so don't point to things with your foot or sit in such a way that the sole of your foot is visible. If you're invited to someone's home you should take your shoes off before going inside. Don't admire any one object in your hosts' home too much. They may feel obliged to give it to you.

V: Something that sometimes surprises business travellers to Venezuela is that we expect people to arrive on time for meetings. Venezuelan business people are often extremely busy so they expect the meeting to start on time and that not too much time is taken up with preliminaries, so get straight to the point. You probably won't be invited to your host's house for a meal, since most entertaining is done outside the home, but if you are, it's polite to send flowers beforehand – and to send a note to say 'thank you' afterwards. Oh … and if your hosts don't tell you where to sit, don't sit at the head of the table. That's the place reserved for the mother or the father in the family.

ANSWER KEY

Grammar plus p.21

1 cow's milk 2 members' enclosure 3 handicraft fair 4 a three-hour exam 5 chocolate cake 6 shop window 7 boys' school 8 A cat's whiskers 9 Spain's National Parks 10 desk drawer 11 two-month holiday 12 My mother's cousin 13 a book exhibition 14 cashmere sweater

English in Use p.22

1 the 2 are 3 to 4 which 5 ✓ 6 it 7 like 8 for 9 is 10 have 11 they 12 as 13 ✓ 14 can 15 because 16 ✓

Writing p.23

1 A would produce the better information sheet. B is too personal.

UNIT 3

Reading pp.24–25

3 1 A 2 D 3 C 4 C 5 A 6 C 7 B 8 A 9 D 10 D 11 E 12 B 13 E 14 A

Vocabulary p.26

1 much weight 2 on 3 through 4 your voice 5 off 6 away 7 the motion 8 too far 9 out

Grammar check pp.26–27

1 1 the 2 a 3 the 4 The 5 the 6 0 7 The 8 the 9 The 10 the 11 0 12 0 13 the 14 0 15 a 16 a 17 a 18 the 19 a 20 the 21 a 22 the 23 a 24 0 25 an 26 a 27 0 28 the

2 1 After Sam and Tina won the lottery they went on a luxury cruise in **the** Mediterranean.
2 People are beginning to make **a** lot of money out of the Internet.
3 My sister-in-law works as **an** engineer with a large oil company.
4 What **a** brilliant speech the new finance minister gave at the opening of parliament.
5 Climbing ~~the~~ Mount Everest has become very fashionable among ordinary tourists.
6 In ~~the~~ Newsweek magazine it said he was one of the ten richest people in the USA.
7 The British have had mixed reactions to **the** introduction of a national lottery.
8 Have a look in the newspaper and tell me what time the new film is on at **the** Odeon.

Speaking p.27

5 Kept discussion going, exchanging turns very naturally and developing what the other candidate had said in previous turn. **Nadja**

5 Worked hard to keep interaction going, initiated and picked up on partner's points but had his work cut out for him. **Felipe**

2 Little or no attempt to elicit partner's opinion; just stated own opinion and refused to budge! No desire or effort to take up any of partner's points. **Tania**

5 Exchanged opinions and kept discussion going, always developing partner's points. Seemed genuinely interested in what she had to say. **Henrik**

Tapescript
First candidate
E1 = Examiner 1   N = Nadja   H = Henrik

E1: Now, I'd like you to discuss something between yourselves, but please speak so that we can hear you. I'd like you to imagine that your country has recently set up a new National Lottery, and that you have been asked to make recommendations about what proportion of lottery funds various projects should receive. Here are some proposals for projects. Talk to each other about these projects and then put them in order of priority from first to last according to how much of the fund they should receive. You have three or four minutes for this.

N: OK. Umm. I think that children's charities are very important, don't you?

H: Yes, I suppose so. Children are an investment for the future, after all, but then so are endangered species. If we don't do something to protect the environment then none of us will be umm ... able to survive.

N: That's true. Umm ... and there are so many different environmental projects that the money could go towards. Perhaps, we should put endangered species projects first. What do you think?

H: It's difficult to choose but ... yes, let's put that first and children's charities second. So, now we've got to choose a project for third position. What do you think should go next?

N: Well, considering that we already made sure that people, animals and plants will benefit, I'd suggest putting heritage projects next.

H: Oh, really? Do you think they're more important than ... well, than scientific research?

N: Yes, I do. I mean, there are so many really beautiful old buildings in need of umm, restoration, ... And a bit like the endangered species, we all benefit from it.

H: Mmm, I know what you mean. And repairing a cathedral or medieval castle can cost millions or probably trillions. But I still feel that we should be supporting science.

N: We will be. But we will be making an even more valuable contribution to our national heritage.

H: OK, OK. So we'll put heritage projects third and scientific research fourth.

N: Uh hum, so, now it's a choice between sports and arts in fifth position.

H: Yes, and I feel quite strongly that sports should get the fifth position, actually.

N: Do you? But surely the arts are more important. I mean a play or an opera is a ... well, a work of art ... whereas a football match ...

H: But that's not really a fair comparison. I mean, sponsoring sports can make a big difference to a disadvantaged community.

N: Yes, you do have a point there. I don't suppose there are all that much difference between fifth and sixth position, so shall we put the sports projects fifth and the arts sixth?

H: Yes, I think that would be best. Oh no! I've just realised that we've forgotten completely about health care.

N: So we have. Actually I think that a government should be paying for healthcare from money raised from the taxation.

H: Yes, I'm inclined to agree with you there. And we've already given a high priority to children's charities and scientific research, so perhaps we could put it last.

N: Fine.

Second candidate
E2 = Examiner 2   F = Felipe   T = Tania

E2: Now, I'd like you to discuss something between yourselves, but please speak so that we can hear you. I'd like you to imagine that your country has recently set up a new National Lottery and that you have been asked to make recommendations about what proportion of lottery funds various projects should receive. Here are some proposals for projects. Talk to each other about these projects and then put them in order of priority from first to last according to how much of the fund they should receive. You have three or four minutes for this.

F: Right. Are you ready to start?

T: Yes.

F: OK. What do you think we should put first then?

T: Scientific projects.

F: Yes, yes, that's a good idea. It's very important and industry doesn't generally fund scientific research unless there is some potential product involved. OK. So, how about the second? What do we put in second position?

T: Healthcare. We need better facilities in my country.

F: I see. Yes, healthcare can, can always benefit from some more money. Yeah, OK. So, we've got scientific research and healthcare. I agree that they're both very very important. How would you feel about putting heritage projects next?

T: That's not a good idea. Preserving old buildings isn't as important as children's charities.

F: Perhaps you're right. So, children's charities third and then heritage projects. The reason I suggested it is that there are a lot of wonderful monuments and buildings in my country that will eventually fall down unless something is done, and this seems like an excellent source of funding for that kind of thing.

T: I want to put endangered species after children's charities.

F: Oh, I see. So you are concerned about the disappearance of animals and plants.

T: Not so much, but I'm not interested in old buildings.

F: But many other people are, and it's a way of attracting income from tourists.

T: All right. We will put the heritage projects next. And then endangered species and then sport.

F: In that order?

T: Yes.

F: OK. Right, so that's scientific research, healthcare, then children's charities, heritage projects, endangered species and sports. Are you happy with that order then?

T: Yes.

Vocabulary p.28

1 1 c 2 g 3 f 4 b 5 a 6 h 7 j 8 i 9 e 10 d

2 1 absent-minded 2 air-conditioned 3 self-made 4 last-minute 5 tight-fitting 6 level-headed 7 mass-produced 8 so-called 9 bullet-proof 10 long-standing

4 1 off 2 down 3 up 4 down 5 up 6 out 7 off 8 out

Grammar plus pp.28–29

1 1 have been living 2 I'm living 3 Had you visited 4 am really enjoying 5 are you planning 6 I have perfected 7 I am only joking 8 am thinking 9 have you been living 10 I will have been 11 Are you missing 12 are always phoning 13 sending 14 has not been 15 have been 16 Have you been 17 I am going 18 I am really looking forward

Writing p.29

Suggested answer:

Dear Gianfranco

I've just heard that I've won first prize in the National Lottery! I can't believe that something so absolutely incredible could have happened, but I'm sure I'll get used to it eventually.

I know you've been having a few financial problems, especially with repaying your mortage, so I'm sending you a cheque for £200,000 and I hope you'll accept it. I think this was the amount you had left to pay on the mortgage, wasn't it?

I'll be coming to Brighton some time soon and wonder if we could meet up. How about a drink at the King's Head at eight on Friday 3rd March? If that suits you, could you ring and let me know? Don't worry if you can't make it that night. I'm sure we'll be able to get together soon.

All the best,

Carolina

Grammar check p.30

1 1 pounds, shillings and pence 2 Australian dollars and cents 3 the song on the radio and TV

2 1 which/that 2 which 3 which 4 whose 5 which/that 6 whose 7 which/that 8 which 9 who 10 which

3 1 He consulted his bank manager, who told him it would be unwise to take out a loan.

2 Australian dollars and cents, which are completely different from the US notes and coins, were introduced in 1966. / Australian dollars and cents, which were introduced in 1966, are completely different from the US notes and coins.

3 Even young children can open bank accounts, which they often maintain for the rest of their lives.

4 Banks carry out extensive market research which tends to show that students are attracted by special offers and free gifts.

5 Mortgages, which are special loans for the purchase of property, are offered by most banks.

6 There were several similarities between the old and new Australian currencies, one of which was the size of some of the coins.

7 I always try to deal with one particular bank teller who is always very friendly and helpful.

8 One day I had to do my banking with a new teller who (whom) I had never spoken to before.

English in Use p.31

1 neutral

2 1 A 2 E 3 B 4 G 5 F 6 I

UNIT 4

Grammar check p.32

1 1 to write 2 to come up with 3 to say 4 to find
5 telling 6 to meet 7 getting 8 taking up 9 joining
10 learning 11 taking up 12 to introduce 13 to be
14 meeting 15 living 16 to do 17 being 18 meeting
19 to find 20 following 21 to meet 22 thinking
23 getting 24 to go 25 calling 26 fooling 27 to spend

Vocabulary p.33

1 1 C 2 B 3 B

2 1 he was as cool as a cucumber 2 like a bull in a china shop 3 as strong as an ox 4 was as light as a feather
5 is like a red rag to a bull

Reading pp.33–35

1 1 A 2 B 3 C 4 D

2 1 A 2 A 3 D 4 B 5 A 6 A 7 B 8 B 9 A 10 C
11 A 12 D 13 C 14 C 15 C 16 A

3 a ruling out b guise c punters d plight e hitherto
f leave a hole in (my) pocket g make a killing
h (his) baby i quid

4 Informal c f g h i

Grammar plus pp.36–37

1 1 B 2 A 3 A 4 A 5 A 6 B 7 B 8 B 9 B 10 A

2 1 probably **shouldn't** let you see …
2 nothing **can** possible change …
3 I **might/may** begin …
4 nothing **can** possibly stop …
5 we really **mustn't/shouldn't/needn't** be apart …
6 I **should/ought to** move …
7 you only **need to/have to** say the word/you **only need say** the word

3 1 must 2 should 3 need 4 can 5 must/should
6 can 7 can 8 might 9 can 10 must 11 might/may
12 must 13 need

Speaking p.37

1 Markus

Tapescript

First candidate

I1 = Interlocutor 1 E = Elena

I1: In this part of the test I'm going to give each of you the chance to talk for about a minute and to comment briefly after your partner has spoken.

First you will each have the same set of pictures to look at. They show people and different types of transport. Elena, it's your turn first. I'd like you to describe two or three of these pictures, saying what you think is happening in each picture and how the people might be feeling.
Don't forget you have about one minute for this. All right? So, Elena would you start now, please?

E: Umm … In the first picture we can see a couple kissing in a railway station. The woman has just arrived back from somewhere … but I don't know where … and the man has been waiting for her. Umm … He has been waiting for her for a long absence and has really missed her. They are both very happy to be together again after such a long time. The second picture shows a man waving goodbye to somebody who is going away somewhere on a bus. We can't see the people on the bus so I don't know if it is his girlfriend or his child or even his mother or father. Er, it is not possible to see the bus's destination either so I can't say where it's going or where the picture has been taken. The man is feeling very sad because he is saying goodbye to someone he loves. Umm … The third picture is very different. In this picture we have a honeymoon couple drinking champagne as they fly off to some ex, exotic destination. Umm … They are together and they are very happy. I can't really say …

Second candidate

I2 = Interlocutor 2 M = Markus

I2: In this part of the test I'm going to give each of you the chance to talk for about a minute and to comment briefly after your partner has spoken.
First you will each have the same set of pictures to look at. They show people and different ways of communicating. Markus, it's your turn first. I'd like you to describe two or three of these pictures, saying what you think is happening in each picture and how the people might be feeling.
Don't forget you have about one minute for this. All right? So, Markus, would you start now, please?

M: Umm … Well, it looks to me as if the woman in this picture has just received a letter from someone she loves. I suppose it could be from one of her children

ANSWER KEY

but it seems more likely that it was from someone she once loved … someone she hasn't heard from for a long time. So, the letter might be asking her to meet up with him again and, and she could be wondering whether she should or not. I think it's pretty obvious that in this picture here the girl has just had some very bad news of some kind. I reckon she, she might have tried to phone her boyfriend and he's got his mobile switched off. She might know that that means he's with someone else. Anyway, she's clearly very upset and doesn't even seem to notice the rain. Perhaps someone will stop and ask her if she's all right. And the third picture … well, well, I suppose it's just possible that they don't know each other or even know the other person is leaning on the other side of the lamp post, but I think it's more likely that they've just had a, a row of some kind. I bet he's feeling really terrible. I think there's a good chance that a few seconds later one or other of them walked off … or perhaps they … perhaps they might have reached out a hand to each other, kissed and made up.

Vocabulary p.38

1 B 2 A 3 B 4 D 5 D 6 C 7 B 8 A 9 C 10 A
11 B 12 C

UNIT 5

Speaking pp.39–40

3 If I understand you correctly … So what you really mean by that is … What I understand by that is …

4 What changes do you both hope will take place over this century?

Guillermo: Yes. Just following on from what you were saying, I also feel …

Gloria: Whilst generally agreeing with Guillermo, I must say that I think …

Guillermo: Yes, that attitude really makes me angry. Adding to what Gloria just said, I think …

Tapescript

GO = Guillermo GA = Gloria I = Interlocutor

GO: OK. Shall we start?

GA: Yes. OK. I think they'd all make really fascinating programmes, don't you?

GO: Yes, I do. Or rather I think they'd all make OK programmes … . Well, maybe not 'the aging population'. I don't think that's a very attractive theme. I, I mean, when you're young it's kind of difficult to even imagine getting older. It's like 'What do I know about being old. I'm only eighteen'.

GA: If I understand you correctly, then you think a programme on the aging population would be boring for young people because it's outside their range of experience. I'm not sure I agree with you though. Surely a lot of young people have lived with older relatives or in close contact with them.

GO: Yes, I suppose you've got a point, but I'd personally rather see a programme on entertainment or exciting stuff like what sports are going to be like in the future. You know, if there will be new world records broken or how the things we use to play sport can make us play better.

GA: So what you really mean by that is that you feel young people are keen to know about new developments in sports equipment technology so they can improve their own performance. I suppose that *would* make an interesting programme, though not *everyone* is interested in sport, you know.

GO: You're right, of course. My brother is an example of that. He hates watching sports programmes on TV, but fashion appeals to almost everyone. I mean, we all wear clothes, so we have to be a bit interested in fashion even if we don't think we are, yeah?

GA: What I understand by that is that you feel that, although not everyone is conscious of it, we all inevitably take an interest in fashion.

GO: Yes, that's it. I mean I wouldn't want people to think I was always reading fashion magazines and that, but I still kind of follow fashion.

I: What changes do you both hope will take place over this century?

GA: Well, I'm sure we'd all like to see an end to wars and poverty, and of course to environmental damage, but actually I think it's not a question of dramatic change but we have to follow through what we've already started with positive changes.

GO: Yes. Just following on from what you were saying, I also feel that a lot of changes that have already begun, on a small scale, need to be developed and extended worldwide. I think a good example is the way people resisted the introduction of genetically modified food. It just shows that ordinary people can say to scientists, 'No thanks, we don't want that'.

GA: Whilst generally agreeing with Guillermo, I must say that I think genetically modified foods might have benefited people in developing countries. You know, if the companies that produced the seeds hadn't been so greedy. I think people in rich countries they often want to prevent poorer countries developing, and it's very selfish. For example, we spent centuries cutting down trees in Europe, but now we tell people in Latin

153

America that they shouldn't do exactly what we were doing ourselves.

GO: Yes, that attitude really makes me angry. Adding to what Gloria just said, I think there's a lot of selfishness and hypocrisy in developed countries and that's certainly something I'd like to see disappear or at least diminish as this century progresses. I think it's beginning to happen already… I mean …

Grammar check p.40

1 1 become   2 will know   3 had done   4 keep   5 are
   6 feel   7 did not spend   8 would benefit
   9 would not feel

2 a) 1 4 5 6
   b) 2
   c) 7 8 9
   d) 3

Writing pp.40–41

1 D C B A

2 profoundly moving, excruciatingly tedious, hugely impressive

3 1 successful   2 absolutely   3 profoundly

Reading pp.42–43

4 1 G   2 E   3 F   4 D   5 C   6 H   7 A

Grammar plus p.44

1 A 1a   B 3a   C 5a   D 4a   E 2a

2 a 7   b 2   c 5   d 6   e 4   f 3   g 1

3 1 Supposing I told you I was thinking of leaving my job, what would you say?
   2 Had scientists realised the damage their discovery would do, they would almost certainly have suppressed the information.
   3 If you will take the time to read the instructions, you will see that the machine should never be immersed in water.
   4 If you happen to pass a chemist's while you're out, could you buy me a bottle of aspirin?
   5 If you were to win first prize in a lottery, would you move to Monte Carlo?
   6 If you require further information, please do not hesitate to contact me.

Vocabulary p.45

1 a 4 hold your breath
   b 2 drum your fingers
   c 6 shrug your shoulders
   d 7 wrinkle your nose
   e 9 crack your knuckles
   f 3 purse your lips
   g 11 clench your fist
   h 12 twist your ankle
   i 10 pull *a* muscle (odd one out)
   j 1 raise your eyebrows
   k 5 shake your head
   l 3 lick your lips

2 1 holding your breath
   2 drumming your fingers
   3 shrugged his shoulders
   4 wrinkled his nose
   5 shook their heads
   6 cracking your knuckles
   7 raised her eyebrows
   8 clenched his fist
   9 pulled a muscle
   10 twist your ankle
   11 purse her lips
   12 licking their lips

English in Use p.46

1 predictions, we   2 that heal   3 ✓   4 ✓   5 ✓
6 European's   7 unusual   8 ninety   9 therapeutic
10 resistance   11 ✓   12 responsible   13 whether
14 rate at   15 inevitable

Vocabulary p.45

1 scientific   2 cloning   3 fertilisation   4 embryonic
5 genetic   6 reproduction   7 unethical   8 Physicists
9 development   10 threaten   11 destruction

UNIT 6

Grammar plus p.47

1 1 f   2 g   3 e   4 a   5 c   6 b   7 d

2 1 won't have heard   2 will be having   3 are to reprint
   4 is to be   5 'll be demanding   6 is due to retire
   7 will have been ruling   8 was on the point of resigning
   9 will have got   10 will be coming

3 a Will Susi be coming
   b will be attempting
   c will be beating
   d are not to be worn
   e is due to start
   f will have been thrashed yet again
   g is about to
   h will have scored

154

Reading pp.48–49

1 New Zealand is not mentioned.
2 1 C 2 A 3 B 4 D 5 C 6 C 7 A 8 C 9 B
10 B 11 B 12 B 13 A 14 B 15 C 16 A 17 D
18 C 19 A 20 B

Grammar check p.50

1 B 2 A 3 A 4 B 5 A 6 B 7 A 8 A 9 A
10 A 11 A

English in Use p.51

1 successfully 2 unforgettable 3 mastery 4 coaching
5 advice 6 length 7 decision 8 shaky 9 confidence
10 ability 11 enjoyment 12 otherwise 13 elusive
14 deterrent 15 variety

Vocabulary p.52

1 1 d 2 b (is manned) 3 h 4 g 5 a 6 c 7 e 8 f (Man)
2 1 everyone for themselves 2 is staffed
   3 as one person 4 a person of my word
   5 one of the people 6 be your own person
   7 person in the street 8 Humanity

3

Writing pp.52–53

The letter is too short (123 words) and the e-mail message too long (83 words).

The letter: begins 'Dear Sir' but the task says 'Write to her'; The writer does not ask for her money back and there are several further omissions from the task (comments on opening times, fitness programme, fitness trainers and pool and sauna); some of the information from the task is repeated word-for-word in the answer ('old and badly damaged' 'never managed to get on'); poor use of linking devices e.g. 'finally, furthermore'.

E-mail message: begins like a formal letter. Since it is a reply to Sara's message it would probably just warn her not to join and say that you have written to complain.

English in Use p.54

1 his mind 2 having done 3 (he) expected 4 using it
5 has to 6 not allowed 7 put 8 have finished
9 be put 10 introducing

UNIT 7

Speaking p.55

1 1 I didn't know your father came from Greece.
2 How long have your family been living in Canada?
3 Do you think of yourself as Greek or Canadian?
4 Have you got any older brothers and sisters?
5 What does your sister do?
6 Has your sister-in-law finished university?
7 How many children do your sister-in-law and brother have?
8 Do you think they'll have any more?
9 How old are the children?

Vocabulary p.55

1 striving for 2 satisfied with 3 influence on 4 ✓
5 depends on 6 According to 7 ✓ 8 reduction in
9 lead to 10 respect for

Grammar check p.55

1 1 could have 2 hadn't got 3 waited 4 would visit
   5 were 6 had not got 7 could go 8 started 9 did
   10 had had

Reading pp.56–58

2 1 A 2 C 3 D 4 B 5 C 6 B 7 B
3 a 3 b 8 c 10 d 9 e 2 f 6 g 1 h 4 i 7 j 5

Grammar plus p.58–59

1 1 'did' and 'do so' have replaced 'survived'
   2 'did' has replaced 'turned 21'
   3 'sympathy' has been left out
   4 'ones' has replaced 'years'
   5 'hand' has been left out
   6 'there were' has been left out

2 Suggested answer:

It is a fact of modern life that in Europe and the USA people are having fewer children than their parents and grandparents did. In the States the current birth rate is 2.1 children per woman. In Europe the average rate is 1.5: Spain has the lowest rate at 1.24. Italy is not far behind and Germany and Greece follow with 1.35. So the birth rate is falling, but why? In a recent poll, many people said that they wanted to have more children but believed that they could not afford to. When they were asked how many they intended to have some said one, though the majority said two. A few said that they intended to have four or more. Of course some of those who want to are unable to have children or unable to have more than one. One woman who was interviewed by the researchers said she would like to have more children but was worried about not having enough money to pay for their education. When asked if she would have more if she inherited a million dollars, she said that she thought she would, but wasn't sure. A young man said that his parents and grandparents had produced a lot of children because they had been farmers and children were a benefit on a farm. In the city, however, they are not. He had therefore decided that he did not want to have a family, though his wife was very keen to. Another man with no children said his wife did want to have a family but that he didn't. Why not? Because his parents had been divorced and he didn't want to inflict this on his children.

3 1 c   2 d   3 a/d   4 c/d   5 d

English in Use p.60

1 C   2 A   3 B   4 B   5 D   6 A   7 C   8 C   9 A   10 D
11 A   12 B   13 C   14 C   15 A

Vocabulary p.61

1 childishly   2 lose   3 alone   4 hard   5 canal   6 worthless
7 especially   8 imply   9 Souvenir   10 principle
11 stationery   12 practising   13 ensure   14 raise   15 lying
16 effect

Writing p.61

1 key words and phrases: Student Counselling Service/students/improve their relationships/parents and brothers and sisters/given to students who use the Counselling Service/weeks leading up to the summer holidays/explain why problems occur/why particularly acute during the holidays/how to cope.

2 Your leaflet should have four sections (1. Introduction 2. Why problems occur 3. Why problems are particularly acute during the holidays 4. How to cope) and it should be written in an informal style.

UNIT 8

Reading pp.62–63

1 1 B   2 C   3 B   4 A   5 B   6 C   7 D

2 1 turned the house upside down   2 self-fulfilling
3 prior to   4 succumbed   5 pick up on   6 throwback

Grammar plus p.64

1 2 to trail/trailing   3 develop/developing   4 make
5 eating   6 to confront/confronting

2 1 I detest **being** kept waiting.
2 He encouraged me **to** apply for a promotion.
3 She is threatening **to** reveal everything to the press.
4 Although he seemed familiar, we couldn't remember **meeting** before.
5 Even though we don't remember their origins, many superstitions continue **to** have considerable influence.
6 I think I will always regret not **celebrating** the end of the millennium.
7 I wouldn't risk **going** out in this weather if I were you.
8 ✓
9 Many people have attempted **to** explain coincidence.
10 You neglected **to** inform me that there would be a delay with the delivery.
11 I was already at the checkout when I realised I'd forgotten **to** get any bread.
12 ✓
13 He could see the wall in front of him but somehow he couldn't avoid **hitting** it.
14 ✓

Vocabulary p.65

1 a3   b1   c2
2 a2   b1   c3
3 a2   b1   c3
4 a1   b2
5 a3   b1   c2

Listening p.65

1 1 G   2 D   3 A   4 F   5 C
2 6 B   7 H   8 C   9 F   10 E

Tapescript

1

During the last war my husband was called into the armed forces and sailed overseas in December 1941. I was in bed one night – and to this very day I'm, I'm convinced I wasn't actually asleep – but I heard this tapping on the window pane. I thought it was probably the branch of a tree or something. But then I heard a key put into my front door and someone coming along the hall to the bedroom. I was terrified and hid under the bedclothes, but when I looked up, I saw my husband standing at my bedside, gazing at me. I was too astonished to speak. He kissed me on the cheek, held my hand and then vanished. It wasn't until 1945 that I received the news that he had died in a prisoner-of-war camp in the Far East on April 3rd 1942. That was the day before I had this experience.

2

A patient came to me complaining of vivid recurring nightmares in which he and a woman were being pursued by angry villagers, who were trying to capture and kill them. He could describe the people and the place in great detail. The strange thing was that I had another patient – a woman – who had described – again in great detail – very similar nightmares. That Christmas someone gave me a book that had just been published on a religious persecution that had taken place in France in the 12th century. Now, as I read the book it became clear to me that the events my patients were describing had actually occurred. They couldn't have known this – I'm absolutely certain of that – and neither of them had read the book – it was published months after they started having the dreams. The patients had never met. I'm also certain of that. D'you know, I really don't know how to explain it.

3

Everyone says dreaming in a foreign language shows you've really mastered that language. Well, that certainly wasn't my case, I promise you. We'd only been in Spain for a couple of weeks when I had the dream. In my dream I was standing on the platform of a railway station waiting for a train and staring at the tracks, when I realised that I had left my suitcase behind. I said to myself … *in Spanish*, 'How absent-minded can you get?' … now here's the weird part … the Spanish for 'absent-minded' is '*despistada*'. '*Des*' is a prefix and '*pista*' means track, though it's not what they say for a railway track. As I said it to myself in my dream I was aware of all this. Anyway, something woke me and I wrote '*despistada*' down on a piece of paper I had next to the bed. When I woke up next morning I saw it written there but I didn't even recognise, it let alone know what it meant. It was only when I looked it up in a dictionary that I remembered my dream.

4

I was driving a passenger through a city somewhere in Latin America when there was this terrible grinding noise. The road kind of lifted the cab and all the other cars up like some gigantic animal stretching itself. The odd thing was that the passenger I was carrying wasn't the slightest bit perturbed by this. He said, 'Seems to be another one of these damned earthquakes! Doesn't look as if you're going to get me the airport in time for my flight so you may as well take me to the hospital.' I turned round and saw that his head was bleeding. That's about all I remember. Next morning I was on the point of going out to get a paper when my friend phoned. 'Did you feel it?' she asked. 'Feel what?' I said. 'The earth tremor! It was one of the worst for years … nearly six on the Richter scale.' 'I may not have felt it,' I told her, 'but I did dream it.'

5

I had a dream a couple of weeks ago I couldn't make head or tale of. It was an extremely vivid and pleasant dream. Two women with long red hair were walking along the bank of a river. The women seemed to be in perfect harmony, but then something seemed to go wrong and one of the women sort of faded away. The other woman walked on alone, looking sad and constantly looking around her as if searching for someone. Then the second woman reappeared and walked towards the first woman with her hands held out. The two women embraced and continued walking together. A couple of weeks later I was describing this dream in a writing workshop I run, and a member of the group 'recognised' the women in my dream as her sister and herself. Apparently, they'd had a row many years before and hadn't spoken since then. She phoned her sister that night and they made it up … all thanks to my dream.

Grammar check p.66

1 1 The science teacher explained that water freezes/froze at 0°C.
   2 Marie asked Clare if she would be able to come to the lecture that evening.
   3 He asked me if I needed a lift to the airport tomorrow/the following day/the next day.
   4 The woman asked her who she spoke/had spoken to when she phoned/had phoned last week/the week before.
   5 Christine said she was thinking of going to France next summer/the following summer.
   6 Tim asked Lynette if she had seen the new Keanu Reeves film.
   7 Simon explained that he might have to leave early this/that afternoon.
   8 The man asked where the nearest petrol station was.
   9 The doctor said I should take a few days off.

10 My mother is always asking me what time I will be back.

2 1 Her boyfriend promised he would take her out to dinner on her birthday this/that year without fail.
2 The girl denied breaking/having broken the vase.
3 Sarah admitted to spending/that she had been spending a lot of time with Andrew.
4 His teacher suggested (that) he take/he took/he should take out a subscription to an English magazine.
5 Her personal assistant reminded her to buy her husband a present for their wedding anniversary.
6 The woman warned her husband that sitting in the sun would make his head cold worse.
7 John accused Sarah of seeing someone else all the time they had been together.
8 Jane agreed to cook the dinner for a change.
9 The head of department apologised for having spoken so rudely to them all the day before.

Vocabulary p.66

1 autobiography immature irrelevant overcome monologue unbelievably illogical misconceptions pseudo-intellectuals disloyal

2 1 anti-social   2 over-population   3 irresponsible
4 rewrite   5 postscript   6 monosyllabic   7 overdone
8 illegal

English in Use p.67

1 C   2 D   3 A   4 B   5 A   6 C   7 D   8 A   9 B   10 A
11 B   12 C   13 D   14 C   15 A

Writing p.68

1 1 a) stumbled   b) dripping wet   c) stunned   d) shatter
e) jagged   f) without giving it a second thought
g) pitch black   h) thumped   i) fell on deaf ears
j) to no avail   k) rushed

2 No sooner had I …

3 sequence of events in real time

4 –

UNIT 9

Vocabulary p.69

2 1 D   2 A   3 D   4 B   5 B   6 D   7 A   8 C   9 C   10 A
11 B   12 C

3 1 do   2 do   3 make   4 do   5 make   6 make   7 make
8 do   9 make   10 do   11 make, do

Listening p.70

1 G   2 F   3 D   4 H   5 B   6 D   7 C   8 E   9 F   10 G

Tapescript

1

I started when I was about fifteen, but I think it only became a habit as such when I was a medical student in the 1950s. There wasn't such a negative attitude to it then. Of course I've always said to my patients, 'Do as I say, not as I do.' They could smell it, of course, though I only ever had one or two at the end of the afternoon surgery. Anyway, the end of a century and a millennium were finally a big enough incentive to make me do it. It wasn't easy at first, I can promise you, but I'm hardly ever even tempted now. The great thing is that I can tell my patients to give up without feeling like a hypocrite.

2

All my friends just went out and got theirs without thinking twice about it, but somehow I just didn't get around to it, and as time went by it just seemed more and more of a hurdle. Of course, living in central London I barely missed it. I mean, I'm only five minutes walk from the tube and there's a bus stop round the corner as well. I think what finally made me promise myself I'd do it this year was having Max. I mean, with a small baby it's completely different. I think you've really got to be able to get around independently, and taxis are not always so easy to come by. I kept asking myself what I'd do in an emergency if David was at work.

3

My father was quite heavy as he grew older, so I suppose I must have inherited his constitution, but as a profession we're notoriously unhealthy. You fly off to some crisis point somewhere or other at a moment's notice and are holed up in a hotel for days or weeks at a time waiting for a story to break. Inevitably you end up eating and drinking all the wrong things and not getting much exercise. Anyway, I went to the doctor about something completely different and she immediately said, 'Hmm, I think we'd better take your blood pressure.' It was terrifyingly high. What's involved is a major change of lifestyle. So I've promised myself. Next time you see me these trousers will be swimming on me.

4

So I actually made it one of my New Year's resolutions … I had a list of them about as long as my arm. We were so close when we were at university together, but when Katherine went off to Scotland and I stayed here, we kind of drifted apart. It was no one's fault, really. Just one of those things, but the friendship is still really important to both of us, we realise now. So we've decided we'll get together at least once every six months, and that we'll 'correspond' via e-mail and stuff once a month or more and, of course, there's the phone as well.

5

I read the other day that some appalling percentage of people in the United States resolve to make more money every New Year's Eve. That just seems such a terrible reflection on our times, if you ask me. Anyway, I decided that I'd make this year a year where I actually spend more money … .on helping other people. I suppose I'm in quite a good position financially … so it won't involve much of a sacrifice to put aside a couple of hundred pounds a month to help support the wonderful work these people are doing literally all over the globe. I sometimes wish I could actually get out there and do something myself, but then again I'm not a doctor, so I don't think I'd be much good to them really.

Grammar plus pp.70–71

2 a 7 b 3 c 8 d 2 e 4 f 1 g 5 h 6

4 1 What happened
 2 What you need
 3 What really gets on my nerves
 4 What I can't understand
 5 What I admire most about him

Speaking p.71

1 Ingrid

2 The first photograph … . The other photograph … . Whereas in the first photograph …, in the second … . Another important difference is … in the first photograph … antique furniture, while the furniture in the second photograph looks brand new …

Tapescript
First candidate

I1 = Interlocutor 1 I = Ingrid C = Carlos

I1: Now in this part of the test, I'm going to give each of you the chance to talk for about a minute and to comment briefly after your partner has spoken. You will each have two different pictures showing working environments. Ingrid, it's your turn first. Here are your pictures. Please let Carlos see them. I'd like you to compare and contrast these two pictures, saying what kind of person you think works in each of these rooms.
Don't forget, you have about one minute for this.
All right? So, Ingrid, would you start now, please?

I: Yes. Er, the first photograph shows a room that is full of all kinds of … objects … . There are books and papers all over the desk, photographs and decor …

well, I mean ornaments on the mantelpiece, and, umm, on the chest of drawers, and I think I can even see, yes, I think I see a, a teddy bear on the chair, but it could be a doll or perhaps a cushion. The other photograph shows a room that is too tidy … well, at least it is for me. Whereas in the first photograph you can't even see the surface of the desk and er, there's a, a sweater hanging over the back of the chair, in the second it looks as if it has never even been used. Er, I'm not sure, but I think it could be an architect's or perhaps a … umm … perhaps a designer's er … room because it's very carefully … very carefully designed and very modern. And as for the person who works in the other room, well, I think he or she could perhaps be a writer. Maybe that's why there are so many books and papers everywhere. Another important difference is the style of the furniture. In the first photograph it seems mainly to be antique furniture, while the furniture in the second photograph looks brand new … to me it almost looks like a photograph in a design magazine or something like that.

I1: Thank you, Ingrid.
Now, Carlos, can you tell us which of the rooms you would prefer to work in?

C: The second one. I am a very tidy person and I cannot concentrate if there's a lot of stuff on the desk as there is in the first photograph.

Second candidate

I2 = Interlocutor 2 A = Adam R = Rafak

I2: In this part of the test I'm going to give each of you the chance to talk for about a minute and to comment briefly after your partner has spoken.
You will each have two different pictures showing working environments. Adam, it's your turn first. Here are your pictures. Please let Rafak see them. I'd like you to compare and contrast these two pictures, saying what kind of person you think works in each of these rooms.
Don't forget, you have about one minute for this.
All right? So, Adam would you start now, please?

A: Well, they're both photographs of rooms … and people, er, work in these rooms … doing what? It's a bit hard to say, actually. Umm … I guess the first room could be the workplace of a professor … I'm not sure really … er, there … there are a lot of books and papers everywhere … I suppose it could be a writer or … perhaps … no … . And the other room … well, that is much tidier and, in my opinion, nicer … I like this room very much because it is so stark and clean … Anyway, it could be the room of … umm … an engineer or an architect perhaps … . There is a computer so it could be a Silicon Valley millionaire

159

even … . Yes, I think I will go for that … a Silicon Valley millionaire. Someone who has enough money to pay a famous designer to make a perfect workspace for them. It could be Bill Gates' room … . No … I saw a photograph of his house once and it wasn't the same as this.

I2: Thank you, Adam.
Now Rafak, can you tell us which of the rooms you would prefer to work in?

R: The first one is more like my room at home, but I think it would be easier to work in the second room.

Vocabulary p.72

2
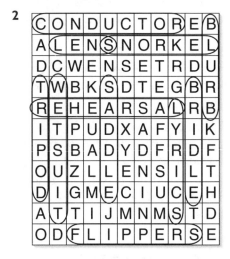

3 1 lenses, tripod   2 flippers, wetsuit   3 rehearsal, conductor   4 saddle, bridle   5 lyrics   6 blurb

Grammar check p.73

1 A   2 B   3 B   4 B   5 A   6 A   7 C   8 A   9 C
10 A   11 C   12 B   13 C   14 A   15 A   16 C   17 C
18 B   19 A   20 B

English in Use p.74

1 ✓   2 opportunity   3 knew   4 which   5 healthier,
6 society's   7 ✓   8 hommage   9 ✓   10 Two   11 loose
12 ✓   13 ambitious   14 resolutions?   15 especific

UNIT 10

Vocabulary p.77

1   a 4   b 3   c 8   d 2   e 5   f 1   g 6   h 9   i 7

2   1 download   2 crashed   3 keyboard   4 on-line
5 downloading   6 Internet Service Provider   7 hacker
8 software   9 deleted

Grammar plus pp.77–78

1 1 It is a pity that the Internet is plagued by hackers, virus writers and hoaxers.
2 It is vital to make back-ups of all your files.
3 It is surprising how dependent people have become on computers.
4 It seems obvious that you must have deleted an important file.
5 It can be difficult to choose a good Internet Service Provider.
6 It is important for people to warn each other about dangerous computer viruses.
7 It is stated in the regulations that you should not tell other people your password.

2 1 The new computer made **it** easier for her to finish the project.
2 He made **it** clear that she was not going to get the promotion.
3 I find **it** surprising that there are still plenty of people who have never used a computer.
4 The constant power failures made **it** difficult to use a computer.
5 Most people consider **it** unwise to download files from suspicious websites.

3 1 ✓
2 I can't stand **it** when people keep me waiting.
3 I found **it** very odd that he didn't even phone to say he wouldn't be coming.
4 I don't think you should have made **it** so obvious that you didn't like what she was wearing.
5 I wish you wouldn't always leave **it** up to me to make the travel arrangements.
6 Let me put **it** to you that you were not at home with your wife on the night of 23rd September, but in Joe's Bar.
7 Our neighbours are making **it** impossible for us to sleep at night.
8 ✓
9 Would you consider **it** an insult if someone pretended not to see you in the street?
10 ✓

Speaking p.78

1   3, 1

2   As far as I can work out, it's some kind of …
I could be wrong, but …
I can just about make out …

160

Tapescript

I = Interlocutor   R = Renate

I: In this part of the test I'm going to give each of you the chance to talk for about a minute, and to comment briefly after your partner has spoken.
First, you will each have the same set of pictures to look at, but your pictures are in a different order. They show people using computers. Please do not show your pictures to each other. Renate, it's your turn first. I'd like you to describe two of these pictures in detail, saying why you think the people might be using the computers.
Don't forget, you have about one minute for this.
I'd like you, Nelson, to listen carefully and tell us which three photographs Renate has not described.
All right? So, Renate would you start now, please?

R: Yes. Umm. Well, both the pictures I'm going to describe show people *working* with computers as opposed to playing. I could be wrong, but in the first one I think the two people are architects because I can just about make out some architect's plans on the screen of the computer, and one of the men seems to be holding a copy of the plans in his hand. The other man is pointing out something in the plans on the screen with his glasses. Perhaps they're discussing changes they should make to the plans before they send them to a client. The second photograph is similar in that again we see people working together. This time though instead of one computer screen we can see … well, I'm not sure exactly how many there are, but I can just about make out two over by the window, and then there are at least seven others. I don't know what kind of work they're doing or where they are, but as far as I can work out it's some kind of control tower, so they might be air traffic controllers. One of the men is wearing headphones, so … yes … I, I think they could be air traffic controllers. Umm … another similarity between this picture and the first and the, er, the first one I described is that the, the woman seems to have pointed something out on one of her screens and her colleague seems to be looking at it. So once again perhaps there's some kind of problem that needs to be corrected. The woman has something next to her but I'm not quite sure what it is. Perhaps it's a microphone of some kind …

Listening p.79

1 problem-solving   2 fantasy   3 negative consequences/complaints   4 dishonest   5 interrupted   6 dreams   7 time limits   8 30 days

Tapescript

Increasing numbers of people here in the United States and elsewhere in the world are the victims of computer game obsessions or addiction to Internet chat rooms. What's more, the problem is, I'm afraid to say, much more serious than the media would have us think. They're inclined to emphasise the positive side of computer games – that they're very entertaining – something almost no one would deny. Journalists are right to point out that they can also help people develop skills, such as concentration and problem-solving. Unfortunately, however, for between six to ten per cent of users, games and Internet chat lines become a problem. They spend hours of their time sitting at their computers – in the worst cases users will play games non-stop for whole weekends. Sooner or later this begins to jeopardise their professional and personal lives, and even their physical health. In fact, a person who is unable to control their use of the computer is in a very similar situation to a drug user.

There are two main reasons that people become addicted to computer games and the Internet in this way. The first of these is what we term 'avoidance': in this case the person is trying to ignore other problems, such as marital strife or financial trouble. Like drug addicts, they try to create a world free from stress, pain and worry. A second reason is fantasy: the person escapes, or gains self-esteem, by adopting online personalities. They can be an airline pilot one minute, and 15 minutes later the director of a company, or a warrior.

It's important to emphasise that being on the computer a lot doesn't make you an addict, just like drinking a lot doesn't necessarily make you an alcoholic. So, what are the warning signs? The number 1 symptom is a loss of control – an inability to stop yourself using the computer, even when there are negative consequences such as complaints from relatives or friends. Partly as a reaction to this, there's also often a tendency to be dishonest about or to minimise the amount of time spent on the computer and to be defensive about your right to use it as much as you want. Experiencing a rush of adrenaline when connecting to the Internet or feeling guilty after periods of protracted use are also clear symptoms of addiction, along with signs of irritability when you are interrupted and, of course, dreams about computer games.

Once that point is reached then some kind of help is needed. In some cases the addicted player can break the addiction by stopping abruptly. Others need to be taught to set time limits on computer game sessions until they have got their behaviour back under control. In the worst cases, they need to be admitted to a special clinic for a period of treatment. We usually recommend 30 days away from home and, of course, the temptation of the computer.

And, in most cases, this will solve the problem …

English in Use p.80

1 little/nothing   2 is   3 to   4 has   5 allows   6 like
7 been   8 than   9 be   10 take   11 makes   12 Another
13 it   14 as   15 no

Grammar check p.81

1 **the** latest   2 **most** successful   3 **as** they
4 three times **as**   5 longer **than**   6 **the** second biggest
7 four times **more**   8 **the** most contrived
9 far **more** subtle   10 the **most** parent-friendly

Vocabulary p.81

1   1 origami   2 duvet   3 siesta   4 chauffeur   5 drama
    6 mammoth   7 confetti   8 mattress   9 marmalade
    10 kindergarten

2   1 kindergarten, chauffeur   2 marmalade, duvet/
    mattress   3 origami, confetti   4 siesta, mattress
    5 mammoth, drama

English in Use p.82

1   1 I   2 F   3 A   4 G   5 B   6 E

Writing pp.82–83

1   1 F   2 T   3 F   4 T   5 T   6 T   7 F

UNIT 11

Listening p.84

1   1 researching   2 writing   3 loneliness   4 three or four
    5 relationships   6 run down   7 two or three weeks
    8 pyjamas   9 restaurants   10 expenses

Tapescript

Well, at the beginning, it was tremendously exciting knowing that my opinions and experiences would end up in print. Also, researching a book forced me to explore off the beaten track, wander down alleys I wouldn't normally wander down, and generally find places I might not otherwise visit if I was on holiday. What most people don't realise, though, is that I spend maybe a quarter of my time travelling, and the rest researching and writing. Even when I'm on the road, the job has its drawbacks. Number one would be loneliness. I can be travelling for three or four months on my own, and you have to cover so much ground in that time that you don't have the opportunity to hang around and forge relationships. It's exhausting too: you get up early in the morning, and don't stop all day. Everything you see and feel may filter into the book. If you don't note it all down at the time, you'll probably never get another chance. So, it's enjoyable but it's easy to get run down. I always have two or three weeks off when I get back because I'm so tired and I almost always say to myself 'never again'. And then there's the writing. The next eight or nine months may be a pretty intense experience and I spend days in my pyjamas, putting the work off.

People often ask me what qualities make a good Rough Guide writer. I think the first thing you need is a prodigious appetite for new places and information – you should be a bit like a sponge, absorbing all sorts of cultural and sociological information – and you must also love language, the nuts and bolts of writing. When you're on the road it's important to remain 'undercover', but sometimes it's just not possible. For example, I've done several books on Goa, on the west coast of India, so I'm pretty well known there. I try not to tell restaurants who I am so that I don't get preferential treatment, but being known can sometimes be advantageous; if I have a chat with the hoteliers it can give me the sort of local details that make a guide seem less like it's written by someone just passing through. Mainly, though, you just have to cope with being on your own, and be able to put up with having very little money. You get paid a portion of your royalties in advance, which just about covers your expenses on the trip but not much more. After that, it just depends on how many books you sell.

Grammar check p.85

1 because **of** our often superficial attitude   2 To start with
3 **In** the first place   4 As **a** result   5 In spite **of the fact
that**   6 Package tourists on **the** other hand
7 In conclusion/Finally   8 and **thus/so** do less damage
9 Despite **the fact that** they have

Vocabulary p.85

1   1 wooded   2 wind-blown   3 tongue-twisting
    4 stumble upon   5 deserted   6 idyllic   7 tucked away
    8 the middle of nowhere   9 lined   10 inching your way
    11 tree-shaded   12 meanders

2   suggested answer

   Halfway through the morning we **stumbled upon** a path that **meandered** though the valley to the village of Saint Batholomew, **tucked away** just beyond Mount Saint Clare in **the middle of nowhere**. Since it was Sunday morning there were no people in the village square when we first arrived, but when the morning church service finished there was a parade and we found ourselves in the middle of a large crowd. We **inched our way** along village streets with **tongue-twisting** names, **lined** with picturesque cottages. Finally, we found ourselves in a pleasant **tree-shaded** park and sat down to eat our picnic lunch.

Reading p.86–87

2 1 G 2 D 3 B 4 C 5 F 6 E 7 B 8 C 9 A
10 C 11 C 12 D 13 A 14 C

Grammar plus p.88

1 1 defining 2 non-defining 3 defining 4 defining
5 non-defining 6 non-defining 7 defining 8 defining
9 non-defining 10 non-defining 11 defining

2

> In **1973, which** was the year I visited the city for the first **time, I** was completely bewitched by London. My friend Gillian and I found a small hotel just off Holland Park Road, By an amazing coincidence it was the same **hotel in which** Gillian's father had stayed five years before – and they remembered him! Near the hotel there were several **buses, none** of which ran particularly regularly in those days. Every morning we would catch one of these buses to Oxford Street and spend hours looking in shop windows at the wonderful things, which two young women on a shoe-string budget could not afford. Gillian also liked to go to **Knightsbridge, where** there were even more expensive shops such as Harvey Nicholls and the famous Harrods. The only things we could afford to buy there were beautiful linen **handkerchiefs, which** we gave to our friends when we got back to Canada. Gillian's older **brother, who** had visited London earlier that **year, had** given us a list of the **places that** he had visited. We happily retraced his steps, sometimes stopping for a cup of tea in one of the **cafés which** he had recommended.

3 1 whom 2 whose 3 which 4 which/that 5 whose
6 who/that 7 whom 8 whom

4 1 that 2 what 3 what 4 that 5 what 6 that
7 what

English in Use p.89

1 cheaper/more economical 2 to become 3 over
4 allows you 5 variety/range 6 require you 7 a ban
8 not allowed/prohibited 9 sell 10 consumption
11 discourage/not allow 12 be purchased 13 departure

Writing p.90

1 1 A 2 A 3 A and B 4 B 5 B 6 A 7 A

2 1 A 2 No, nothing on night life. 3 Yes, though use of more complex and expressive language would make it more attractive. 4 Yes, though the Section headings are not very interesting. 5 No. There is far too much lifting of language from the task. 6 No.

UNIT 12

English in Use p.91

1 magical 2 recurring/recurrent 3 relationship
4 observer 5 invisible 6 intriguing 7 reflection

Reading pp.92–93

2 1 B 2 E 3 G 4 D 5 A 6 F

3 A 7 B 9 C 2 D 8 E 4 F 5 G 3 H 6 I 1

Speaking pp.94–95

	Grammar and Vocabulary	Discourse Management	Pronunciation	Interactive Communication
Carmen	G	P	E	G
Piotr	E	E	G	E

Tapescript

I = Interlocutor C = Carmen P = Piotr

Part 1

I: Good afternoon. My name is Nuala MacMahon and this is my colleague Jeremy Neilsen. And your names are Carmen and Piotr?

C and P: Yes, that's right.

I: Can I have your mark sheets, please? Thank you. First of all we'd like to know a little about you. Where are you both from?

M: I'm from Mexico.

P: And I'm from Poland.

I: And how long have you been in this country?

C: Since October.

P: I've been here for nearly two years.

I: Now I'd like you to ask *each other* something about life in your two countries and the places of interest you've visited here in Britain.

P: So you're from Mexico. Where did you grow up?

C: In Mexico City. It's one of the biggest cities in the world. There are 17 million people living there. And you?

P: I'm from quite a small village in Poland. I can't imagine what it would be like to grow up with so large number of people around me. What was it like?

163

C: Well, for me, quite normal, of course. It takes a long time to get from one side of the city to the other and the traffic is really crazy. Like many big cities it's very contaminated, unfortunately, so I suppose you would say that's one of the disadvantages, but I like living there and I miss quite a lot. Umm …

P: Yes, I miss my village too, though I've managed to go back a couple of times while I've been living here. There are quite a lot of differences between how people live in Poland and here in England, though there are things in common too, especially because of the climate. Have you noticed many differences?

C: Oh yes, too many. One is that I think the family is much more important in Mexico than it is here.

P: Have you had many … I mean much … opportunity to travel around Britain so far?

C: Yes. I've been to Scotland and I've also been to Bath and Bristol, to Oxford and Cambridge and to Devon and Cornwall.

P: Wow. You've seen a lot more than I have. I haven't been to the half the places you mentioned. I'd love to go to Scotland. Did you find it interesting?

C: Yes. But a bit cold.

I: Piotr, how would you feel about living abroad permanently?

P: I'd quite like it, actually. I spent six months in Spain on an exchange programme when I was a student and I've been travelling almost the whole time since then. Of course, I want to be able to go back to Poland sometimes too.

I: What about you, Carmen?

C: No, I miss my family too much. I couldn't live away from Mexico.

I: Thank you.

Part 2

I: In this part of the test I'm going to give each of you the chance to talk for about a minute and to comment briefly after your partner has spoken. First, you will each have the same set of pictures to look at. They show different traditional celebrations.
Carmen, it's your turn first. I'd like you to compare and contrast two or three of these pictures, saying why people might enjoy traditional celebrations like these and how important it is to preserve them.
Don't forget, you have about one minute for this. All, right? So, Carmen, would you start now, please?

C: Umm … vamos a … In the … There is a photograph of a marriage … or I suppose they get married … but I don't know really. They are a couple surround by a group of other people. It seems they are seated on a special chair and they wear special dresses. I'm not sure where they are from … I don't know … . Then there is another photo which is more familiar to me. It is a group of people in traditional Scottish costumes, they are playing the … umm … I can't remember what it is called in English … a musical instrument typical of Scotland, and they wear … a kilt … a special Scottish skirt worn by men. It is very funny. May be they perform for tourists in Edinburgh Castle but I'm not sure … (SILENCE)

I: How important is it to preserve traditional celebrations like these?

C: Not so important for me. I think they are fine but … well, I don't think is so important.

I: Thank you.
Now, Piotr, can you tell me which of these celebrations you would most like to take part in or attend?

P: I would really like to see the Scottish celebration, but I think I'd look a bit strange if I tried to take part.

I: Thank you.
Now I'm going to give each of you another set of pictures to look at. They show aspects of life in the city.
Now, Piotr, it's your turn. I'd like you to compare and contrast two or three of these situations, saying what aspects of city life are shown and what they have to tell us about life in the city today.
Don't forget, you have about one minute for this. All right? So, Piotr, would you start now please?

P: OK, well I'm going to describe the park and the bridge. The first photograph shows a summer's day in a city park in … well, I'm not sure … but I think it could be New York … or, well, perhaps it's Central Park. Anyway, there are people taking advantage of the glorious weather and lying in the sun. It might be during the lunch hour because there really are a lot of people. The other photograph is similar – there are also a lot of people, but this time it's people on the move in … well, er, must be London … I think it's Waterloo Bridge. Rather than lunchtime I think this is probably the rush hour. I get the impression that the people are hurrying to get the tube or bus home from work. It's, it's hard to tell what time of year it is but whereas in the first photograph I described it is definitely summer, here something makes me think it's autumn, though I suppose it could just be a rather grey and mserable summer's day. So, while one photograph shows people in the city taking a few moments of leisure, the other shows people getting to or from work. I think they both tell us important things about life in modern cities. What I mean is that cities are places people come to spend their leisure time, shopping, or going to the cinema or theatre or, as in the photograph, just enjoying a city park. At the same time, they are places people come to to work, and because of that transport takes on a very important role. In the park, you can forget for a while that you're even in a city … the traffic noise is just a distant hum … but in a situation like the second photograph the noise and smell of the traffic would be very noticeable … so that's another difference between the two scenes … relative peace and quiet in the first one, and the noise and smell of the city in the other.

I: Thank you.

Now, Carmen, can you tell us which situation you would least like to find yourself in?

C: I don't like any of them too much. The park is OK for me, I suppose.

I: Thank you.

Part 3

I: Now I'd like you to discuss something between yourselves, but please speak so that we can hear you.

I'd like you to imagine that a trip around the world by bicycle to raise money for charity is being planned. Here are some pictures showing various aspects of the trip.

Talk to each other about the problems and opportunities they represent, and then decide which aspect of the trip would be most difficult and which one would be the most rewarding.

P: OK. Er, shall we start?

C: If you want.

P: Well, I think planning the trip would be very interesting, though rather difficult, don't you? (PAUSE) I mean you would need to get a lot of information about the climate, about places to stay and the state of the roads and so on, and I guess you would have to learn a lot about bicycle repairs and also about first aid.

C: Yes. (PAUSE)

P: That kind of information could prove really essential if you had some kind of accident, and I suppose on such a long trip it's almost inevitable that something would go wrong at some point. I think that would be quite hard to cope with, don't you?

C: Yes. I think it would be terrible to be so far from home and have an accident like that. I think saying goodbye to your friends and family is really horrible too. I cry a lot when I left Mexico.

P: Yes, but you would probably also feel excited about the, about the prospect of doing something really important, like raising money for charity, and also seeing the whole world. So although it would be one of the more difficult parts of the trip, I think it would also be kind of exhilarating. I suppose the best part would be meeting people in other countries. What do you think?

C: I suppose it could be OK, but for me the best would be getting home and seeing my family again after so, so long time away. 800 days is too long time. It's almost three years.

P: Yes, it is a long time … but I suppose nowadays you would be able to stay in touch with people quite easily, or at least more easily than in the past. I mean with the Internet and so on. So for me that would not be so hard. I think I would find it quite tough to write a whole book about my experiences, though. That would be a lot of work. How would you feel about that?

C: I don't know. I think you are right.

P: (PAUSE) Perhaps the best thing about the trip would be riding through spectacular countryside, and on a bicycle you could really see things a lot better, if, er, than, than you could if you were travelling by car or train. Would you enjoy riding a bicycle do you think?

C: Not so much. I don't know ride a bicycle.

P: You could learn. It's easy. Of course being able to give the money you'd raised to charity would be fantastic. How do you think you'd feel?

C: OK, I suppose.

P: I think it would probably be the best thing about doing something like this, knowing that you had been able to help … of course, I suppose you could be worried about raising less money than you had originally hoped, but at least you'd know that you had really made an effort. (PAUSE)

I: So, which aspects have you chosen?

P: We think leaving home would be very sad and difficult. The most rewarding would be the contact with the other cultures and having raised money for charity.

Part 4

I: What kind of people enjoy this kind of experience?

P: I, I think in some ways you would have to be rather egotistical and perhaps even a little obsessed. I mean, there are all sorts of other ways of raising money apart from going on what could be even a quite dangerous journey.

C: But surely people who do these things ... who want to raise money ... to help other people ... they have good intentions.

P: Yes, I think that's a good point. What, what I mean is that, though one of their reasons for doing this might be to raise money, to, to keep going over such a long journey with so many possible problems, you would need to be a very special kind of person ... with, with a rather special personality.

I: Could you see yourself going on a trip like this?

C: Definitely, no. I think it would be terrible to have to ride a bicycle all that way and to be in danger places so far from everyone you know.

I: What about you, Piotr?

P: Well ... yes, I *could* imagine doing something like this ... maybe not on a bicycle, but I really like walking and I could see myself going on a long walk, perhaps to raise money or something. I think it would be very satisfying, but I wonder how I might be feeling after it was over. I suppose I could write about it.

I: Why do you think people enjoy reading accounts of trips like these?

P: Well, because most of us are really not so adventurous but we like to experience danger and excitement ... but second hand.

C: Yes, I think people like to read about other people's experiences, and then you don't have to have the experience yourself.

I: Thank you. That is the end of the test.

Grammar plus p.96

1 **No sooner had I sat** down to eat my supper, **than** I heard someone knocking at the door.
2 **Never before has this city been** in greater need of cheap public transport than it is today.
3 **Never had I met** such a fascinating and intelligent person as Medallion.
4 **Not only does he forget** people's names, he also finds it difficult to remember the words for common objects.
5 **Under no circumstances should you let** people in if they don't have identification on them.
6 **Hardly had she opened her mouth to speak** when someone in the audience shouted 'fire'.
7 **Only after she had posted the letter did she realise** that she had forgotten to enclose the cheque.
8 **At no time did she doubt** that he would come home.
9 **Scarcely had she found** her seat on the plane **when** a flight attendant asked her if she would mind moving.

Listening p.97

1 90 minutes   2 20 minutes   3 rapid eye movement
4 in colour   5 ten minutes   6 half an hour   7 external sounds   8 stimulation

Tapescript

What exactly is dreaming? Well, during the night our brains are still mainly concerned with whatever we were thinking about and doing during the day. We spend most of our sleeping time on this, and it's a pretty dull slow business without much visual interest. Just to liven matters up every 90 minutes or so, the curtain rises on what I like to call 'the cinema of the mind'. I mean dreaming sleep. It lasts for 20 minutes or so at a time. Sleep researchers also use the term 'rapid eye movement' or R.E.M., REM sleep for dreaming sleep. This is because the eyes move rapidly, in much the same way as they do when we look around a room or at a landscape when we're awake. The big difference, of course, is that our eyes are closed when we're asleep.

Another important difference between sleeping and waking is that while we're dreaming our brain paralyses our body and stops all movement, except for a bit of twitching in the hands and feet. Apart from paralysing you, a typical dream has four characteristics. Firstly, it's in colour. Secondly, it fades from our memory in about ten minutes, unless, of course, we happen to wake up and make a real effort to remember it, that is. Thirdly, it lasts quite a long time. Dreams are not over in a flash as some people believe; they can last for more than half an hour. Finally, a typical dream includes some of the things that are going on around us, like certain kinds of physical discomfort and external sounds. We incorporate these things into our dreams because we are actually sleeping quite lightly and are vaguely aware of our surroundings.

So why do we dream? My theory goes like this. During non-dreaming sleep the brain probably rests and recovers from the wear and tear of wakefulness, but it doesn't like being unconscious for too long and needs periodic stimulation. Rather than having to wake up repeatedly to get this, the brain finds substitute stimulation in REM sleep and dreaming. And if you ask me, it's the most sophisticated entertainment there is.

ANSWER KEY

Vocabulary p.97

2 1 hiss   2 flash   3 flicker   4 crash   5 screech
   6 sparkle   7 bang   8 roar   9 beam   10 thud
   11 twinkle   12 glow   13 hum

Grammar check p.98

1 a

2 2 How long had you been having the recurring 'bad dream'?
   3 What did the place in the dream look like?
   4 Were you alone (in the dream)?
   5 Where did you stop for the night?
   6 Was it like/similar to/the same as the inn in the dream?
   7 Why did you have to stay in the annexe?
   8 Who slept/who did you choose to sleep in the haunted room?
   9 How did you sleep that night?
   10 Do you still have nightmares

3 2 Who ~~did show~~ showed you to your rooms in the annexe?

4 ~~About~~ What were you worried about?

6 Did your husband know why ~~did you choose~~ you chose the room with the view of the valley?

UNIT 13

Grammar check p.99

1 is often called   2 refuses   3 settles   4 was produced
5 bolted   6 called   7 was given   8 always felt   9 be marketed   10 be applied   11 become   12 did not possess   13 put   14 were marred   15 was killed
16 died   17 persevere   18 were brought   19 earned
20 was left   21 founded   22 was employed   23 made
24 convince   25 were banned   26 were loosened
27 climbed   28 allow   29 was started   30 made

Grammar plus p.100

1 1 Having finally got a job at Johnson and Barnet, I was anxious that my first campaign should be effective.
   2 He sold all his shares in Burchfield Books, having realised/realising that the company was in trouble.
   3 Having gone into debt to traders, the people in the village missed out on what they should have been earning.
   4 Closing/Having closed the door quietly behind me, I tip-toed into the room.
   5 The drilling in the street continued throughout the three-hour exam, completely destroying his concentration.

2 1 There are 2.3 million snowboarders in the United States representing nearly 20% of the people who visit ski resorts annually.
   2 Burton spent the summer of 1978 in Europe testing his boards on Austrian glaciers.
   3 Burton Snowboards still dominates the industry, selling more than 100,000 snowboards a year in North America.
   4 Sometimes key ingredients for a product are not available locally, making it necessary to find alternatives.
   5 He remembers getting very excited while teaching his students in Bangladesh how economic theories provided solutions to problems.
   6 Manufacturers throughout the world have patented just about every imaginable car name, making it extremely difficult to find a suitable name for a new model.

English in Use pp.100–101

1 1 from   2 often   3 far   4 as   5 must   6 especially
   7 with   8 of   9 for   10 if   11 to   12 on   13 which
   14 around   15 rather

Vocabulary pp.101–102

1
F	L	E	X	I	-	T	I	M	E	S
S	L	A	Y	O	F	F	A	T	M	E
D	O	G	B	H	C	R	T	Y	U	S
I	C	P	O	B	B	O	R	S	X	A
V	U	S	L	E	A	V	E	H	O	I
I	T	O	Y	R	N	L	Y	A	D	U
D	U	P	R	S	K	A	E	R	Y	S
E	R	E	T	I	R	E	M	E	N	T
N	N	P	J	B	U	K	N	S	R	R
D	O	J	K	P	P	O	U	B	F	I
I	V	P	I	H	T	M	S	A	C	K
S	E	C	O	U	N	G	H	V	F	E
A	R	D	J	K	Y	T	R	B	V	W

2 1 share   2 Turnover   3 laid off   4 flexi-time   5 leave
   6 bankrupt   7 sacked   8 retirement

Vocabulary p.102

1 1 I missed some classes at the beginning of the course and it took me ages to catch **up** with the others.

167

2 Trying to cut **down** on the number of cigarettes you smoke won't work. You should give up completely.
3 Would you like to use the bathroom to freshen **up** before we go out?
4 I managed to track (**down**) a copy of his first album (**down**) in a second-hand record shop.
5 Would you mind speaking **up** a bit? We can't hear you at the back of the room.
6 I was only away for a week but the work has really piled **up** in my absence.
7 The pickpocket must have sneaked **up** behind me and taken my wallet while I was waiting in the queue.
8 They're going to spend the money Tony inherited on having their house done **up**.
9 Calm **down**, will you! There's no point getting angry about it.
10 I can't keep **up** with Anna. She's got so much energy she never seems to stop to draw breath.
11 I thought the film was a rather watered **down** version of the story in the book. It wasn't nearly as powerful.
12 he's gone to the hairdresser to have her highlights touched **up**.
13 They had to interview everyone on the list, but they've managed to narrow it **down** to five applicants.
14 I wish you'd liven **up** a bit. You seem so miserable lately.
15 When Andrew was younger it was impossible to imagine him ever getting married and settling **down**.
16 The police have managed to pin (**down**) the time of the murder (**down**) to between ten and ten-thirty.

English in Use p.103

1 C 2 A 3 D 4 A 5 B 6 B 7 C 8 A 9 C 10 B
11 D 12 C 13 A 14 B 15 D

Writing pp.104–105

Dear Ms Henning,
I am writt~~i~~ng to apply for ~~the~~ MBA course at the University of ʻHarlow. It ~~had~~ has been my intention for some time to continue my studies in the field of business administration and because ~~of~~ my employer, Rambler Cars, is now willing to allow~~ed~~ me take study leave, I have decided to apply to begin your course in September.
Despite the fact that I do not hold/not holding/not being a holder of a degree from a British university, I have a Diploma in Banking and Finance from the Institute of European Business Studies and a Certificate in Direct Market~~t~~ing from the same institution. I have enclosed copies of both the diploma and certificate.
In addition, I ~~am~~ have been working for just over nine months with Rambler as a trainee manager. Prior to taking up this post, I had been an Assistant Manager at English Court, a major clothing manufacturer.
I feel certain that your programme would ~~be~~ suit my needs particularly well as my main interests ~~lay~~ lie in investment, marketing and corporate finance. Your flexi-study programme and the study visits also ~~called~~ attracted my attention. I would probably choose to study part-time.
I look forward to hearing from you.
Yours sincerely,
Lucía Rubio Sanchez

UNIT 14

Vocabulary p.106

1 1 for 2 of 3 of 4 to 5 about 6 by

3 1 We have every reason to be ashamed **of** our treatment of the other species on this planet.
2 The National Park is open **to** all visitors who undertake to obey the rules.
3 Sheldrick was baffled **by** the behaviour of the elephant.
4 The keeper was absent **from** the stall where he should have been sleeping with the elephant.
5 There's nothing wrong **with** punishing an elephant as long as you remember to make friends afterwards.
6 Conservationists are very anxious **about** the falling tiger population.

Grammar check p.106

1 ✓
2 He published some ground-breaking research on apes and language recently.
3 Can I give you some advice?
4 ✓
5 There was some very interesting news in the paper yesterday about pandas.
6 ✓
7 They're both dark but their little girl has got lovely red hair.
8 Did you have a good time at Tina's party?
9 ✓
10 If we're going to have children we'll need more space.

English in Use p.107

1 doubtless 2 concealment/concealing 3 confusing
4 threatening 5 accidental 6 evolution 7 protective
8 survival

Reading pp.108–109

2 1 A 2 B 3 B 4 D 5 A 6 B 7 C

Grammar plus p.110

1 2 could be very naughty, competitive and disobedient.
3 that you had to be careful to make friends with them again.
4 had done something to the elephant which they'd forgotten but the elephant hadn't.
5 had died of a broken heart.
6 they will come flying back to their human keepers.
7 she was very flattered that a completely wild elephant would come and talk to her.

2 1 a 2 b 3 b 4 a 5 b 6 a

3 1 It is thought that the universe is expanding.
2 It is believed that the breakthrough in genetics will lead to a cure for cancer.
3 It is feared that there are as few as fifteen tigers left in the region.
4 It was thought that the volcano was dormant.
5 It has been suggested that building barriers might protect the city from eruptions.
6 It was announced earlier today that the use of insecticides was to be banned.

4 1 whisper 2 concede 3 mutter 4 boast 5 stress
6 claim 7 urge 8 retort

Vocabulary p.111

1 1 situation 2 topic/question/issue 3 opinion/view
4 question 5 issue 6 problem 7 aspect 8 trend

Listening p.111

1 the Park rules 2 is illegal 3 seeds and insects
4 uninhabited islands 5 fearless 6 feed 7 litter
8 souvenirs 9 your guide's instructions

Tapescript

If I could just have your attention please. In a moment, you'll be starting your tour, but there are just a few things I'd like to run through before you meet your guides. Right. I'm sure you're all very much aware that these islands are absolutely unique and extremely delicate, and that we all need to make a special effort to preserve them in their natural state. Well, The Galápagos Islands National Park has come up with some rules which I'm going to read to you now. If you've got any questions, then please ask. You'll all be given a printed copy of the Park rules later. I can't emphasise enough how essential it is that you follow the rules … *to the letter*. You can expect your guide to be quite strict about enforcing them too. All the guides love the islands and do their best to protect them. We don't bend the Park rules for anybody!

The most important rule is that no plants or animals or any other natural objects are to be removed from the park. Doing this could harm the ecological balance of the park and it's also illegal. So don't even think about it. Also … be careful not to transport any live material, such as seeds and insects, to the islands or from one island to another. This too is against the law. All the islands have their own unique flora and fauna, and any introduced species could destroy these ecosystems, so please be careful and check your clothing for seeds and insects before each landing and departure. Now, if you're going to one of the uninhabited islands, please don't take any food with you … if you drop as much as an orange seed it could grow into a tree and damage the existing ecosystems. Humans are only temporary visitors to these islands, and we want to make sure the only thing we leave behind is our footprints.

Now, moving on to the wild life in the park … please don't touch the animals under any circumstances. It might seem tempting, because some of the animals are remarkably fearless, but remember that they will quickly lose this fearlessness if they're approached by humans. So … don't touch the animals, and although it seems blindingly obvious I will say it … don't feed the animals. You can put yourself in danger and destroy the animals' social structure and breeding habits by offering them food, so please don't. Remember. You came here to see a completely natural situation. Please don't interfere with it. OK. And for the same reason, don't leave litter on the islands or throw any off your boat. Carry along a bag of some sort if you're going to need to dispose of litter such as film wrappers or Kleenex.

And at the end of your visit don't buy any souvenirs made of plants or animals from the islands. If anyone offers you any, please advise the National Park Service. Unfortunately this problem is on the increase and we need your full cooperation if we want to put a stop to it.

So finally, follow your guide's instructions at all times, and you'll have a fantastic, trouble-free visit to the The Galapagos Islands National Park … Now, are there any questions before we go and meet the guides?

Writing p.112

Content: no recommendation for action to be taken.
Irrelevancy: final sentence of section on oil refinery

Vocabulary: repetition of 'terrible'

Register: final sentence too informal

Accuracy: every day we face ~~with~~ more and more noise …;
all the other things people throw **away** are taken …;
frightful pollution (not '**a** frightful **contamination**') …; we must **make** sure that … .

UNIT 15

Listening p.113

1 A 2 C 3 C 4 A 5 C 6 B 7 A 8 B 9 A 10 C

Tapescript

1

I'm not much of a photographer as you can see, but I had it enlarged and framed. I don't know how many times she's begged me to put it in a cupboard or something, but I'd never do that, particularly since we don't see her so often now. I really do think it captures the essence of her. I mean it's such a characteristic gesture … tilting her head to one side like that. Even though she's so grown up now, she still does exactly the same thing when she's concentrating. Her mother does it too and so did *her* mother.

2

I know who some of them are … my two aunts are the ones with the big bows in their hair … and this rather wicked looking boy here in the front row is one of my uncles, actually … my Aunt Nora married her first love and she met him when she was five! … And, yes, Miss Blackham, I think it was … she looks very strict but she was their favourite. They often talked about her … but the others … well, I wouldn't have a clue now. But I can remember looking at it when I was a child and being told all their names and what they were like and so on.

3

We're in the garden of our old house. My parents sold it after we'd all left home, which was a pity I always thought. I don't remember it being taken, but I've always imagined it was my mother who was holding the camera and that my father was telling me to look at her. I do remember being given the doll, though. It must have been that day my father came back from America and brought it for me. I was absolutely thrilled with it as you can see, and he was very pleased to be home again after such a long time away from us.

4

In those days they had all these backdrops with different landscapes and scenes from classical antiquity, and so on, to make the photograph look grand. It looks like some kind of villa in the background, doesn't it? The dress is in an old chest at my aunt's. It's beautiful silk but it's far too fragile to wear. Mum inherited the necklace and earrings, and Aunt Maria has her ring. He left his gold watch to me. I suppose they were happy in their own way, though they used to have some terrible rows and refuse to speak to each other for days on end. Still, they did manage to stay together for almost sixty years.

5

Doesn't the street look so much wider without any cars? When they went to live there it had only just been built. That's why there are so few trees in the front garden. They can't have been married for more than a couple of months when he took the photo, because as far as I know they lived there all their married lives. It seemed terrible to have to move her out into the home, but she really couldn't manage on her own. Oh, we were terrified she'd have a fall or something. And she'd always been so proud of the house and the garden. You can see how thrilled she is, even though she's trying not to show it.

Reading pp.114–115

1 G 2 D 3 E 4 A 5 F 6 B

Vocabulary p.116

1 get 2 talk 3 making 4 gave 5 get 6 say 7 got
8 talk 9 make 10 talking

Grammar plus p.116

1 1 a/d 2 a 3 c 4 a/d 5 a/d 6 d 7 b

2 1 The bill seems **to have been added up incorrectly**.

2 It **has been known** for some time that smoking causes lung disease.

3 **The front door was left unlocked** last night.

4 **It is often said** that things were better in the 'good old days'.

5 **I am frequently asked** if parapsychology is recognised by universities.

6 **More than forty students from the university are going to be sent abroad to study**.

7 **I've been told** you are planning to get married.

8 **We had been warned** that it was difficult to find somewhere cheap to stay in Rome.

9 **The power must be switched off** before you connect the screen to your computer.

10 Transformation not possible.

English in Use p.117

1 ✓ 2 could 3 ✓ 4 the 5 who 6 as 7 had 8 such
9 ✓ 10 (first) of 11 it 12 quite 13 that 14 much
15 out 16 ✓

ANSWER KEY

Grammar check p.118

1 1 don't get it done   2 have/get it cut   3 Get that bed made   4 have your suitcase packed   5 would get/have the aerial on the roof fixed   6 have/get it stolen   7 had the windows cleaned   8 will have you thrown out

2 1 c   2 a   3 d   4 e   5 a   6 b   7 a   8 a

Vocabulary p.119

Practice exam

Paper 1 Reading

PART 1   1 A   2 A   3 A   4 D   5 C   6 C   7 D   8 A
         9 E   10 B   11 B   12 D   13 A   14 A   15 E

PART 2   16 E   17 F   18 D   19 A   20 G   21 C

PART 3   22 A   23 C   24 D   25 B   26 A   27 C   28 D

PART 4   29 A   30 B   31 A   32 C   33 D   34 E   35 D
         36 D   37 E   38 B   39 A   40 C   41 C

Paper 3 English in Use

PART 1   1 C   2 B   3 D   4 D   5 C   6 B   7 B   8 C
         9 C   10 A   11 B   12 A   13 C   14 D   15 D

PART 2   16 other   17 because   18 on   19 what
         20 the   21 their   22 as   23 rather   24 in
         25 had   26 more   27 every/each   28 for
         29 way   30 at

PART 3   31 are   32 bit   33 little   34 ✓   35 the
         36 ✓   37 have   38 they   39 ✓
         40 (second) of   41 some   42 ✓   43 out   44 ✓
         45 a   46 more

PART 4   47 loss   48 restlessness   49 treatment
         50 advice   51 unsuitable   52 allergic
         53 sensitivity   54 continuously   55 pianist
         56 unheated   57 legendary   58 rivalry
         59 artistic   60 vacancy   61 timing

PART 5   62 like   63 let them   64 try   65 much/enough
         66 get/take   67 rush   68 bit/little cheaper
         69 free   70 risk of / danger of   71 ban
         72 good idea   73 leave   74 ready

PART 6   75 E   76 F   77 A   78 C   79 I   80 B

Paper 4 Listening

Tapescript

PART 1

A: Dreams have always fascinated us but have remained outside our control. This afternoon, scientist Dr Silvia Johnson explains that this need not be so.

B: Late for work in the morning? Forget that old excuse about the alarm clock not working. I believe that we can wake up at any time in the morning we choose, simply by making a decision to do so the night before. Until quite recently, sleep researchers assumed that sleep was not conscious, but controlled by automatic hormonal mechanisms – known colloquially as 'the

171

body clock' – and that these in turn reacted to environmental influences such as the number of daylight hours. However, now we're beginning to see that sleep can also be affected by the conscious brain. In effect, this means that we can, if we try hard enough, decide when to wake up.

In our most recent study, two groups of volunteers were told before going to bed that they had to wake up at different times. As they slept, my team measured the levels of a particular stimulating hormone in each of the volunteers. This hormone is released around the body shortly before we wake up. In both groups the levels of the hormone started to rise about an hour before the time they had been told they would have to get up. This suggests that anticipation – which is a conscious activity – can actually influence bodily mechanisms that we once thought were entirely unconscious.

Of course one of the problems with this kind of research is that we can't ask the subjects of the study why they woke up when they did. We have to make the assumption that it was because they anticipated having to wake up at a certain time. Generally a sleeping person is out of contact and unable to indicate what, if anything, is going on inside their mind. But there's a curious condition in which a person is partly awake and partly asleep. In this state, the conscious part of the mind can actually observe some of its unconscious mechanisms. I'm talking about lucid dreaming.

What happens in a lucid dream is that a person 'wakes up' while dreaming, but continues to dream. All the strange fantasies that the brain concocts seem to be as solid as the real world, but because the dreamer's brain is in full waking mode, he or she realises that the effects must be hallucinations.

And what makes lucid dreams really different from ordinary dreams is that we can control them. Experienced lucid dreamers can learn to create extraordinary physical sensations, such as leaving their bodies and flying.

Most people are likely to experience a fleeting lucid dream at least once, and some people have them at least once a month. Anyone can learn to do it. The trick is to tell yourself repeatedly while awake that you will watch out for oddities in your dream and 'wake up' when you notice them.

PART 2

If I could call you all to order. Right. We'll get started. First of all, a few apologies. Er, Greg Wilson, our treasurer, can't be with us tonight because, as many of you know, he's representing the club in the tennis final which is being played over at Goring Heath. I'm sure we all wish him all the best of luck. Doug and Nancy Peppard are currently in the United States attending their daughter Julie's wedding. Congratulations to Julie and her husband. Right, the first item on the agenda is actually the treasurer's report, but, as I've just told you, our treasurer is doing battle on the tennis court, so he's asked me to present his report for him. If you'll just bear with me. Erm, right, here it is. You may recall that we began the year with over £1,000 in the bank … umm … £1,265.79 to be precise … revenue from your membership fees and the interest on some investments that we'd made. At last year's AGM we agreed that we'd use a proportion of this year's membership fees to pay for some minor repairs in the clubhouse. Now, these included a new burglar alarm, replacement keys for several of the lockers, new shower curtains for the changing rooms and new nets for the tennis courts. Well, we went ahead with each of these, and, as you'll see on the balance sheet that Sandy is giving out … if you'd be so kind Sandy … thank you … the new burglar alarm came to a little over £200 … . Now that might seem like quite a bit, but I should point out that it's a state-of-the-art alarm … any sign of anyone attempting to enter the building illegally will result in an alarm going off at the local police station. Mmm. Andrew was anxious that I should point out that the £200 included the cost of the installation of the alarm as well. A very sound investment I think. We've also had to spend a bit more than we anticipated on the replacement keys for the lockers since we ended up actually having to replace the locks. Well, er, the replacement locks came to … umm … and fitting them of course … came to … umm … oh, yes there it is, £55. The shower curtains … and I think you'll agree they look very smart … were a good deal cheaper than we anticipated, since one of our members is in the interior decorating trade and managed to get us a substantial discount. All ten shower curtains for only £80. Not bad at all. … Apart from that we had to spend another £100 on new nets for the tennis courts, and we also took the liberty of buying a wedding gift for Julie Peppard on behalf of you all. Sandy chose the gift, which was a delightful set of glasses. That came to er £69.75 including the glasses themselves and the cost of postage to California. What was left of that thousand has been divided equally between our investment fund …

PART 3

P: Well, I have with me today someone who first made a name for himself as the lead singer in the group Metamorphosis, but is now almost certainly better known to you as the brains behind the famous Voyager music festivals. I'm talking, of course, about Andrew Brodsky. Welcome, Andrew.

A: Hello.

ANSWER KEY

P: Andrew, when you parted company with Metamorphosis at the end of the 1970s, you made a statement to the effect that you didn't see a future for yourself in the music industry in any capacity. You were thoroughly disillusioned, basically.

A: Well, that's putting it mildly. I didn't care if I never saw another guitar as long as I lived!

P: But today you're back right in the thick of the same business. What happened?

A: I grew up! No, no, seriously, umm, the other guys in the band and I had known each other since we were children. We lived in the same neighbourhood and we went to the same schools, and then we went on to play music together and to form Metamorphosis. We umm … I was about to say we'd grown up together, but I think er instead we'd kind of held one another back. Years of playing together, of touring, living in one another's pockets, er, well, it had meant we really hadn't had a chance to develop individual interests. One of mine had always been world music … music from other cultures and traditions … and once Metamorphosis split up I finally had a chance to realise just how important that interest was to me, er, well … to kind of see that I didn't just want to play rock music, but to explore what it means to be a musician, like from lots of different perspectives. And, and then, I met my wife.

P: Who is also here with us in the studio. Welcome Juliet Dreyfus.

J: Thanks. It's great to be here.

P: Well, Juliet, you've just heard Andrew give you much of the credit for his second career as a musical entrepreneur. What did you do?

J: I think, if I did anything at all, and let me say I'm not sure that I do deserve so much credit, it was to arrange for Andrew to meet some African musicians … people I'd known and worked with in Africa before I came to this country. Until then Andrew's interest in world music had been largely academic: he enjoyed listening to the music but he didn't actually know any musicians and had never played any of the instruments. Through my contacts he got to sit down and play with some of the great masters of African music and to learn from them.

P: And now you both perform with musicians from all over the world. But it's not just performing you do, is it?

A: No, no, that's just a small … but very enjoyable … part of what we do. We spend most of our time organising music festivals. As you know, we hold two each year, one in the summer and one in the late autumn.

P: One of these has just taken place and once again it was hugely successful. What makes a festival work so well?

A: Well, I think there are two essential ingredients. Er, excellent music … and that's almost guaranteed because we now have access to some of the world's greatest musicians … and the second thing … and I have to say that this is far more difficult … is er, perfect organisation.

P: You make it sound like a military campaign. What does it involve?

A: Well, everyone … people on the gate, stewards, lighting people, sound people, even the people who run food stalls … they all have to know exactly what they're supposed to be doing and when. Er, we always run a full rehearsal two days before the festival begins … not so much for the musicians who, as I said before, they're almost always very well prepared anyway … but for the 300 or so people we employ to run the festival. Everyone has a chance to run through what they'll have to do and er, well, to anticipate where problems might arise.

P: How do you go about getting the people you want to work for you?

J: Well, the musicians are people we've met and have heard performing. We often learn about new musicians from those we already know well, and we go and kind of track them down wherever they happen to be. So we spend half the year doing that, just travelling and going to concerts all over the world. So that's the musicians. The other staff are hand-picked as well, though. Andrew and I interview every single one of them, right down to the person who fries the hamburgers and the guys who put up the big tents. Actually we're already recruiting for our next festival which will take place in August. So if there are people listening who have skills to offer, they should keep an eye out for our press advertisement. It should be appearing in the next couple of days.

P: Thank you very much Andrew Brodsky and Juliet Dreyfus.

PART 4

Speaker 1

My parents ran a printing business, and when I turned 15 they took it for granted that I'd go and work for them in my summer holidays. Both my sisters had done when they were younger, but they both had their own lives and so it was my turn. Dad always said they were short-staffed over the summer months but it wasn't really true. I think he just wanted me to feel needed. It was a bit of a shock to the system working nine to five like that, but the work itself wasn't all that demanding – mostly helping out help out

173

with filing and taking orders over the phone – but I got to do a bit of everything really, which meant I was hardly ever bored.

Speaker 2

… I got this holiday job this summer in a beach resort … I thought it would be fun, you know, lots of sun and swimming and going out clubbing at night. But it was really hard work … we hardly saw the sea! To begin with as far as the cooks and other kitchen staff were concerned student waiters like me were the lowest of the low. They gave us hell. We had only one day off a week and the other days we had to be on duty to serve breakfast from 7 to 10, lunch from 12 to 3 and finally dinner from 6 to 9. But we were free to do what we wanted in between and at night, and we made the most of every minute, I can promise you.

Speaker 3

It was door-to-door sales work basically, though we had to go on this very elaborate training course first … and pay for our accommodation and food while we were doing it, into the bargain. Umm. The course was very convincing though, and I think we were all pretty sure we'd make a fortune. I signed up straight away on the basis of the course, and so did most of the others. As it turned out, there was no salary as such. It was all on a commission basis, so what you made depended entirely on how much you sold. The first couple of days it seemed I couldn't put a foot wrong. I could hardly believe my luck. Most of the people were not what you'd call welcoming, and some of them were downright rude, but every householder agreed to talk to me, and once I got them talking I almost always made the sale. Fifteen on the first afternoon alone. The next day it was twenty, and so on.

Speaker 4

The local council set up a scheme whereby volunteers helped elderly people with er shopping, preparing meals, cleaning and anything else they needed doing. Er, I'd already decided I wanted to go on to study nursing and perhaps specialise in working with older people, so it offered me the possibility of getting some valuable experience. We er, we were each assigned a person who was to be our exclusive responsibility, though the council staff popped in from time to time to see how we were getting along. We, we were expected to go round every Saturday morning and two or more afternoons a week to see if they wanted anything done. Er, sometimes this was more a question of spending time with the people, having a chat over a cup of tea, or perhaps going out for a walk with them.

Speaker 5

I think I would actually have enjoyed the job if it hadn't been for the supervisor. There wasn't actually a lot of work to do once the summer sale had finished, but we always had to kind of pretend to be busy. You'd get told off if you were caught standing around talking. The only way we could manage to have a decent chat was to start doing something completely pointless like re-folding piles of T-shirts that were already in perfectly neat piles. The supervisor also took it amiss if you spent too long with one customer. As far as she was concerned, you should take the money and give the customer the goods, and that was that. If you were civil enough to thank them and say goodbye, she'd look daggers at you from the other side of the shop and then tell you off once the customer had gone.

Paper 4 Answer key

PART 1 1 wake up   2 conscious   3 daylight hours
4 measured their levels   5 anticipation
6 inside their minds/brains/heads
7 can control them   8 flying

PART 2 9 tennis final   10 £1265.79
11 membership fees   12 police station
13 installation of   14 locks   15 £80
16 (new) nets   17 (set of) glasses

PART 3 18 disillusioned   19 individual interests
20 important   21 African musicians
22 organising   23 hugely successful
24 excellent music   25 full rehearsal
26 interview/hand-pick

PART 4 27 A   28 B   29 A   30 B   31 C   32 A
33 C   34 B   35 C   36 B

Paper 5 Speaking

Tapescript

PART 1

Interlocutor: Good morning. My name is Sheila McLeod and this is my colleague John Munroe. And your names are …? (*bleep*)

Can I have your mark sheets, please? Thank you.

First of all we'd like to know a little about you.

Where do you both live? (*bleep*)

Do you study English together? (*bleep*)

Now I'd like you to ask each other something about your reasons for studying English. (*bleep*)

I'd also like you to ask each other about your interests and leisure activities. (*bleep*)

What have you both enjoyed most about studying English? (*bleep*)

Thank you.

PART 2

In this part of the test, I'm going to give each of you the chance to talk for about one minute and to comment briefly after your partner has spoken.

First, you will each have the same set of pictures to look at. They show situations in which people have to be as quiet as possible.

Candidate A, it's your turn first. I'd like you to describe two or three of these pictures, saying why people need to be as quiet as possible in these situations and what might happen if they made a noise. (*two bleeps*)

Now, Candidate B, can you tell us in which of the situations you would find it most difficult to keep quiet? (*two bleeps*)

Now I'm going to give each of you another set of pictures to look at. They show people running in different situations. Now, Candidate B, it's your turn. I'd like you to compare and contrast two or three of these pictures, saying how you think the people are feeling and what might have happened to make them feel like this. (*two bleeps*)

Now, Candidate A, can you tell us in which situation you think the people seem the most anxious? (*bleep*)

PART 3

Now I'd like you to discuss something between yourselves, but please speak so that we can hear you.

I'd like you to imagine that the countries of the world are producing a set of international postage stamps. Here are some designs that have been put forward.

Talk to each other about the suitability of these designs for a set of world postage stamps, and then decide which two would be most acceptable to all countries.

You have three or four minutes for this. (*bleep*)

Thank you.

So which two designs have you chosen? (*bleep*)

PART 4

What would be the advantages of an international postage stamp system? (*bleep*)

Perhaps in the future people will no longer send letters. What's your opinion? (*bleep*)

How important is it to write letters and postcards in this age of technology? (*bleep*)

On what kinds of occasions are people particularly likely to send letters or cards? (*bleep*)

Are there other ways of communicating that are more effective than sending letters or cards? (*bleep*)

Thank you. That is the end of the test.